A Man's World? Changing Men's Practices in a Globalized World

Edited by Bob Pease and Keith Pringle

Much work has been produced in recent years regarding critical studies of men's practices utilizing various feminist and pro-feminist perspectives. This book seeks to widen what has hitherto been a dialogue primarily within the Western democracies. The Editors have sought to achieve this by bringing together a number of established as well as new scholars in order to provide a broader critical analysis of men's practices across a wide range of socio-cultural settings. Particular attention is given to the fact that most studies of globalization and transnational social policy have tended not to encompass issues of men's practices at all.

Issues covered within this volume include: men as carers of children; men as professional welfare workers; men's health; men's violence; and men's involvement in gender equality projects. Several contributions explore the complex transnational intersections and interactions which are occurring in the way men's practices are developing across the globe. In addition to this comparative analysis, a carefully selected and wide range of national studies are included from Europe (the UK, Ireland, Sweden and Finland); the Americas (the USA, Brazil and Nicaragua); Asia (India and Hong Kong); as well as Australia and South Africa.

A Man's World? will be invaluable reading for academics and students of sociology, gender studies, comparative social policy, social and community work, and development studies.

Global Masculinities – a new series from Zed Books
Series Editor: Michael S. Kimmel

Men face common issues – the balance between work and family, fatherhood, defining masculinity in a globalizing economy, health and reproduction, sexuality and violence. But they are experiencing these all over the world in very different contexts and are coming up with different priorities and strategies to address them. This new international series will provide a vehicle for understanding this diversity, and reflect the growing awareness that analysis of masculinity will be greatly impoverished if it remains dominated by a European/North American/Australian matrix. A number of regional and thematic cross-cultural volumes are planned.

The editor, Michael S. Kimmel, is a well-known educator on gender issues. His most recent book, *Manhood in America: A Cultural History*, was published in 1996 to significant acclaim. His work has appeared in dozens of magazines, newspapers and scholarly journals, including the *New York Times Book Review*, the *Harvard Business Review*, the *Nation* and *Psychology Today*, where he was a contributing editor and columnist on male–female relationships. His teaching examines men's lives from a pro-feminist perspective. He is national spokesperson for the National Organization for Men Against Sexism (NOMAS) in the United States.

Already published:

Robert Morrell (ed.), *Changing Masculinities in a Changing Society: Men and Gender in Southern Africa*

Bob Pease and Keith Pringle (eds), *A Man's World? Changing Men's Practices in a Globalized World*

In preparation:

Frances Cleaver (ed.), *Making Masculinity Matter: Men, Gender and Development Policy and Practice*

A Man's World? Changing Men's Practices in a Globalized World

edited by Bob Pease and Keith Pringle

Zed Books

LONDON • NEW YORK

*A Man's World? Changing Men's Practices in a Globalized
World* was first published by Zed Books Ltd, 7 Cynthia Street,
London N1 9JF, UK and Room 400, 175 Fifth Avenue,
New York, NY 10010, USA in 2001.

Distributed in the USA exclusively by Palgrave, a division of
St Martin's Press, LLC, 175 Fifth Avenue, New York,
NY 10010, USA

Cover designed by Andrew Corbett
Set in Monotype Ehrhardt and Franklin Gothic by Ewan Smith
Printed and bound in Malaysia

A catalogue record for this book is available from the British
Library

Library of Congress Cataloging-in-Publication Data: available

ISBN 1 85649 911 1 cased
ISBN 1 85649 912 X limp

Contents

Acknowledgements

Bob Pease would especially like to thank Jacques Boulet for challenging him to internationalize his teaching and research on men's practices. Keith Pringle would like to thank especially Shahida Ali, Rick Bowler and Maria Eriksson for helping him to develop thinking about one or several of the following: sexism, racism, the world beyond Europe.

Contributors

Chan Kam Wah is an associate professor in the Department of Applied Social Studies, Hong Kong Polytechnic University. He has been involved in the feminist movement in Hong Kong since the mid-1980s. His books include: *Social Construction of Gender Inequality in the Housing System* (1997); *Hong Kong Women's File* (co-author; 1993), and *Women and Social Welfare in Hong Kong* (co-author; 1990).

Alastair Christie is a lecturer in the Department of Applied Social Studies, University College Cork and an honorary research fellow in the Department of Applied Social Science, Lancaster University. He has worked as a social worker and social work manager in England and Canada. He is the editor of *Men and Social Work: Theories and Practices* (2001).

Harry Ferguson is Professor of Social Policy and Social Work at University College Dublin. He has taught, researched and published widely on gender and men's issues, child protection and family life. He is currently engaged in a major research project, 'The Lives of Irish Men', from which a book will eventually be published. His most recent book is *Changing Fathers? Fatherhood and Family Life in Modern Ireland* (with K. McKeown and D. Rooney).

Jeff Hearn is Research Professor in Sociology at the University of Manchester as well as Guest Professor at Svenska Handelshogskolan, Finland and Visiting Professor II, Oslo University, Norway. His major publications include *The Gender of Oppression* (1987), *Men in the Public Eye* (1992), *Men as Managers, Managers as Men* (co-editor, 1996), *Violence and Gender Relations* (co-editor, 1996), *Men, Gender Divisions and Welfare* (co-editor, 1998), *The Violences of Men* (1998), and *Gender, Sexuality and Violence in Organisations* (co-author, 2001).

Ira Horowitz worked as a public interest lawyer for twenty-six years before becoming a social justice trainer and consultant. He currently facilitates gender-sensitivity workshops for men under the sponsorship of the Gender Education and Training Network in Cape Town.

Michael Kaufman is the former deputy director of the Centre for Research on Latin America and the Caribbean at York University in Toronto. He is editor of *Beyond Patriarchy*, author of *Cracking the Armour: Power, Pain and the Lives of Men* and co-editor (with Harry Brod) of *Theorising Masculinities*. He is a founder of the White Ribbon Campaign and now works full-time as a public educator on gender issues and writer of both non-fiction and fiction i oks.

Michael S. Kimmel is Professor of Sociology at SUNY at Stony Brook. His books include *Changing Men* (1987), *Men Confront Pornography* (1990), *Men's Lives* (4th edn, 1997), *Against the Tide: Profeminist Men in the United States, 1776–1990* (1992), *The Politics of Manhood* (1996), *Manhood: A Cultural History* (1996) and *The Gendered Society* (2000). He edits *Men and Masculinities*, an interdisciplinary scholarly journal, a book series on Men and Masculinity at the University of California Press, and the Sage series on Men and Masculinities. He is the spokesperson for the National Organization for Men Against Sexism (NOMAS) and lectures extensively on campuses in the United States and abroad.

Gary L. Lemons is Director and Professor in the Program in Literature at Eugene Lang College, New School for Social Research, New York. He has published widely on issues associated with the historic, current and future relationship of African American men to pro-feminism/womanism.

Jorge Lyra is a Fellow of the MacArthur Foundation in the Population Program in Brazil. He is currently researching 'Adolescent Fatherhood' in the city of Recife in partnership with the Federal University of Pernambuco.

Sven-Axel Månsson is Professor of Social Work at Goteborg University in Sweden. He has written several books and articles on issues of gender and sexuality in social work. His latest book deals with the issue of women exiting prostitution.

Benedito Medrado is undertaking doctoral research on the topic 'The Concept of Risk and the Social Construction of Masculinity in Adolescent Socialisation Processes' at São Paulo Catholic University in Brazil. He is a Fellow of the Young and Adolescent Father Support Program (PAPAI); and a Fellow of a Study Group on Paternity and Masculine Sexuality (GESMAP), based in São Paulo, and co-editor of the book *Men and Masculinities: Other Words*.

Marko Monteiro is currently undertaking a Master's degree in the Department of Anthropology at the State University of Campinas in Brazil. He is a Fellow of the Group for the Study of Masculinity and

Fatherhood and since 1997 has run an internet site dedicated to the study of masculinity.

Bob Pease is Associate Professor in Social Work at RMIT University in Melbourne. He has been teaching in the area of men and masculinities since 1989. He is the author of *Men and Sexual Politics: Towards a Pro-feminist Practice* (1997) and *Recreating Men: Postmodern Masculinity Politics* (2000) and is co-editor of *Transforming Social Work Practice: Postmodern Critical Perspectives* (1999) and *Working with Men in the Human Services* (2001). He has been involved in anti-sexist men's politics for over twenty years and is a co-founder of Men Against Sexual Assault in Melbourne.

Keith Pringle is Professor in Comparative Social Policy and co-director of the International Centre for the Study of Violence and Abuse at the University of Sunderland. He is also a visiting professor at the Institute for Housing Research, Uppsala University. He has published widely on men's practices, child welfare and comparative social welfare. His major publications include *Men, Masculinities and Social Welfare* (1995), *Protecting Children in Europe: Towards a New Millennium* (co-editor with Margit Harder, 1997), *Children and Social Welfare in Europe* (1998) and *Through Two Pairs of Eyes: A Comparative Study of Danish Social Policy and Child Welfare* (with Margit Harder, 1999).

Graeme Russell is an Associate Professor in Psychology at Macquarie University, Australia. He is an internationally recognized researcher and industry consultant on work–life balance and is the author of two books on fathers, *The Changing Role of Fathers* and *A Practical Guide for Fathers*, and over fifty research papers on fatherhood, gender and work/family issues. He was the co-director of a recent major government-funded project on men's roles as parents, 'Fitting Fathers into Families', and joint editor of a recent book on families and workplace issues, *Organisational Change and Gender Equity*.

Siddhartha lives in Bangalore, India, and is a writer and social activist. He is a board member of the South–North Network Cultures and Development (Brussels) and the editor of *Butterfly Futures: The Asia-Pacific Journal of the Alliance for a Responsible and United World*. He is the director of Pipal Tree, an Indian organization concerned with cultural conflict and sustainable development.

Ben Wadham co-ordinated the development of the South Australian draft men's health policy, 1996. He is currently a consultant in South Australia working largely on issues of men and violence. His current research includes a PhD project on 'White Strategies of Aboriginal Reconciliation'.

He is also the editor of *XY: Men, Sex, Politics*, a magazine about masculinity and social justice.

Patrick Welsh works for CANTERA, a Nicaraguan non-governmental organization that specializes in the methodology of popular education. He has been involved in the development and implementation of a methodology for gender analysis with and between men. Since 1994, he has been involved in running courses on masculinity and popular education.

Introduction: Studying Men's Practices and Gender Relations in a Global Context

Bob Pease and Keith Pringle

Over the last fifteen years a considerable body of work has been produced regarding critical studies of men's practices utilizing various feminist and profeminist perspectives (for instance, Brod 1987; Kimmel 1987; Segal 1990; Connell 1995; Mac an Ghaill 1996). More recently, specific studies of men and various aspects of social welfare have developed, building on these more general analyses (Pringle 1995; Pease 1997a; 2000; Popay et al. 1998). Within those studies considerable debate focuses on a range of issues relating to men's practices, including the following: men as carers of children or adults; men as professional welfare workers; men as pro-feminist activists; men's well-being (encompassing topics such as employment/ unemployment and health); crime; sexual violence; and men's practices in organizations. Many of these debates also have relevance to some very current and central tensions within the spectrum of feminist/profeminist perspectives:

1. The extent to which critical studies of men's practices should focus on men's violence as a prime site where patriarchal relations are generated and performed. For instance, certain commentators (Hearn 1996b; Pringle 1998a; 1998b) have suggested that those profeminist perspectives sometimes defined as 'Men's Studies' have tended to lack sufficient focus on those issues.

2. The ways in which we can try to understand the complex inter-sections of gender with 'race', disability, sexuality, class and age in the practices of men. For instance, some commentators from within the 'Men's Studies' tradition (Messner 1997) have suggested that analyses more heavily influenced by radical feminist perspectives may over-generalize the commonality of men's practices.

3. The extent to which critical studies should contextualize men's practices within the frame of gender relations. Some commentators (for instance Hearn 1996b; Pease 1997a; 1977b; Pringle 1998b) have suggested

that such conceptualization is not always given the central importance that it requires. Part of this debate has come to centre on the utility or otherwise of the concept of 'masculinities'. There is no doubt that the shifting of the conceptual focus from 'masculinity' to 'masculinities' a decade ago, primarily by Bob Connell (1987; 1995), represented a major step forward in assisting feminist and profeminist commentators to encapsulate both the diversity and potential fluidity of the processes involved in men being men. Moreover, Connell himself has always emphasized the centrality of locating the study of masculinities within a clear gender relational frame. However, with the pervasive use of the concept over the years, some concern has developed (see especially Hearn 1996b) about whether it may militate against gender relational analysis. At the same time, Hearn (1996b) has also suggested that the prolonged focus on masculinities may have become too abstract, thereby diverting critical attention away from the materiality of what men are actually doing in their relations with women, children and other men. Consequently, Hearn advocates greater conceptual emphasis being placed on men's practices rather than masculinities. Throughout this introductory chapter, and the one that concludes the book, we ourselves generally follow Hearn's advice on this matter.

Returning to the aims of this volume, we want to stress that these important contemporary themes outlined above have primarily derived, and are mainly continuing to develop, from dialogues between commentators located within a relatively narrow band of socio-cultural structures and/or discourses: those which are predominant in what we might collectively term the 'western democracies'; especially the United States and, to varying lesser extents, the United Kingdom, Australia and Canada

At the same time, most studies of globalization and transnational social policy tend not to specifically encompass issues of men's practices, while a transnational literature on women's experiences has been developing over a period of time (for instance Dominelli 1991; Rai et al. 1992). A few texts have attempted some form of cross-cultural perspective on the topic of masculinity but all have limitations

In this volume we carry forward within a global perspective the current debates on men's practices identified above. Even more crucially, the book seeks to fill those gaps in the literature that we have just highlighted via the process of encouraging a broader critical analysis of men's practices. This concept of breadth is not purely geographical in nature given the following objectives which it seeks to fulfil:

1. To provide critical studies of men's practices across a wide range of socio-cultural settings within the context of a clear gender relational framework

2. By means of these studies, to provide comparative analyses of the debates and themes mentioned above. This includes consideration of how relevant these concerns (derived largely from 'western' discourses about men) are within a variety of socio-cultural frames of reference – and whether other themes and debates emerge from broader geographical surveys.

3. The studies in this volume explore, within a social context, the complex transnational intersections and interactions that occur in the way men's practices are developing across the globe. This comparative exploration will draw partly upon similar transnational analyses that are beginning to develop in relation to men's practices more generally.

Clearly this whole enterprise is predicated upon the utility and validity of comparative approaches to social analysis. Consequently, in this introductory chapter we begin by addressing some of the advantages and difficulties of such approaches.

Comparative Approaches to Social Analysis[1]

In recent years a comparative perspective has been applied to various aspects of study within the fields of sociology, social policy and social welfare. There are probably many reasons for this tendency, some being more legitimate in scholarly terms than others. Perhaps one of the most convincing reasons for adopting a comparative approach is the potential offered for deconstructing the assumptions that underpin social practices and policies in different countries. In turn, such a process of deconstruction may facilitate a reconstruction of more effective policies and practices. There is also an awareness that such practices and policies increasingly interact transnationally; consequently, research may seek to explore the processes and outcomes of those interactions and connections.

In many cases where specific social issues have been studied transnationally, attempts have been made to apply various general theoretical categorizations to particular issues: unfortunately much of this work – or at least much of this work which has gained the widest academic circulation – has been confined largely to the European context.

In the case of the study of differential welfare regimes, the most common general model applied in this specific fashion is that devised by Esping-Andersen (1990; 1996) which did at least seek to look beyond Europe, albeit to those parts of the world most associated with 'western capitalism'. There has now been an extensive critique of such models in terms of their insufficient attention to gender relations (Lewis and Ostner 1991; Leira 1992; Orloff 1993; O'Connor 1993; Sainsbury 1994). In turn, some commentators have gone further and offered critiques of these more gender-sensitive comparative analyses on the grounds that they too ignore important dimensions of inequality including heterosexism (Carabine 1996), ageism, racism and disablism (Pringle 1998a).

Some commentators have also taken a variety of positions regarding the analytic value of these applications from the general to the particular (for instance, Anttonen and Sipilä 1996; Harder and Pringle. 1997; Pringle 1998a; 1998b; Pringle and Harder 1999), partly depending upon the issue being studied. Furthermore, there is a need for considerable open-mindedness in the assumptions that are brought to bear in such analyses. For example, Trifiletti (1999), through a feminist perspective on the relationship between gender and welfare system dynamics, has provided detailed arguments that southern European welfare regimes may not in fact be more sexist than those in northern and western Europe.

As noted earlier, one field of social enquiry which has to a considerable extent escaped specific comparative scrutiny is the critical study of men's practices, although the latter has received important attention within broader and relatively established transnational feminist surveys of gender relations (for instance, Dominelli 1991; Rai et al. 1992). Yet, the limited amount of work devoted specifically to men's practices transnationally suggests there is immense scope for extending critical analysis in that particular area.

White (1994), Cornwall (1997), Cornwall and Lindisfarne (1994), Moser (1993), Sweetman (1997) and Dudink (1998) all converge on the need to add the critical study of men's practices to the attempts at understanding gender regimes in various parts of the world. However, comparative work on men, masculinities and patriarchies has only recently begun to be addressed (UNDP 1995).

Gilmore (1990) has perhaps provided the most comprehensive research on how men in different cultures perceive and experience manhood. He set out to explore whether there were continuities of masculinities across different cultural boundaries by examining ways in which boys and men prove their manhood. However, because Gilmore assumes that maleness is unitary, he fails to recognize the plurality of masculinities and men's practices within any of the cultures he studied (Conway-Long 1994). Connell (1995: 32) notes that Gilmore's framework is based on a positivist model of social science, where 'multiple cases are put together in attempts to arrive at cross-cultural generalization and overall laws about human society'. Thus his aim was to discover a broad base for generalizations about manhood. Gilmore's study reflects the weakness of cross-cultural psychology where western researchers transport mainstream tests to different cultures to explore the universality of hypotheses derived from developed societies (Moghaddam and Studer 1997: 189).

Connell (1995: 34) indicates the 'futility' of creating a positivist science of masculinity 'by cross-cultural generalization', but later (1998), while agreeing with the importance of ethnographic 'in-depth' work, he equally suggests the need to locate such work in 'global history' and to engage in 'comparative studies from different parts of the world'.

We believe that Connell's (1987) concept of a gender regime provides a useful framework for analysing the diversity of men's practices. His framework comprises three main structures: a gendered division of labour within the state apparatus, a gendered structure of power in the state apparatus and a gendered structure of cathexis (emotional attachment). While Connell's analysis is confined to states, as Peterson and Runyan (1993: 218) note, 'it could be extended to the relations between different states and the gender regimes produced through new forms of regionalization'.

In the field of social welfare there are complex patterns of convergence and divergence between men's practices internationally which await further interrogation (Pringle 1998b). Similarly, Connell's initial enquiries re garding the global transactions which occur in processes of masculinity formation have opened up a whole range of possibilities for exploration and contestation (Connell 1991; 1995; 1998; Hearn 1996a). These studies have begun to conceptualize broad transnational categories of men and masculinities, such as 'global business masculinity' (Connell 1998) and 'men of the world' (Hearn 1996a).

In this introductory chapter we now want to expand upon some of these themes within a 'global' frame, thereby setting the context for the contributions which follow in this book. We begin by considering the existing global perspectives on women.

Globalizing Women[2]

Studies in international social development have noted the continued existence of profound inequalities and relative disadvantage on a world scale within the societies of both the so-called developed and developing worlds (Esping-Anderson 1996; Bissio 1997; Deacon 1997). Scholars studying gender relations, while acknowledging modest improvements in some societies in women's living conditions and structural position, have pointed to the collective worsening of their situation in many countries of the world (Mies 1986; White 1994; 1996; Duggan et al. 1997; Foreman 1999). The global dimension of violence against women has also now been widely recognized, although its form, extent and intensity vary between countries

(Pettman 1996: 209) and the rapid growth of sex tourism and prostitution has moved on to the global agenda (Steans 1998: 137).

While unequal wages, gender-segregated jobs, the 'feminization of poverty', inequalities in health and social care, 'housewifeization' (Mies 1986) and gender-related violence are all issues that impinge on women, they are centrally concerned with men's practices (Connell 1987; Hearn 1998). Questioning dominant forms of masculinity and gender oppression in particular locations is a necessary step in addressing these global inequalities. If the global situation of women is to improve, men must change their subjectivities and practices.

Brethell and Sargent (1993: 64) observe that women's status is highest in societies in which the public–domestic spheres are only weakly differentiated. Thus, the most egalitarian societies will be those in which men participate in the domestic sphere. But how do we create positive, equality-oriented changes among men? What are the obstacles? Why is it that so many men are reluctant to support women's rights or oppose them? Changes in men's practices and experiences, while being acknowledged, have only recently begun to be investigated in non-western contexts, in their own right (see, for example, White 1994; 1997; Cornwall 1997).

The field of men's studies has meanwhile, in the western world at least, become a generic term for much theoretical and empirical work and, although the term is not without controversy, it has matured to the degree that there are now clearly distinguishable paradigmatic approaches to the conceptualization and investigation of men's practices. The theoretical approach taken here is located within the critical sociological tradition (Hearn 1992; 1998; Kimmel 1996; Messner 1997; Connell 1995; Pringle 1995; Pease 1997b) which emphasizes the importance of locating the study of men's lives within the context of patriarchy, class relations, hegemonic masculinity, cultural domination and the social divisions between men. Although this form of gender analysis has been developed largely within a framework of western sociological gender theory, it is our view that it has relevance to the experience of gender relations in semi-industrialized societies and those undergoing westernization or modernization.

Women, Gender and Development

In the 1950s most development projects were technically oriented and neither women nor gender were explicitly addressed. The term Women and Development (WAD) emerged in the late 1970s to identify how women have been left out of development (Moser 1993: 2). The Women and Development discourse was based on a premise that women as a general category could be added to the traditional approach and that this would be sufficient to change development outcomes to improve women's position (Elson 1991: 1).

The limitations of this approach soon became evident in that it was based on the view that women's issues can be addressed in isolation from their relationship to men. The term Gender and Development (GAD) was later introduced to represent a shift towards a gender relations analysis. Moser (1993: 3) notes that 'GAD maintains that to focus on women in isolation is to ignore the real problem which remains their subordinate status to men'. She says that women are only 'half the story' and to focus on gender facilitates an analysis of the way in which relations with men are socially constructed. Thus the aim of GAD was to explore the social construction of gender roles, with particular attention to the situations of both women and men in their social context. This enabled a shift from promoting women's integration into development projects to researching the social structures, processes and relations that position women in disadvantaged positions. The implication of GAD was that men would need to relinquish some of their economic, political and social power.

While this represented an important theoretical shift, Moser (1993: 3) observes that the terms WAD and GAD 'are all too often used synonymously'. Gender awareness training programmes focus on women and rarely speak to men's experiences as men (Cornwall 1997: 8). Thus the move from WAD to GAD did little to alter the overwhelming preoccupation with women.

Furthermore, post-colonial and postmodern feminists challenged many of the assumptions of GAD as well. Instead of concentrating on grand theories of gender and development, they argued that research should focus on 'the historically and culturally specific experiences of different groups of women' (Steans 1998: 152–4). They emphasized the importance of focusing on gender relations that operate in specific situations and how they are affected by both international and local factors. Steans (1998: 175) argues that gender subordination can be understood only in the context of particular cultural practices by demonstrating the extent to which gender relations are constantly influenced by global and local processes. Thus, in this view, gender relations must be understood in terms of both specific practices and global power relations.

Men, Gender and Development

The focus on gender rather than women is a reminder that men must also be targets of attempts to redress gender inequality and that their interests are also socially constructed and thus amenable to change (Steans 1998: 149). As White (1994: 102) argues, 'if gender is about relations between men and women, then men's experience must also be taken into account'. Furthermore, if women's gender identities are to be changed, then men's must also change. Women's task will be made impossible unless men begin to 'question their personal practices and the ideologies of masculinity which they embody' (White 1997: 15). This means focusing not only on men but also on the institutions, culture and practices that sustain gender inequality.

Men are often excluded from being part of the processes of changing and confronting gender inequality (Cornwall 1997: 11). However, because hegemonic masculinity can also be oppressive to those men who either refuse or fail to conform, women's liberation can also benefit men. Men's dominance over women is also related to the dominance of some men over other men. The hierarchy between men means that some men are also disadvantaged by the existing system of gender relations. These men may choose to struggle against the dominant model of gender relations and be open to forming alliances with women to bring about change (White 1997: 107). Such men who have already begun to embrace change can be allies and opportunities could be provided to involve them in gender and development work (Cornwall 1997: 12).

Ethnographic Studies of Men's Practices

While development research and practice have tended to marginalize issues of men and masculinity, anthropology has recently taken an interest in studying men's practices in non-western contexts. There have been a number of important studies, including Herdt's (1982) study of the boy-inseminating rituals among the Sambia of New Guinea; Herzfeld's (1985) study of sheep stealing as masculine ritual in Cretan mountain villages, and Silberschmidt's (1991) study of the changing gender roles in Kenya. Gutmann (1996) examines what it means to be a man in Mexico City, and Almeida (1996) poses the same question in a small Portuguese town. There have also been a number of recent studies of gender relations in Asia that have addressed the changing subjectivities and practices of men (Karim 1995; Ong and Peletz 1995).

Connell (1995: 34) makes the point, however, that 'ethnographic knowledge about masculinity is valuable to the extent we understand it as part of a global history'. While Connell (1998: 6) recognizes the importance of the 'intellectual fruits' of the 'ethnographic moment' in research on men and masculinity, he urges us to complement this localist orientation with historical and analytic research, focusing on 'whole countries' and ultimately 'the whole world'. He even suggests that 'thinking about masculinity as a feature of world global structure and dynamics of gender' will help us to use the findings of ethnographic and comparative research more adequately. Such an approach needs to be able to incorporate and validate locality-oriented ethnographic approaches and requires the establishment of a contextual framework that substantially allows us analytically to link both specific national/regional data of an historical and socio-structural nature as well as relevant elements reflecting the globalizing processes at work.

Globalizing Men

Connell (1998: 10) argues that certain hegemonic masculinities have now been globalized. By this, he means that the making of masculinities is shaped by global forces. Thus, to understand masculinities in specific local contexts, we need to think in global terms.

Globalization is a concept that is difficult to define. However, there seems to be some general agreement that it involves increased economic interdependence (Trevillion 1999: 64). The term 'globalization' has been used to describe the ever-intensifying networks of cross-border human interaction. As Pettman (1996: 23) observes, globalization 'draws our attention to the increasing permeability of state borders and the growing power of non-state borders such as transnational corporations in determining much that goes on within it'.

However, the level of integration and interdependence is not unprecedented. For instance, to give only one example, historical analysis from the 1960s and 1970s (Braudel 1967; Davis 1973) opened up the complex socio-economic and geographical interconnections operating in the European expansion outwards in the fifteenth and sixteenth centuries. On these grounds we should perhaps be a little wary of potential academic 'hype' around the concept of 'globalization'.

Moreover, there are other reasons for exercising care before embracing the concept too readily or too extensively. For instance, it has been suggested (see Clarke 2000) that a post-Fordist accumulation regime associated with the global economy has set in train a relative convergence of welfare systems towards more neo-liberal agendas (Gray 1998). However, as has recently been pointed out by Hirst and Thompson (1999: 51): 'Globalization has not eliminated the scope for extensive welfare, and even within the constraints of the EU, states have clear options if they have the political resources.' This highlights the fact that the influence of local and/or national cultural and socio-economic factors may well have far more leverage in shaping the welfare configurations within a particular country or region than some advocates of globalization have allowed. For example, in a comparative analysis of child welfare, one of us has demonstrated (Pringle 1998a) that the alleged demise of the Nordic welfare states under the pressure of global neo-liberal trends is rather premature; a judgement borne out more recently by Kvist's (1999) statistical analysis. Similarly, Harris and McDonald (2000) warn against over-simplistic applications of globalization perspectives by comparing the personal social services for elders in Australia and Britain.

Thus, both historically and politically it may well be that the concept of globalization has been rather over-extended. Nevertheless, we may still see the present process as to some extent being characterized by a 'deepening' of capitalist integration. As Kofman and Youngs' reader (1996) points out, globalization has 'generated a new geography of centrality and power, on the one hand, and marginality and decline, on the other'. Friedman (1994) argues that this results in deep-seated processes of identity change and should be analysed with cultural sensitivity and in a multidisciplinary fashion as well as simultaneously on the local and global level of process and phenomena. It is globalization, though, that provides us with 'the possibility of a systematic and comparative study of the relationship between felt experience, culture, technology and social networks' (Trevillion 1999: 79) and this enables us to explore the different subjectivities and practices that emerge in the global context.

Connell (1998) points out that the historical process of globalization led to 'a partially integrated, highly unequal and turbulent society, in which gender relations are partly but unevenly linked on a global scale'. He further points out that while 'the culture and institutions of the North-Atlantic countries are hegemonic within the emergent world system', the world gender order is 'not simply an extension of a traditional European–American gender order'. All of this clearly converges on and confirms the need for a systematic and contextualized but culturally-sensitive investigation of interconnected but also quite idiosyncratic experiences and practices of men within distinct but interrelated gender regimes across the various regions of the world. This book represents our attempt to respond to this challenge.

Overview of the Book

The book is divided into two parts. Part I provides transnational and transcultural analyses of various thematic issues, including: men's practices in the context of globalization, men's violence, men's domestic practices and men's health. Part II surveys the past, current and likely future terms of debates on men's practices in eleven specific countries: Finland, United Kingdom, Ireland, Sweden, United States, Brazil, Nicaragua, Australia, Hong Kong, India and South Africa.

The first section begins with Michael S. Kimmel's overview of right-wing movements around the world that use masculinity as a discursive strategy to explain their position and to mobilize men. He observes, for example, that ethnic nationalists seek to reclaim their homelands and that right-wing militias rail against emasculating national governments and the problematized masculinity of various 'others' – gays, Jews, immigrants, blacks – who threaten white men's entitlement to possession of white women. Underlying these contemporary right-wing movements, he says, are ideologies of racism, sexism, anti-Semitism and homophobia.

In Chapter 3 Michael Kaufman analyses the complexities of men's violence against women, pandemic in most countries of the world. He argues that men's involvement is critical if men and boys are to be successfully addressed on this issue and he explores the possibilities for large-scale anti-violence educational and awareness campaigns by men and boys aimed at their peers. He discusses the potential of the White Ribbon Campaign, which began in Canada in 1991 and which has now spread to at least a dozen countries, as an example of an international effort that is aimed at ending men's violence against women.

Graeme Russell's chapter analyses the impact of globalization on the practice of fatherhood in different cultural contexts, with particular reference to Australia, Canada, United States, Europe, Japan and Korea. He explores the similarities and differences in the practice of fatherhood in these cultural contexts and considers the future of fatherhood practices in light of changes in workplace expectations and changes in the opportunities fathers have to become more involved in parenting.

In the final chapter in this section, Ben Wadham examines how western discourses of men's health have excluded and violated the needs of men in marginalized locations. He explores the links between the western crisis in masculinity, the processes of globalization and the remaking of hegemonic masculinity and the health needs of men in non-western countries. His intention is to broaden the understanding of men's health needs, official responses to those claims and to highlight the strategic operation of hegemonic masculinity in the framing of the men's health discourse.

In the first chapter in Part II, Jeff Hearn examines the broad connections that can be drawn between men, masculinities and gender relations; nation, state and territory; and more specific questions concerning the welfare state. He places special emphasis on the importance of men's relations to family and fatherhood, and to personal violence and war. In the second part of his chapter, he uses case studies of Finland and the United Kingdom to analyse contemporary constructions of men's relations to not just nation, state and welfare, but the social relations of class, gender, race and sexuality more generally.

In Chapter 7 Alastair Christie discusses the identities of men as social workers in the United Kingdom. He argues that men may transgress gendered boundaries by working in a 'caring' profession and a profession in which most of the workers and service users are women. However, he says men's over- and under-representation in particular areas of social work may also reinforce dominant constructions of masculinities. Drawing on research with men and women social workers, he investigates the way in which men's professional identities and practices are discursively produced in the UK.

Harry Ferguson's chapter examines some forms that masculinities are taking in Ireland and provides an overview of what is known about men's lives, in terms of such core issues as work, sexuality, fatherhood, social exclusion and marginalization. He argues that the Irish case exemplifies changes in how masculinities are configured in the western world. In the final section of the chapter, he focuses on the implications of changing configurations of masculinities for men's practices in Ireland.

It is the contention of Sven-Axel Månsson's chapter that one of the central questions for understanding prostitution must deal with men's motives for going to prostitutes. In recent years, Scandinavian research on prostitution has begun systematically to show interest in this question. The chapter starts by giving a résumé of the main findings of this research. It then relates these research findings to the ongoing international debate on prostitution containing different ideological and political perspectives.

Chapter 10 by Gary L. Lemons advocates a profeminist reconceptualization of black manhood and masculinity as a critical practice in the social, political and economic framework of black liberation. He argues that since the achievement of women's suffrage and other gains for women in the United States, there has been a recent resurgence of pro-male, nationalist sentiment in black communities that supports a patriarchal vision of black political movements. However, he notes that concurrently there has been a new sign of black male support for women's rights and it is this burgeoning movement that this chapter addresses, contemplating its implications for the future direction of black self-determination in North America.

In Chapter 11 Benedito Medrado, Jorge Lyra and Marko Monteiro identify and analyse the depiction of masculinity in Brazilian television advertisements, based upon the idea that the commercials are discursive practices. The authors argue that 'masculinity' in merchandising is almost exclusively associated with a hetero-erotic pattern of relations, in which men and women perform traditional cultural roles. They stress the importance of building up new definitions of masculinity and femininity and of spreading new repertoires about gender and sexual relations so as to broaden the possibilities of people's actions.

Patrick Welsh's chapter reports on the processes of training and awareness-raising on masculinity carried out over five years in Nicaragua. As well as adopting positions of solidarity with women's rights, some men linked to feminist NGOs began to meet on a regular basis to reflect upon issues related to their own masculinity and in particular male violence, giving birth in 1993 to the Men Against Violence Group, based in Managua. Since then, activities organized by men to help them to reflect critically upon their masculinity and begin to 'unlearn machismo' have proliferated in Nicaragua, extending to other countries in the region.

In Chapter 13 Bob Pease explores the implications of the definitively Australian style of masculine behaviour, called mateship, for gender relations in Australia. Mateship, he says, is part of the Australian male heritage, a heritage born in colonial days and glorified in war and sport. It functions to protect the interests of groups of men through the exclusion of others. He argues that the celebrated culture of silence and emotional repression embodied in mateship is a major issue facing Australian men and is related to men's violence against women. The feminist movement in Australia has challenged the dominant form of masculinity inherent in mateship and the basic rationale for male–female relations that flow from it. In this chapter he discusses Australian men's responses to the feminist challenge and documents the efforts of a small group of men to construct pro-feminist subjectivities and practices.

Chan Kam Wah's chapter notes that the men's movement in Hong Kong is virtually non-existent, in spite of the existence of an indigenous feminist movement that has been active since the early 1980s. He acknowledges that it is very difficult to change men living in the strong patriarchal culture of a Chinese society like Hong Kong. In this context, he traces the social and cultural background leading to the self-detachment of men from gender-conscious practice. He emphasizes the importance of including men in the pursuit of gender equality, by paying more attention to changing men in welfare services and developing pro-feminist men's services in Hong Kong.

In Chapter 15 Siddhartha analyses the impact of globalization processes on Indian masculinity. He says that while the citadels of Indian masculinity are still intact, in that Indian men enjoy a range of privileges which are denied to women, women's increased political participation and the spread of the electronic media have led to some rethinking on the part of a small number of Indian men. His chapter points to the need for dialogue between men and women on the oppressive nature of Indian patriarchy and illustrates how humanizing discussions on gender relations can liberate men from centuries of cultural conditioning.

In the final chapter in this section, Ira Horowitz outlines the cultural practices of masculinity in post-apartheid South Africa. He draws upon information generated at a number of gender-awareness workshops held for men that took place in South Africa between 1996 and 1999. During those workshops, the participants engaged in a series of exercises in which they described how they were taught to behave as men, and they told stories about early experiences relating to their male identity. The chapter illustrates how key elements of this identity were shaped by cultural and religious forces.

In the concluding chapter, we provide a comparative overview of the issues raised in the previous chapters in terms of the process of comparative study and the content on men's practices in specific socio-political contexts. We illustrate how the book will contribute to national and international debates and research about diversity and difference in men's subjectivities and practices, and about differential gender regimes and, finally, about the interplay between global and local processes in both these areas.

Notes

1. Parts of the section 'Comparative approaches to social analysis' were originally drafted by Keith Pringle and incorporated within the successful application to the European Commission for the Thematic Network entitled 'The Social Problem and Societal Problematisation of Men and Masculinities' (Pringle et al. 1998). This European Commission Network is now operative under contract HPSE-CT-1999-0008. The website for the Network is www.cromenet.org

2. Parts of this section were originally drafted by Bob Pearce and Jacques Boulet as part of an application to the Australian Research Council for a project entitled 'Changing Men in a Global Context'.

References

Almeida, M. (1996) *The Hegemonic Male: Masculinity in a Portuguese Town*, Providence, RI: Berghahn Books.

Anttonen, A. and J. Sipilä (1996) 'European Social Care Services: Is It Possible to Identify Models?', *Journal of European Social Policy*, Vol. 6: 87–100.

Bissio, R. (ed.) (1997) *The World Guide 1997/98*, Oxford: New Internationalist Publications.

Braudel, F. (1967) *Civilisation matérielle et capitalisme*, Paris: Armand Colin.

Brethall, C. and C. Sargent (1993) *Gender in Cross-Cultural Perspective*, Engelwood Cliffs, NJ: Prentice Hall.

Brod, H. (ed.) (1987) *The Making of Masculinities: The New Men's Studies*, London: Allen and Unwin.

Carabine, J. (1996) 'A Straight Playing Field or Queering the Pitch: Centring Sexuality in Social Policy', *Feminist Review*, Vol. 54: 31–64.

Clarke, J. (2000) 'A World of Difference? Globalization and the Study of Social Policy', in G. Lewis, S. Gewitz and J. Clarke (eds), *Rethinking Social Policy*, London: Sage.

Connell, R. W. (1987) *Gender and Power*, Cambridge: Polity Press.

— (1991) 'The Big Picture – a Little Sketch: Changing Western Masculinities in the Perspective of Recent World History', paper presented at the conference on 'Research and Masculinity and Men in Gender Relations', Sydney, 7–8 June 1991.

— (1995) *Masculinities*, Sydney: Allen and Unwin.

— (1998) 'Masculinities and Globalization', *Men and Masculinities*, Vol. 1, No. 1: 3–23.

Conway-Long, D. (1994) 'Ethnographies and Masculinities', in H. Brod and M. Kaufman (eds), *Theorizing Masculinities*, Thousand Oaks, CA: Sage.

Cornwall, A. (1997) 'Men, Masculinity and "Gender in Development"', *Gender and Development*, Vol. 5, No. 2: 8–13.

Cornwall, A. and N. Lindisfarne (1994) 'Introduction', in Cornwall and Lindisfarne (eds), *Dislocating Masculinity*.

— (eds) (1994) *Dislocating Masculinity: Comparative Ethnographies*, London: Routledge.

Davis, R. (1973) *The Rise of the Atlantic Economies*, London: Weidenfeld and Nicolson.

Deacon, B. (1997) *Global Social Policy*, London: Sage.

Dominelli, L. (1991) *Women Across Continents: Feminist Comparative Social Policy*, London: Harvester Wheatsheaf.

Dudink, S. (1998) 'The Trouble with Men: Problems in the History of Masculinity', *European Journal of Cultural Studies*, Vol. 1, No. 3: 419–31.

Duggan, L., L. Nisonoff, N. Visvanathan and N. Wiegersma (eds) (1997) *The Women, Gender and Development Reader*, London: Zed Books.

Elson, D. (1991) 'Male Bias in the Development Process: An Overview', in D. Elson (ed.), *Male Bias in the Development Process*, Manchester: Manchester University Press.

Esping-Andersen, G. (1990) *The Three Worlds of Welfare Capitalism*, Cambridge: Polity Press.

— (ed.) (1996) *Welfare States in Transition: National Adaptations in Global Economies*, London: Sage.

Foreman, M. (1999) *AIDS and Men: Taking Risks or Taking Responsibility*, London: Zed Books.

Friedman, J. (1994) *Cultural Identity and Global Process*, London: Sage.

Gilmore, D. (1990) *Manhood in the Making: Cultural Concepts of Masculinity*, New Haven, CT: Yale University Press.

Gray, J. (1998) *False Dawn: The Delusion of Global Capitalism*, London: Granta Books.

Gutmann, M. (1996) *The Meaning of Macho: Being a Man in Mexico City*, Los Angeles: University of California Press.

Harder, M. and K. Pringle (eds) (1997) *Protecting Children in Europe: Towards a New Millennium*, Aalborg: Aalborg University Press.

Harris, J. and C. McDonald (2000) 'Post-Fordism, the Welfare State and the Personal Social Services: a Comparison of Australia and Britain', *British Journal of Social Work*, Vol. 30: 51–70.

Hearn, J. (1992) *Men in the Public Eye*, London: Routledge.

— (1996a) 'Deconstructing the Dominant: Making the One(s) the Other(s)', *Organization*, Vol. 3, No. 4: 611–26.

— (1996b) 'Is Masculinity Dead? A Critique of the Concept of Masculinity/masculinities', in M. Mac an Ghaill (ed.), *Understanding Masculinities*

— (1998) *The Violences of Men*, London: Sage.

Herdt, G. (1982) *Rituals of Manhood: Male Initiation in Papua New Guinea*, Berkeley, CA: University of California Press.

Herzfeld, M. (1985) *The Poetics of Manhood: Contest and Identity in a Cretan Mountain Village*, Princeton, NJ: Princeton University Press.

Hirst, P. and G. Thompson (1999) *Globalization in Question: The Myths of the International Economy and the Possibilities of Governance* (2nd edn), Cambridge: Polity Press.

Karim, W. (ed.) (1995) *'Male' and 'Female' in Developing Southeast Asia*, Oxford: Berg.

Kimmel, M. (1996) *Manhood in America: A Cultural History*, New York: Free Press.

— (ed.) (1987) *Changing Men: New Directions in Research on Men and Masculinity*, Newbury Park, CA: Sage.

Kofman, E. and G. Youngs (eds) (1996) *Globalization: Theory and Practice*, London: Frances Pinter.

Kvist, J. (1999) 'Welfare Reform in the Nordic Countries in the 1990s: Using Fuzzy-set Theory to Assess Conformity to Ideal Types', *Journal of European Social Policy*, Vol. 9, No. 3: 231–52.

Leira, A. (1992) *Welfare States and Working Mothers: The Scandinavian Experience*, Cambridge: Cambridge University Press.

Lewis, J. and I. Ostner (1991) 'Gender and the Evolution of European Social Policies', paper presented at CES Workshop on 'Emergent Supranational Social Policy: The EC's Social Dimension in Comparative Perspective'. Center for European Studies: Harvard University.

Mac an Ghaill, M. (ed.) (1996) *Understanding Masculinities*, Milton Keynes: Open University Press.

Messner, M. (1997) *Politics of Masculinities: Men in Movements*, Thousand Oaks, CA: Sage.

Mies, M. (1986) *Patriarchy and Accumulation on a World Scale: Women in the International Division of Labour*, London: Zed Books.

Moghaddam, F. and C. Studer (1997) 'Cross-cultural Psychology: The Frustrated Gadfly's Promises, Potentialities and Failures', in D. Fox and I. Prilleltensky (eds), *Critical Psychology: An Introduction*, Thousand Oaks, CA: Sage.

Moser, C. (1993) *Gender Planning and Development: Theory, Practice and Training*, London: Routledge.

O'Connor, J. S. (1993) 'Gender, Class and Citizenship in the Comparative Analysis of Welfare State Regimes: Theoretical and Methodological Issues', *British Journal of Sociology*, Vol. 44, No. 3: 501–18.

Ong, A. and M. Peletz (eds) (1995) *Bewitching Women, Pious Men: Gender and Body Politics in South East Asia*, Berkeley, CA: University of California Press.

Orloff, A. S. (1993) 'Gender and the Social Rights of Citizenship: State Policies and Gender Relations in Comparative Research', *American Sociological Review*, Vol. 58, No. 3: 303–28.

Pease, B. (1997a) *Men and Sexual Politics: Towards a Pro-feminist Practice*, Adelaide: Dulwich Publications.

— (1997b) 'The Sexual Politics of Men's Health', paper presented at the Second National Men's Health Conference, Fremantle, 29–31 October 1997.

— (2000) *Recreating Men: Postmodern Masculinity Politics*, London: Sage.

Peterson, V. and A. Runyan (1993) *Global Gender Issues*, Boulder, CO: Westview Press.

Pettman, J. (1996) *Worlding Women: A Femininist International Politics*, Sydney: Allen and Unwin.

Popay, J., J. Hearn and J. Edwards (eds) (1998) *Men, Gender Divisions and Welfare*, London: Routledge.

Pringle, K. (1995) *Men, Masculinities and Social Welfare*, London: UCL Press.

— (1998a) *Children and Social Welfare in Europe*, Milton Keynes: Open University Press.

— (1998b) 'Pro-feminist Debates on Men's Practices and Social Welfare', *British Journal of Social Work*, Vol. 28: 623–33.

Pringle, K. and M. Harder (1999) *Through Two Pairs of Eyes: A Comparative Study of Danish Social Policy and Child Welfare Practices*, Aalborg, Aalborg University Press.

Pringle, K., J. Hearn, U. Mueller and E. Oleksy (1998) Application to European Commission Research Directorate Framework 5 Thematic Network entitled 'The Social Problem and Societal Problematization of Men and Masculinities', unpublished.

Rai, S., H. Pilkington and A. Phizacklea (eds) (1992) *Women in the Face of Change: The Soviet Union, Eastern Europe and China*, London: Routledge.

Sainsbury, D. (ed.) (1994) *Gendering Welfare States*, London: Sage.

Segal, L. (1990) *Slow Motion: Changing Masculinities, Changing Men*, London: Virago.

Silberschmidt, M. (1991) *Rethinking Men and Gender Relations: An Investigation of Men, Their Changing Gender Roles within the Household and the Implications for Gender Relations in Kisii District, Kenya*, Copenhagen: Centre for Development Research.

Steans, J. (1998) *Gender and International Relations: An Introduction*, Cambridge: Polity Press.

Sweetman, C. (1997) 'Editorial', *Gender and Development*, Vol. 5, No. 2: 2–7.

Trevillion, S. (1999) 'On Being a Social Worker: Globalization and the New Subjectivities', in P. Chamberlayne, A. Cooper, R. Freeman and M. Rustin (eds), *Welfare and Culture in Europe: Towards a New Paradigm in Social Policy*, London: Jessica Kingsley.

Trifiletti, R. (1999) 'Southern European Welfare Regimes and the Worsening Position of Women', *Journal of European Social Policy*, Vol. 9, No. 1: 49–64.

UNDP (United Nations Development Program) (1995) *Human Development Report 1995*, New York: Oxford University Press.

White, S. (1994) 'Making Men an Issue: Gender Planning for the "Other Half"', in M. Macdonald (ed.), *Gender Planning in Development Agencies*, London: Oxfam.

— (1997) 'Men, Masculinities and the Politics of Development', *Gender and Development*, Vol. 5, No. 2: 14–22.

Part I

Transnational Contexts

Global Masculinities: Restoration and Resistance

Michael S. Kimmel

It has become almost axiomatic that gender is inextricably implicated in the development process. 'Human development, if not engendered, is endangered' was a central message of the 1995 Human Development Report.

The pioneering efforts of feminist scholars over the past three decades have established that development is an uneven process, not only within and between nations, but between the sexes. Women and men are differently situated culturally and economically, with unequal access to material and cultural resources, different and unequal relationships to the provision and consumption of material goods, and different and unequal access to the political process that guides economic development. Thus we read, for example, of the global 'feminization of poverty', that women represent approximately 70 per cent of the 1.3 billion poor people in the world (Beneria and Bisnath 1996: 6). We examine the impact of women's fertility and marital status on their access to economic and political power, the ways in which women's unpaid domestic labour remains statistically invisible in efforts to reduce or eradicate poverty.

It is still the case that when we think or read about gender, we think and read about women. In part, of course, this is as it should be. It was women scholars and policy-makers who first brought gender to our attention, through the hidden costs and statistical invisibility of women's participation. It was women who made gender visible as a category of analysis, as a variable that must be factored into any discussion of development. Today, although we understand that development is a gendered process, the impact of development on men remains relatively less well understood.

This 'invisibility' of masculinity in discussions of development has political dimensions. The processes that confer privilege on one group and not another group are often invisible to those upon whom that privilege is conferred. Thus, not having to think about race is one of the luxuries of being white, just as not having to think about gender is one of the 'patriarchal dividends' of gender inequality.

The invisibility of masculinity reproduces gender inequality, both materially and ideologically. Thus any initiative to improve the condition of women must include efforts to involve men. In fact, I believe that any effort to further gender equality that does not include men is doomed to failure. Of course, most initiatives towards gender equality must and will continue to focus on women's empowerment. But achieving the vision of gender equality is not possible without changes in men's lives as well as in women's.

If our first task is to make masculinity visible in the development process, this necessitates that we recognize the ways in which definitions of masculinity vary. The various social and behavioural sciences have elaborated the differing meanings of masculinity over time (history), across cultures (anthropology), over the course of a man's life (developmental psychology), and within any one culture among different social groups (sociology). Masculinity, in this view, is not a constant, universal essence, but rather an ever-changing fluid assemblage of meanings and behaviours that vary dramatically. Thus we speak of *masculinities*, in recognition of the different definitions of manhood that we construct. By pluralizing the term, we acknowledge that masculinity means different things to different groups of men at different times.

Speaking specifically about the American case, for example, we understand that within any one society at any one moment, there are multiple meanings of manhood. Simply put, not all American men are the same. Our experiences depend on class, race, ethnicity, age, region of the country. Each of these axes modifies the others. For example, what it means to be an older, black, gay man in Cleveland is different from what it means to a young, white, heterosexual farm boy in Iowa.

However, to pluralize the term does not mean that all masculinities are equal. Typically, each nation constructs a model of masculinity against which each man measures himself. This hegemonic image of manhood is constructed often through articulation of differences with a variety of 'others' – racial or sexual minorities and, of course, women. The hegemonic definition of masculinity is 'constructed in relation to various subordinated masculinities as well as in relation to women', writes sociologist R. W. Connell (1987: 183). As the sociologist Erving Goffman once wrote:

> In an important sense there is only one complete unblushing male in America: a young, married, white, urban, northern, heterosexual, Protestant, father, of college education, fully employed, of good complexion, weight, and height, and a recent record in sports ... Any male who fails to qualify in any one of these ways is likely to view himself – during moments at least – as unworthy, incomplete, and inferior. (Goffman 1963: 128)

In each society, then, there are multiple definitions of masculinity, some more valorized than others. In all cases, masculinities are constructed in relation to femininities and express the multiple ways in which gender identity is articulated through a gender *order*, in which gender is not only a property of individuals but a process of institutions and a dynamic of power relations between groups. That is, the gender order expresses men's power over women (male domination) and the power of some men over other men (by race, sexuality, ethnicity, age, able-bodiedness).

Masculinities and Power

Any discussion of gender necessitates such a discussion of power. Men's power over women is expressed in two arenas:

Public patriarchy refers to the institutional arrangements of a society, the predominance of males in all power positions within the economy and polity, both locally and nationally, as well as the 'gendering' of those institutions themselves (by which the criteria for promotion, for example, appear to be gender-neutral, but actually reproduce the gender order)

Domestic patriarchy refers to the emotional and familial arrangements in a society, the ways in which men's power in the public arena is reproduced at the level of private life. This includes male–female relationships as well as family life, child socialization and the like.

Both public patriarchy and domestic patriarchy are held together by the threat, implicit or explicit, of violence. Public patriarchy, of course, includes the military and police apparatus of society, which are also explicitly gendered institutions (revealed in their increased opposition to women's entry). Rape and domestic violence sustain domestic patriarchy.

These two expressions of men's power over women are neither uniform nor monolithic; they vary enormously, are constantly under flux. Equally, they are not coincidental, so that increases or decreases in one invariably produce increases or decreases in the other. Nor are they so directly linked that a decrease in one automatically produces an increase in the other, although there will be pressures in that direction. Thus women's entry into the workforce or increased representation in legislatures undermine public patriarchy and will likely produce both backlash efforts to reinforce domestic patriarchy (covenant marriage, tightening divorce laws to restrain women's exit from the home, increased domestic assault) or even a virulent resurgence of domestic patriarchy (the Taliban). At the same time, increased public presence will also undermine domestic patriarchy (shared parenting and housework).

The Global Context

Equally crucial for our understanding of the integration of masculinity into the study of development, however, is to recognize the ways in which globalization reconfigures and reshapes the arena in which these national and local masculinities are articulated, and transforms the shape of domestic and public patriarchies.

Globalization disrupts and reconfigures traditional, neo-colonial, or other national, regional or local economic, political and cultural arrangements. In so doing, globalization transforms local articulations of both domestic and public patriarchy. Thus, for example, globalization includes the gradual proletarianization of local peasantries, as market criteria replace subsistence and survival.

Local small craft producers, small farmers and independent peasants traditionally stake their notions of masculinity on ownership of land and economic autonomy in their work; these are increasingly transferred upwards in the class hierarchy and outwards to transnational corporations. Proletarianization also leads to massive labour migrations – typically migrations of *male* workers – who leave their homes and populate migrant enclaves, squatter camps, labour camps.

Globalization thus presents another level at which hegemonic and local masculinities are constructed. Globalization was always a gendered process. As Andre Gunder Frank (1968) pointed out several decades ago in his studies of economic development, development and underdevelopment are not simply stages through which all countries pass; there is no single continuum along which individual nations might be positioned. Rather, he argued, there is a relationship between development and underdevelopment; in fact, the development of some countries implies the specific and deliberate underdevelopment of others. The creation of the metropole was simultaneous and co-ordinated with the creation of the periphery.

As with economic development, so too with gender, with the historical constructions of the meanings of masculinity. As the hegemonic ideal was being created, it was created against a screen of 'others' whose masculinity was thus problematized and devalued. Hegemonic and subaltern emerged in mutual, but unequal, interaction in a gendered social and economic order.

Thus, for example, colonial administrations often problematized the masculinity of the colonized. In British India, Bengali men were perceived as weak and effeminate, though Pathas and Sikhs were perceived as hyper-masculine, as violent and uncontrolled (see Sinha 1995). Similar distinctions were made in South Africa between Hottentots and Zulus, and in North America between Navaho or Algonquin on the one hand, Sioux, Apache and Cheyenne on the other (see Connell 1998: 14). In many colonial situations, the colonized men were called 'boys' by the colonizers (see Shire 1994).

Today, although they appear to be gender-neutral, the institutional arrangements of global society are equally gendered. The marketplace, multinational corporations and transnational geo-political institutions (World Court, United Nations, European Union) and their attendant ideological principles (economic rationality, liberal individualism) express a gendered logic. The 'increasingly unregulated power of transnational corporations places strategic power in the hands of particular groups of men', while the language of globalization remains gender neutral so that 'the "individual" of neo liberal theory has in general the attributes and interests of a male entrepreneur' (Connell 1998: 15).

As a result, the impact of global economic and political restructuring is greater on women. At the national and global level, the world gender order privileges men in a variety of ways, such as unequal wages, unequal labour force participation, unequal structures of ownership and control of property, unequal control over one's body, as well as cultural and sexual privileges. What's more, in the economic South, for example, aid programmes disproportionately affect women, while in the metropole, the attack on the welfare state generally weakens the position of women, domestically and publicly. These effects, however, are less the result of bad policies or even less the results of bad – inept or evil – policy makers, and more the results of the gendered logic of these institutions and processes themselves (Enloe 1990; Connell 1998).

Hegemonic Masculinity and Its Discontents

In addition, the patterns of masculinity embedded within these gendered institutions are also rapidly becoming the dominant global hegemonic model of masculinity, against which all local, regional and national masculinities are played out and to which they increasingly refer. The emergent global hegemonic version of masculinity is readily identifiable: he sits in first-class waiting rooms or in elegant business hotels the world over, wearing a business suit by a famous international designer, speaking English, eating 'continental' cuisine, talking on his cellphone, his laptop computer plugged into any electrical outlet, while he watches CNN International on television. Temperamentally, he is increasingly cosmopolitan, with liberal tastes in consumption (and sexuality) and conservative political ideas of limited government control of the economy. This has the additional effect of increasing the power of the hegemonic countries within the global political and economic arena, since everyone, no matter where they are from, behaves in the same way.

These processes of globalization, and the emergence of a global hege-monic masculinity, have the ironic effect of increasingly 'gendering' local, regional and national resistance to incorporation into the global arena as subordinated entities. Scholars have pointed out the ways in which religious fundamentalism and ethnic nationalism use local cultural symbols to ex-press regional resistance to incorporation (see especially Juergensmeyer 1993; 2000; Barber 1992). However, these religious and ethnic expressions are often manifest as gender revolts, and include a virulent resurgence of domestic patriarchy (as in the militant misogyny of Iran or Afghanistan); the problematization of global masculinities or neighbouring masculinities (as in the former Yugoslavia); and the overt symbolic efforts to claim a distinct 'manhood' along religious or ethnic lines to which others do not have access and which will restore manhood to the formerly privileged (white militias and skinhead racists in Europe).

Thus gender becomes one of the chief organizing principles of local, regional and national resistance to globalization, whether expressed in religious or secular, ethnic or national terms. These processes involve flattening or eliminating local or regional distinctions, cultural homogeniza-tion as citizens and social heterogenization as new ethnic groups move to new countries in labour migration efforts. Movements thus tap racialist and nativist sentiments at the same time as they can tap local and regional protectionism and isolationism. They become gendered as oppositional movements also tap into a vague masculine resentment of economic dis-placement, loss of autonomy and collapse of domestic patriarchy that accompany further integration into the global economy. Efforts to reclaim economic autonomy, to reassert political control, and revive traditional domestic arrangements thus take on the veneer of restoring manhood.

To illustrate these themes, we could consider several political movements of men, in North America or elsewhere. Indeed, Promise Keepers, men's rights and fathers' rights groups all respond to the perceived erosion of public patriarchy with an attempted restoration of some version of domestic patriarchy. The mythopoetic men's movement responds instead to a per-ceived erosion of domestic patriarchy with assertions of separate mythic or natural space for men to experience their power – since they can no longer experience it in either the public or private spheres. (For more on the movements of men, see Kimmel 1996a; 1996b; and Messner 1998.)

Right-wing Militias: Racism, Sexism and Anti-Semitism as Masculine Reassertion

Far-right organizations in the United States have generated significant scrutiny, especially since the bombing of a federal office building in

Oklahoma City. In these groups, racism, nativism, anti-Semitism, hetero-sexism and sexism blend in a virulent and violent reassertion of the eroding privileges of middle-class, straight, white, Protestant, native-born men. Like other fringe groups on the far right, these rural-based small-town organizations – from the John Birch Society, Ku Klux Klan and the American Nazi Party, to Holocaust deniers, neo-Nazi or racist skinheads, White Power groups such as Posse Comitatus and White Aryan Resistance, and radical militias such as the Wisconsin Militia or the Militia of Montana – are almost entirely composed of white men, sons of former independent farmers or small-town shopkeepers and artisans. Buffeted by the global political and economic forces that have produced global hegemonic masculinities, they have responded to the erosion of public patriarchy (displacement in the political arena), and domestic patriarchy (their wives now work away from the farm) with a renewal of their sense of masculine entitlement to restore patriarchy in both arenas. Ideologically, what characterizes these scions of small-town rural America – both the fathers and the sons – is (1) their ideological vision of producerism, threatened by economic transformation; (2) their sense of small-town democratic community, an inclusive community that was based on the exclusion of broad segments of the population; and (3) a sense of entitlement to economic, social and political and even military power.

To cast the middle-class straight white man as the hegemonic holder of power in America would be fully to miss the daily experience of these straight white men. They believe themselves to be *entitled* to power – by a combination of historical legacy, religious fiat, biological destiny and moral legitimacy – but they believe they do not have power. That power has been both surrendered by white men (their fathers) and stolen from them by a federal government controlled and staffed by legions of the newly enfran-chised minorities, women and immigrants, all in service to the omnipotent Jews who control international economic and political life. 'Heaven help the God-fearing, law-abiding Caucasian middle class,' explained Charlton Heston to a recent Christian Coalition convention, especially,

> Protestant or even worse evangelical Christian, Midwest or Southern or even worse rural, apparently straight or even worse admittedly [heterosexual], gun-owning or even worse NRA card-carrying average working stiff, or even worst of all, male working stiff. Because not only don't you count, you're a downright obstacle to social progress. (quoted in *Freedom Watch* 1999)

Downwardly mobile rural white men – those who lost the family farms and those who expected to take them over – are squeezed between the omnivorous jaws of capital concentration and a federal bureaucracy which is at best indifferent to their plight and, at worst, facilitates their further demise. By framing state policies as emasculating and problematizing the masculinity of these various 'others', rural white militia members seek to restore their own masculinity. The entire rhetorical apparatus that serves this purpose is saturated with gendered readings of the problematized masculinity of the 'others', of the emasculating policies of the state, and of the rightful masculine entitlement of white men.

Each of these themes pivots on retrieving manhood. First, they believe the state has been captured by evil, even Satanic forces; environmental regulations, state policies dictated by urban and northern interests, the Internal Revenue Service, are the outcomes of a state now utterly controlled by feminists, environmentalists, blacks and Jews. They call it the 'Nanny State', and a constant barrage of jokes describe how 'President Clinton, and her husband Bill', have done something or other. One book sold by the Militia of Montana well illustrates these themes. In *Big Sister is Watching You: Hillary Clinton and the White House Feminists Who Now Control America – And Tell the President What to Do*, Texe Marrs argues that Hillary Clinton and her feminist co-conspirators control the country and are threatening Americans' rights and national sovereignty. Marrs describes 'Hillary's Hellcats' and 'Gore's Whores' – a 'motley collection [including] lesbians, sex perverts, child molester advocates, Christian haters, and the most doctrinaire of communists' (Marrs 1993: 11).

The state is now an engine of gender inversion, feminizing men, while feminism masculinizes women. Feminist women, it turns out, are more masculine than men are. Not only does this call the masculinity of white men into question, but it uses gender as the rhetorical vehicle for criticizing 'other' men. Typically, problematizing the masculinity of these others takes two forms simultaneously: other men are both 'too masculine' and 'not masculine enough'. We call this the 'Goldilocks Paradox', after the fairytale heroine who found chairs too big or too small, porridge too hot or too cold. So, too, the 'others' are seen as too masculine (violent rapacious beasts, with no self-control) or not masculine enough (weak, helpless, effete, incapable of supporting a family).

Thus, in the logic of militias and other white supremacist organizations, gay men are promiscuously carnal, sexually voracious and effete fops who do to men what men should only have done to them by women. Black men are both violent hyper-sexual beasts, possessed of an 'irresponsible sexuality', seeking white women to rape (*WAR* 1989: 11) and less than fully manly, 'weak, stupid, lazy' (N. S. Mobilizer cited in Ferber 1998: 81). What can a black man do but 'clumsily shuffle[s] off, scratching his wooley [sic] head, to search for shoebrush and mop' (in *New Order*, cited in Ferber 1998: 91).

Most interesting is the portrait of 'the Jew'. One the one hand, he is a greedy, cunning, conniving, omnivorous predator; on the other, he is small, beady-eyed and incapable of masculine virtue. By asserting the hyper-masculine power of the Jew, the far right can support capitalism as a system while decrying the actions of capitalists and their corporations. According to militia logic, it's not the capitalist corporations that have turned the government against them, but the international cartel of Jewish bankers and financiers, media moguls and intellectuals who have already taken over the US state and turned it into ZOG (Zionist Occupied Government). The US is called the 'Jewnited States' and Jews are blamed for orchestrating the demise of the once-proud Aryan man. In white supremacist ideology, the Jew is the archetype villain, both hyper-masculine – greedy, omnivorous, sexually predatory, capable of the destruction of the Aryan way of life – and hypo-masculine, small, effete, homosexual, pernicious, weaselly. In lieu of brawn power, Jewish men have harnessed their brain power in their quest for world domination. Jews are the masterminds behind the other social groups who are seen as dispossessing rural American men of their birthright. And, towards that end, they have co-opted blacks, women and gays and brainwashed cowardly white men to do their bidding.

Embedded in this anti-Semitic slander is a critique of white American manhood as soft, feminized, weakened – indeed, emasculated. Article after article decries 'the whimpering collapse of the blond male', as if white men have surrendered to the plot (in Ferber 1998: 127). Yet it is there that the far-right organizations simultaneously offer white men an analysis of their present situation and a political strategy for retrieving their manhood. As *National Vanguard* puts it:

> As Northern males have continued to become more wimpish, the result of the media-created image of the 'new male' – more pacifist, less authoritarian, more 'sensitive', less competitive, more androgynous, less possessive – the controlled media, the homosexual lobby and the feminist movement have cheered ... the number of effeminate males has increased greatly ... legions of sissies and weaklings, of flabby, limp-wristed, non-aggressive, non-phys-ical, indecisive, slack-jawed, fearful males who, while still heterosexual in theory and practice, have not even a vestige of the old macho spirit, so deprecated today, left in them. (cited in Ferber 1998: 136)

It is through the militias that American manhood can be restored and revived – a manhood in which individual white men control the fruits of their own labour. It is the militarized manhood of the heroic John Rambo; a manhood that celebrates the God-sanctioned right to band together in armed militias if anyone, or any governmental agency, tries to take it away from them. If the state and capital emasculate them, and if the masculinity of the 'others' is problematic, then only real white men can rescue this American Eden from a feminized, multicultural androgynous melting pot.

Bringing Men into Gender Equity Work: Counter-hegemonic Points of Entry

The far right uses a highly charged rhetoric of masculine reclamation and the restoration of public and domestic patriarchies as a recruiting tool among disaffected, downwardly mobile lower-middle-class white men in both small towns and rural areas across the United States. Masculinity becomes the rhetorical currency through which opposition to global integration, state centralization and increasing ethnic heterogeneity can be mobilized. In such cases, we expect to find ideas of traditional, local masculinities and their accompanying hierarchies reaffirmed. Typically, as Connell notes (1998: 17), 'hardline masculine fundamentalism goes together with a marked anti-internationalism'. It appears equally true that similar groups of men use similar approaches to mobilize their minions in Britain, France, Germany, Austria and other nations that have experienced a right-wing resurgence. Masculinity can become a currency of hegemonic reassertion, an ideology of entitlement to patriarchal privilege.

It can also become a rhetoric of resistance. Transitional moments often reveal openings, possibilities for change, and, most significantly, points of entry for men into the conversations about gender equality. While the specific content of such points of entry may differ in the North and South, we can readily identify several arenas for possible integration of men into the discussion of gender and development. All over the world, there is a growing number of organizations devoted to engaging men in gender-equity work. Organizations, NGOs and volunteer associations have sprung up to engage men in challenging public and domestic patriarchy and men's entitlement to power. Here, I can point to only a few of these organizations before highlighting one of the most successful pro-feminist men's efforts.

For example, in Chile, FLACSO co-ordinates a Network of Studies of Masculinity to help researchers and professionals utilize recent research on masculinity in their professional outreach. The Norwegian-based International Association for Studies of Men (IASOM) is a world-wide network of researchers and activists who are committed to using gender perspectives to promote gender equality. The European Pro-feminist Men's Network, organized by Daniel Welzer-Lang in Toulouse, France, brings together European pro-feminist men. In the United States, the National Organization for Men Against Sexism (NOMAS) is perhaps the most comprehensive pro-feminist men's organization in the world. NOMAS sponsors conferences and workshops, particularly on the connections between racism, sexism and homophobia in the construction of masculinity. Of particular importance are their workshops on violence intervention, where activists who run programmes for men who batter share resources and techniques.

Other efforts concern enquiries into the effects of masculine social-ization on both boys and girls and the transformation of the relationship between home and work occasioned by the overwhelming numbers of women entering the labour force since the end of the Second World War. Increased involvement by fathers has consistently positive effects on both boys' and girls' socialization. There is some evidence of increased domestic activity by men, although women continue to do most of the 'second shift' (Hochschild 1989). Yet the research is clear that the simple presence or absence of the father tells us little about his impact on child development. While 'a nurturing, supportive partner in economic, domestic and child care responsibilities has immeasurable positive effects on the physical, emotional and financial welfare of children', it is equally true that 'non-functioning or abusive men in families can cause tremendous hardship and suffering' (Foumbi and Lovich 1997: 21). In the United States, boys exhibited more empathy for others when their fathers had been actively engaged in child-care (Miedzian 1991)

In schools, attempts to empower girls include new programmes for the teaching of science and maths; strategies to prevent bullying and sexual harassment of girls are vital steps, as are efforts to pay attention to the ways in which male socialization steers boys away from intellectual pursuits, especially the arts and humanities (see Martino 1997; Mac an Ghaill 1997).

In addition, industrial countries have focused on the socialization effects of various mass media and peer groups as agents of socialization for boys. Media images often reinforce traditional stereotypes of masculinity and discredit and undermine images that might promote change. Peer emphasis on acting masculine, adopting a 'tough guise' (Katz and Jhally 1999), puts enormous pressure on young boys to exaggerate traditional masculine stereotypes of strength, false control and risk-taking. Living up to the 'boy code' (Pollack 1997) places boys in a peer-dominated 'culture of cruelty' (Kindlon and Thompson 1998) in which perceived deviation from norms of hyper-masculinity is severely punished. In fact, the pressure on boys to act 'masculine' is significantly greater than it is for girls to act 'feminine', at least in the Anglophone industrial world, where it is, today, far easier these days to be a 'tomboy' than it is to be a 'sissy'.

In the field of health, there is another point of entry for men into counter-hegemonic political arenas. Women and men have different rates of different diseases, seek medical care differently and in differing amounts, and are unequally affected by global health intervention strategies. One of the major obstacles to women's improved health-care is the same obstacle that inhibits men's adequate use of available health-care systems: traditional ideologies of masculinity. Women who seek to improve access to health-care, to avail themselves of existing methods of contraception or to practise safer sex often run 'into a wall of un-cooperation from men' (Meursing and Sibindi 1995). Yet those same ideologies that inhibit women also reduce men's utilization of health-care systems, and discourage safety as part of a sexual repertoire. Health researcher William Courtenay writes that:

> A man who does gender correctly would be relatively unconcerned about his health and well-being in general. He would see himself as stronger, both physically and emotionally, than most women. He would think of himself as independent, not needing to be nurtured by others. He would be unlikely to ask others for help... He would face danger fearlessly, take risks frequently, and have little concern for his own safety. (Courtenay 2000: 21)

Or, as one Zimbabwean man put it, 'real men don't get sick' (cited in Foreman 1999: 22).

This is particularly true in efforts to stop the spread of HIV infection around the world. 'The HIV epidemic is driven by men', commented Calle Almedal, a senior official with the Joint United Nations AIDS Programme (UNAIDS) (cited in Foreman 1999: viii). Of the estimated 30 million people infected with HIV, about 17 million are men (Foreman 1999: 172).

Attempts to integrate men into the international efforts directed towards improving health-care will differ in the economic North and South. For example, HIV risk-reduction efforts must confront very different issues of masculinity. In both cases, the association of masculinity with risk-taking and irresponsibility have been confronted, but with very different intentions. In the North, where well over 85 per cent of all HIV-infected people are men, few public health discussions include reference to the fact that HIV is the most 'gendered' disease in the history of Europe and North America. (Unlike a 'sex-linked' disease that could attack only one biological sex or the other [as does, for example, haemophilia or prostate cancer], a gendered disease is one that could, in principle, affect both women and men equally, but affects one gender disproportionately.) In the North, then, efforts to reduce HIV infection must confront the association of masculinity with risk-taking by encouraging needle exchange programmes (not sharing hypodermic needles) and promoting safe-sex health education campaigns (since men associate unsafe sex with masculine prowess). Thus, for example, in western Europe, Canada and the United States, gay men's organizations have expressly designed safe-sex promotional campaigns and clubs that keep safe sex 'sexy', i.e. allow it to retain the demonstration of masculinity through sexual behaviour (see, for example, Kimmel and Levine 1993).

In the economic South, the rates of HIV infections are on a relative par, or cases among women actually outnumber those among men (Africa, Asia, Latin America). This gender imbalance towards women actually reflects more accurately the epidemiology of the disease in heterosexual non-IV drug-using populations, where women are at greater risk from HIV than are men through unprotected heterosexual intercourse. In sub-Saharan Africa, 60 to 80 per cent of women infected with HIV have had only one sexual partner (Adler et al. 1996), so efforts to decrease promiscuity among females would be wasted.

Here, HIV risk-reduction also requires men to take responsibility for birth control by wearing condoms, when in many cultures ignoring the health risks to one's partner or eschewing birth control and fathering many children are signs of masculine control and power. In Thailand, for example, condoms are seen as appropriate only for casual sex, but not in the context of a relationship (Cash and Anasuchatkul 1993). In Senegal, men may suspect that a woman is a sex-worker or has other lovers if she requests condom use (Niang et al. 1997). In this way, the spread of HIV among women in the South may also be an indirect consequence of masculine resistance – reassertion of domestic patriarchy – to global or national integration.

Efforts to reduce the risk of HIV also run into culturally sanctioned homophobia. In the economic North, where rates of infection are highest among men who have sex with men, homophobia remains a major obstacle to acknowledging potential risks. In some countries, where cultural pre-scriptions against homosexuality are strongest, men who have sex with men remain frightened into secrecy, and rarely are able to seek treatment. In Kenya, for example, officially sanctioned homophobia – the current president, Daniel arap Moi, claimed that 'Kenya has no room or time for homosexuals and lesbians' – has resulted in a very high rate of infection (about 1.2 million) among men who have sex with men as well as among women (see Foreman 1999: 123).

Though intervention strategies in both North and South confront the masculine equation of risk-taking and masculinity, the consequences are different for women and for men. Yet in both cases, masculinity remains the chief risk factor for the spread of this 'gendered' disease, and it is imperative to bring masculinity into the public health discussion about HIV.

Finally, increasing attention is being paid to the association of mascu-linity with violence. In the United States, men and boys are responsible for 95 per cent of all violent crimes. Every day twelve boys and young men commit suicide – seven times the number of girls. Every day eighteen boys and young men die from homicide – ten times the number of girls. From an early age, boys learn that violence is not only an acceptable form of conflict resolution, but one that is admired. Four times more teenage boys than teenage girls think fighting is appropriate when someone cuts into the front of a line. Half of all teenage boys get into a physical fight each year. Cultural acceptance for male violence is widespread. Researchers from the Pan American Health Organization (PAHO) note that '[n]ot only are boys allowed to be openly aggressive and fight with their fists, but this type of behavior is expected of them' (Foreman 1999: 53).

The threat of violence affects all women and provides one of the most serious obstacles to the achievement of women's equality. Violence against women takes a variety of forms, from cultural prescriptions that promote or demand female genital mutilation to rape, spousal assault, sexual harassment in the workplace and in the public sphere more generally.

To diminish men's violence against women, and to reduce the violent confrontations that take place in the name of such mythic entities as nation, people, religion or tribe, we must confront the separation of symbolic and structural spheres. Women's involvement in public life is equally important as men's involvement as parents. And the definition of masculinity must be able to acknowledge a far wider range of emotions, including fear, without having that identity as a man threatened. And we must develop mechanisms to dislodge men's sense of identity from that false sense of entitlement.

In the economic North, pro-feminist men's organizations work alongside women's shelters to confront men's violence. Over 100 men's groups in the United States – including Men Overcoming Violence (MOVE) in San Francisco, St Louis's Rape and Violence End Now (RAVEN), the Massachusetts-based Men's Resource Center, upstate New York's Volunteer Counselling Service, and Boston's EMERGE – actively work to end men's violence against women. Such groups typically conduct batterers' groups, composed of convicted batterers who choose an alternative to incarceration. Many of these groups are affiliated with NOMAS, which conducts annual workshops for men involved in batterers' intervention programmes. In Australia, Men Against Sexual Assault (MASA) is a network of community groups concerned about violence.

Perhaps the most successful intervention programme world-wide is the White Ribbon Campaign. Founded in Canada in 1991 as a specific response by men to the murder of fourteen women in Montreal, the WRC invites men to wear white ribbons for one week symbolizing their opposition to men's violence against women, and to develop local responses to support battered women and to challenge men's violence.

Conclusion

More than two decades ago, Norwegian social anthropologist Signe Howell and Roy Willis (1980) found that the definition of masculinity had a significant impact on the status of women, and especially on levels of violence against both women and other men. In those societies in which men were permitted to acknowledge fear, levels of violence were low. In those societies in which masculine bravado and the repression and denial of fear were defining features of masculinity, however, violence was likely to be high.

The value of such anthropological comparisons is that they provide evidence that it need not be this way, that it can be otherwise. They give empirical solidity to our hopes, a non-utopian concreteness to our vision. Achieving this vision, however, will require a dramatic transformation, in the ideal definition of what it means to be a man, and in the cultural prescriptions that govern the relationships among men and between women and men. Taken together, the projects we have described provide various points of entry to engage men in personal and political discussions about gender and development, and particularly to engage men as women's allies in their struggle for equality.

Note

Much of this chapter was first delivered as the keynote lecture at the conference 'The Challenge of Difference: Articulating Gender, Race, Class', in Salvador, Bahia, Brazil, 8 April 2000. Support for its presentation was generously provided by the Ford Foundation. I am grateful to Cecilia McCallum for the invitation, and to my friends Javier Alatorre, Norma Fuller, Matt Gutmann, Ondina Fachel Leal, Teresa Valdes and Mara Viveros.

Much of the section 'Right-wing Militias' is based on collaborative work with Abby Ferber and portions appear in Kimmel and Ferber (forthcoming).

Much of the material in the section 'Bringing Men into Gender Equity Work' was developed collaboratively with James Lang, and a dramatically different version appears as part of Greig et al. (2000). Much of the material about the White Ribbon Campaign is courtesy of Michael Kaufman.

References

Adler, M., S. Forster, J. Richens and H. Slavin (1996) 'Sexual Health and Care: Sexually Transmitted Infection: Guidelines for Prevention and Treatment', *Health and Population Occasional Paper*, London: Overseas Development Administration.

Barber, B. (1992) *MacDonalds and Jihad*, New York: Simon and Schuster.

Beneke, T. (1982) *Men on Rape*, New York: St Martin's Press.

Beneria, L. and S. Bisnath (1996) *Gender and Poverty: An Analysis for Action*, Gender in Development Monograph series, No. 2, New York: UNDP.

Cash, K. and B. Anasuchatkul (1993) 'Experimental Education Interventions for AIDS Prevention Among Northern Thai Single Migratory Female Factory Workers', *Women and AIDS Research Programme Report-in-Brief*, Washington, DC: International Center for Research on Women.

Connell, R. W. (1987) *Gender and Power*, Stanford, CA: Stanford University Press.

— (1998) 'Masculinities and Globalization', *Men and Masculinities*, Vol. 1, No. 1: 3–23.

Courtenay, W. H. (2000) 'Engendering Health: A Social Constructionist Examination of Men's Health Beliefs and Behaviours', *Psychology of Men and Masculinity*, Vol. 1, No. 1: 4–15.

Enloe, C. (1990) *Bananas, Beaches and Bases: Making Feminist Sense of International Politics*, Berkeley, CA: University of California Press.

Ferber, A. L. (1998) *White Man Falling: Race, Gender and White Supremacy*, Lanham, MD: Rowman and Littlefield.

Foreman, M. (1999) *AIDS and Men: Taking Risks or Taking Responsibility*, London: Zed Books.

Foumbi, J. and R. Lovich (1997) 'The Role of Men in the Lives of Children', New York: UNICEF.

Frank, A. G. (1968) *The Development of Underdevelopment*, New York: Monthly Review Press.

Freedom Watch (3) (1999), Colorado Springs, CO: Citizen's Project.

Goffman, E. (1963) *Stigma*, Englewood Cliffs, NJ: Prentice-Hall.

Greig, A., M. Kimmel and J. Lang (2000) *Men, Masculinities and Development: Broadening Our Work Towards Gender Equality*. Gender in Development Monograph series, No. 10, New York: UNDP.

Hochschild, A. (1989) *The Second Shift*, New York: Viking.

Howell, D. and R.Willis (eds) (1980) *Societies at Peace*, New York: Routledge.

Juergensmeyer, M. (1993) *The New Cold War? Religious Nationalism Confronts the Secular State*, Berkeley, CA: University of California Press.

— (2000) *Terror in the Mind of God: The Global Rise of Religious Violence*, Berkeley, CA: University of California Press.

Katz, J. and S. Jhally (1999) *Tough Guise*, video, available from Media Education Foundation, Amherst, MA; www.mediaed.org

Kimmel, M. (1996a) *Manhood in America: A Cultural History*, New York: Free Press.

— (ed.) (1996b) *The Politics of Manhood*, Philadelphia: Temple University Press.

Kimmel, M. and A. Ferber (forthcoming) '"White Men are This Nation": Right-wing Militias and the Restoration of Rural American Masculinity', *Rural Sociology*.

Kimmel, M. and M. Levine (1993) 'Men and AIDS', *Los Angeles Times*, 2 April.

Kindlon, D. and M. Thompson (1998) *Raising Cain*, New York: Random House.

Mac an Ghaill, M. (1994) *The Making of Men: Masculinities, Sexualities and Schooling*, London: Routledge.

Marrs, T. (1993) *Big Sister is Watching You: Hillary Clinton and the White House Feminists Who Now Control America – And Tell the President What To Do*, Austin, TX: Living Truth Publishers.

Martino, W. (1997) 'Gendered Learning Practices: Exploring the Costs of Hegemonic Masculinity for Girls and Boys in Schools', in *Gender Equity: A Framework for Australian Schools*, Canberra.

Messner, M. (1998) *Politics of Masculinities: Men in Movements*, Thousand Oaks, CA: Sage.

Meursing, K. and S. Sibindi (1995) 'Condoms, Family Planning and Living with HIV in Zimbabwe', *Reproductive Health Matters*, Vol. 5.

Miedzian, M. (1991) *Boys Will be Boys: Breaking the Link Between Masculinity and Violence*, New York: Doubleday.

Niang, C., H. Benga and A. Camara (1997) 'An evaluation of HIV Prevention Interventions Utilizing Traditional Women's Associations in Senegal', *Woman and AIDS Research Programme Report-in-Brief*, Washington, DC: International Center for Research on Women.

Pollack, W. (1997) *Real Boys*, New York: Henry Holt.

Shire, C. (1994) 'Men Don't Go to the Moon: Language, Space and Masculinities in Zimbabwe', in A. Cornwall and N. Lindisfarne (eds), *Dislocating Masculinity: Comparative Ethnographies*, New York: Routledge.

Sinha, M. (1995) *Colonial Masculinity: The Manly Englishman and the Effeminate Bengali in the Late Nineteenth Century*, Manchester: Manchester University Press.

WAR (1989), Vol. 8, No. 2, White Aryan Resistance.

The White Ribbon Campaign: Involving Men and Boys in Ending Global Violence Against Women

Michael Kaufman

The large hall and surrounding rooms were crowded with men from small villages and communities from across Namibia. Many wore a black T-shirt emblazoned with a white ribbon. They were clustered into discussion groups, developing action plans for their return home the next day. The question to them was simple: what can you do, together, to end wife assault and sexual violence in your community? Not grand schemes. Simply, what can you do next week and in the weeks ahead?

The discussion took place at the end of an extraordinary three-day conference that gathered men – farmers, teachers, ministers, community leaders, students, trades-people – from all across this southern African nation of 1.7 million people. As in most countries in the world, violence against women is pandemic. As in most countries, the response to the violence remains inadequate; as in many, concern about, and action to end, the violence is largely that of women.

The need to address men, to challenge them to end the violence, should be apparent. After all, it is men, or at least some men, who are committing the violence, and meanwhile the vast majority of men have remained silent about it. Through this silence, men – as the half of humanity who have controlled social discourse, law-making, religious ideas, the police and courts, and so forth – have allowed the violence to continue.

Although the need for public education campaigns that challenge men to stop the violence seems unarguable, in most parts of the world, efforts of this sort have been infrequent or non-existent.

Public education is critical for tearing away the shroud of silence that has allowed law-makers, health-care professionals, police and judges to disregard the problem. It is essential to shift the discourse on the violence from one that speaks of the private nature of the violence to one that casts it as a public crime in the same way that a 'private' robbery is more than a private affair between the robber and the owner of a store.

Public education is critical if men are to question their own attitudes and behaviour that might be part of a continuum of violence. It is critical if men are to challenge the men around them. However, I'd like to suggest that there are two prerequisites if we are going to address men and boys effectively and successfully on this issue: (1) we must actually involve them in the work to end the violence; and (2) we must do so – without playing down the extent of the problem or the importance of personal responsibility – based not on a vague sense of collective guilt or litanies about those other men who presumably are not as pure or good as us but rather on the basis of love and an appeal to goodness in men. It must be done on the basis of respect for men, even if there is absolutely no respect for the behaviour and attitude of some of those very same men. This latter point is not the focus of this article, but is the note I will end on.

In this chapter I first sketch out an analysis of the complexities of men's violence against women, an analysis that forms the basis for the strategies I am suggesting. Flowing from this analysis, I discuss why men's involvement is critical to addressing boys and men successfully on these issues. Third, I discuss the White Ribbon Campaign, a growing international effort to address and involve boys and men in ending violence against women.

The Complex Puzzle of Men's Violence

An understanding of the complex nature and causes of men's violence must form the basis of any strategic approach. Without such an understanding, we will be left with exhortations from well-meaning men or women that have little or no social or individual impact. (Indeed, I would suggest that the often-discussed high-recidivism rate of North American men who have gone through treatment programmes for violence against women is the result of an incomplete analysis of the problem.)

Let me reprise my analysis of this violence, drawing on my framework of 'the seven Ps of men's violence' (Kaufman 1999).

Patriarchal power: the first 'P' Individual acts of violence by men occur within what I have described as 'the triad of men's violence'. Men's violence against women does not occur in isolation but is linked to men's violence against other men and to the internalization of violence, that is, a man's violence against himself (Kaufman 1985).

Indeed, male-dominated societies are not only based on a hierarchy of men over women but some men over other men. Violence or the threat of violence among men is a mechanism used from childhood to establish that pecking order. One result of this is that men 'internalize' violence or perhaps, the demands of patriarchal society encourage biological instincts that otherwise might be relatively dormant or more benign.

This triad of men's violence – each form of violence helping create the others – occurs within a nurturing environment of violence: the organization and demands of patriarchal or male-dominant societies.

What gives violence its hold as a way of doing business, what has naturalized it as the *de facto* standard of human relations, is the way it has been articulated into our ideologies and social structures. Simply put, human groups create self-perpetuating forms of social organization and ideologies that explain, give meaning to, justify and replenish these created realities.

Violence is also built into these ideologies and structures for the simpler reason that it has brought enormous benefits to particular groups. First and foremost, violence (or at least the threat of violence) has helped confer on men (as a group) a rich set of privileges and forms of power. If indeed the original forms of social hierarchy and power are those based on sex, then this long ago formed a template for all the structured forms of power and privilege enjoyed by others as a result of social class or skin colour, age, nationality, religion, sexual orientation or physical abilities. In such a context, violence or its threat becomes a means to ensure the continued reaping of privileges and exercise of power. It is both a result and a means to an end.

The sense of entitlement to privilege: the second 'P' The individual experience of a man who commits violence may not revolve round his conscious desire to maintain power. His conscious experience is not the key here. Rather, as feminist analysis has repeatedly pointed out, such violence is often the logical outcome of his sense of entitlement to certain privileges. If a man beats his wife for not having dinner on the table on time, it is not only to make sure that it doesn't happen again, but is an indication of his sense of entitlement to be waited on. Or, say a man sexually assaults a woman on a date, it is about his sense of entitlement to physical pleasure even if that pleasure is entirely one-sided. In other words, it is not only inequalities of power that lead to violence, but a conscious or more often unconscious sense of entitlement to privilege.

Permission: the third 'P' Whatever the complex social and psychological causes of men's violence, it would not continue if it did not receive explicit or tacit permission in social customs, legal codes, law enforcement and certain religious teachings. In many countries, laws against wife assault or sexual assault are lax or non-existent; in many others laws are barely enforced; in still others they are absurd, such as those countries where a charge of rape can be prosecuted only if there are three male witnesses and where the testimony of the woman is not taken into account.

Meanwhile, acts of men's violence and violent aggression (in this case, usually against other men) are celebrated in sport and cinema, in literature and warfare. Not only is violence permitted, it is glamorized and rewarded.

The paradox of men's power: the fourth 'P' It is my contention, however, that these first three points – the critical components of most feminist analyses of men's violence – while central, do not adequately explain the widespread nature of men's violence, nor the connections between men's violence against women and the many forms of violence among men. Here we need to draw on the paradoxes of men's power or what I have called 'men's contradictory experiences of power' (Kaufman 1993; 1994).

The very ways in which men have constructed their social and individual power is, paradoxically, a source of enormous fear, isolation and pain for men themselves. If power is constructed as a capacity to dominate and control, if the capacity to act in 'powerful' ways requires the construction of a personal suit of armour and a fearful distance from others, if the very world of power and privilege removes men from the world of child-rearing and nurturance, then we are creating men whose own experience of power is fraught with crippling problems.

This is particularly so because the internalized expectations of masculinity are themselves impossible to satisfy or attain. This may well be a problem inherent in patriarchy, but it seems particularly true in an era and in cultures where rigid gender boundaries are being challenged or where there is a fear of challenge and change. Whether it is physical or financial accomplishment, or the suppression of a range of human emotions and needs, the imperatives of manhood (as opposed to the simple certainties of biological maleness) seem to require constant vigilance and work, especially for younger men.

The personal insecurities conferred by a failure to make the masculine grade, or simply the threat of failure, is enough to propel many men, particularly when they are young, into a vortex of fear, isolation, anger, self-punishment, self-hatred and aggression.

Within such an emotional state, violence becomes a *compensatory mechanism*. It is a way of re-establishing the masculine equilibrium, of asserting to oneself and to others one's masculine credentials. This expression of violence usually includes a choice of a target who is physically weaker or more vulnerable. This may be a child or a woman, or it may be social groups, such as gay men, or a religious or social minority, or immigrants, who seem to pose an easy target for the insecurity and rage of individual men, especially since such groups often do not receive adequate protection under the law.

What permits violence to become an individual compensatory mechanism has been the widespread acceptance of violence as a means of solving differences and asserting power and control. What makes it possible are the power and privileges men have enjoyed, things encoded in beliefs, practices, social structures and the law.

The psychic armour of manhood: the fifth 'P' Men's violence is also the result of a character structure that is typically based on emotional distance from others. As I and many others have suggested, the psychic structures of manhood are created in early child-rearing environments that are often typified by the absence of fathers and adult men – or, at least, by men's emotional distance. In this case, masculinity is codified by absence and constructed at the level of fantasy. But even in patriarchal cultures where fathers are more present, masculinity is codified as a rejection of the mother and femininity, that is, a rejection of the qualities associated with care-giving and nurturance. As various feminist pyschoanalysts have noted, this creates rigid ego barriers, or, in metaphorical terms, a strong suit of armour.

Dr Gabor Maté draws on new research on brain development:

> There is now a large body of evidence suggesting that the infant's emotional interactions with its primary caregivers provide the major influence on the physiological and biochemical development of the brain regions responsible for emotional and behavioural self-control. When infants and young children lack parenting which is emotionally nurturing and consistently available, given in a non-stressed atmosphere, research suggests that problems of self-regulation often result. The greater the deprivation, the less optimally the orbitofrontal cortex is likely to develop and function, which a July 2000 article in *Science* suggests might be a critical factor in developing a proclivity to acts of violence. (Maté 2000)

The result of this complex and particular process of psychological development is a dampened ability for empathy (to experience what others are feeling) and an inability to experience other people's needs and feelings as necessarily relating to one's own. Acts of violence against another person are, therefore, possible.

Masculinity as a psychic pressure cooker: the sixth 'P' Many of our dominant forms of masculinity hinge on the internalization of a range of emotions and their redirection into anger. It is not simply that men's language of emotions is often muted or that our emotional antennae and capacity for empathy are somewhat stunted. It is also that a range of natural emotions have been ruled off-limits and invalid. While this has a cultural specificity, it is rather typical for boys to learn from an early age to repress feelings of fear and pain. On the sports field we teach boys to ignore pain. At home we tell boys not to cry and act like men. Some cultures celebrate a stoic manhood. (And, I should stress, boys learn such things for survival; hence it is important we don't blame the individual boy or man for the origins of his current behaviours, even if, at the same time, we hold him responsible for his actions.)

Of course, as humans, we still experience events that cause an emotional response. But the usual mechanisms of emotional response, from actually experiencing an emotion to letting go of the feelings, are short-circuited to varying degrees among many men. But, again for many men, the one emotion that has some validation is anger. The result is that a range of emotions are channelled into anger. While such channelling is not unique to men (nor is it the case for all men), for some men, violent responses to fear, hurt, insecurity, pain, rejection or belittlement are not uncommon.

The seventh 'P': past experiences This all combines with more blatant experiences for some men. Far too many men around the world grew up in households where their mother was beaten by their father. They grew up seeing violent behaviour towards women as the norm, as just the way life is lived. For some men this results in a revulsion towards violence, while in others it produces a learned response. In many cases it is both: men who use violence against women often feel deep self-loathing.

The phrase 'learned response', though, is almost too simplistic. Studies have shown that boys and girls who grow up witnessing violence are far more likely to be violent themselves. Such violence may be a way of getting attention; it may be a coping mechanism, a way of externalizing impossible-to-cope-with feelings. Such patterns of behaviour continue beyond childhood: most men who end up in programmes for men who use violence either witnessed abuse against their mother or experienced abuse themselves.

The past experiences of many men also include the violence they themselves have experienced. In many cultures, while boys may be only half as likely as girls to experience sexual abuse, they are twice as likely to experience physical abuse. Again, this produces no one fixed outcome, and, again, such outcomes are not unique to boys. But in some cases these personal experiences instil deep patterns of confusion and frustration, boys learn that it is possible to hurt someone you love, and that only outbursts of rage can get rid of deeply-imbedded feelings of pain.

Finally, there is the issue of petty violence among boys that, as a boy, doesn't seem petty at all. Boys in many cultures grow up with experiences of fighting, bullying and brutalization. Sheer survival requires, for some, accepting and internalizing violence as a norm of behaviour.

Why Men's Involvement is Critical

How might such an analysis inform our strategies to end violence against women? We can see, of course, that we must collectively challenge men's social and individual power, men's sense of entitlement to privilege, and the social permission most societies have given to the violence. This requires the sort of legal, judicial, educational, political, cultural, behavioural and attitudinal changes that have been a part of feminist practice and social change over the past thirty years.

But the final four 'Ps' tell us that such an approach will, in a sense, 'rebound' off men's own experiences unless we find ways that link men's experiences with an understanding of the oppression of women.

One way of doing this is through the actual involvement of men and boys as a critical component of public education to end violence against women:

1. The challenge of ending violence against women is not simply a question of providing corrective information as we might, for example, when we educate people about the link between contaminated water and certain diseases. People in those situations – once equipped with information, encouragement and, of course, resources – can and will change their habits.

Violence against women occurs because of a complex and contradictory range of factors deeply imbedded in culture, economy, law and, most intractably, the psychic structures of masculinity. By and large, it is not the result of lack of information, although misinformation may in some cases fuel it.

If the ability to dominate is a display of manhood, only by involving males in a redefinition of manhood will we effectively challenge these patterns of domination and control.

2. Violence against women is not simply an activity easily amenable to behavioural modification. It is very different from, say, educating people about the terrible consequences of drunk driving. Such issues can be addressed largely through media campaigns and the provision of information. Ending the violence requires far more than drumming a message into men's heads.

3. Men must be involved because, more than anything else, men and boys will listen to other men and boys, far more than they will listen to the anger or pleas of women or to a disembodied media voice. This is

because masculinity is created in the eyes of men. In other words, if one's manhood is most critically assessed in a homosocial environment (Kimmel 1996; Burstyn 1999), then it is this environment that can most readily deconstruct and reshape the dominant discourse on masculinity. Simply put, men and boys tend to look to other men and boys for their models of manly activity.

This power of the male voice is part of the sexist reality (and part of our message to men is to listen to the voices of women). But if we are effectively to reach men and boys, then men and boys must be involved. This requires more than having a man's voice used in a radio ad. By involved, I mean the active participation of men and boys in anti-violence efforts, in defining and leading efforts to reach other men.

4. One reason for the effectiveness of such participation is that through participation, men and boys will feel a sense of 'ownership' in the problem. They will feel they have a personal relationship to the issue and a stake in the process of change. Such a feeling, in turn, will unleash greater energies and unlock new resources that can be used to end the violence.

In other words, involving men in this work is, paradoxically, the way to address the very real concern about scarce resources (that now go to women and girls and to women's programmes) being siphoned off by/to men and boys. Developing a sense of ownership means that men will develop a commitment to redirecting resources towards explicit gender issues as well as learning to address the gender dimensions of all issues.

What might such an effort – actually to address and involve men – look like? One approach is that of the White Ribbon Campaign.

The White Ribbon Campaign

In 1991 a handful of men in Canada took the first steps down a pathway whose future we did not know: we decided we had a responsibility to urge men to speak out against violence against women. We knew that most men in Canada were not violent towards women, but we also knew that the vast majority of us remained silent. Through our silence, we allowed the violence to continue.

We adopted a white ribbon as a symbol. Wearing the ribbon would neither be an act of contrition, nor a symbol of misplaced collective guilt; it did not indicate that the wearer was a great guy. Rather, wearing the ribbon was a personal pledge never to commit, condone or remain silent about violence against women. It would be a catalyst for discussion and soul-searching. It would be a public challenge to those many men who may use violence against a wife, girlfriend, family member or stranger. It would be a call on our policy makers, opinion leaders, police and courts to take seriously this national and international epidemic. And it would be an act of love for the women in our lives.

From the start, the primary goal of the WRC has been to encourage men to look at their own attitudes and behaviour and to learn to challenge other men to stop all forms of violence against women. We believe that as more men and boys take responsibility for challenging themselves and others, then the epidemic levels of violence against women will finally end.

In the past decade, we have moved beyond an idea organized from my living room, to active campaigns in schools and communities across Canada. We know of White Ribbon organizations or local White Ribbon campaigns or white ribbon distribution in Asia (India, Japan and Vietnam), Europe (Norway, Sweden, Finland, Denmark, Spain, Belgium, Germany and England), Africa (Namibia, Kenya, South Africa and Morocco), the Middle East (Israel), Latin America (Brazil), Australia and the United States. There may well be others.

The campaign is developing closer contacts with international organizations including ties with various bodies of the United Nations, in particular UNIFEM, with whom we are developing a formal partnership. (UNIFEM has proclaimed 25 November as the International Day for the Eradication of Violence Against Women.) We are working closely with women's organizations in a number of countries.

The central organizing idea of White Ribbon is this: just as the problem of violence against women is not confined to the margins of society, our efforts to reach men cannot be marginal. We know that we must find ways to involve the vast majority of men. This is in contrast to many previous efforts of pro-feminist men. Walking a narrow and cosy pathway can be nice; it is safe and you can be relatively assured that everyone around you agrees on all the important issues of the day. But there's room for only a few of you. White Ribbon wants to make room for hundreds of thousands, millions of men and boys. To do so, we have to find the highways where men travel.

This has a number of implications, in terms of how, when, where and with whom we work.

How White Ribbon functions Concretely, what does it mean to 'make room for millions of men'? For one thing, it means knowing that these men are going to disagree on many important issues of the day. Traditional progressive organizations have insisted (or at least assumed) that their members agree on virtually everything: that is, they must share a worldview. Instead, White Ribbon decided we needed agreement on one point: that men must work together and alongside women to end all forms of violence against women.

This has allowed us to pitch a tent that would bring together men from across the political, economic and social spectrums. To be active in White Ribbon, we do not have to agree on environmental or economic issues, we do not have to agree on which political parties to support, we do not have to agree on labour or poverty issues, and so forth. When some of us feel strongly that the policies of a given national or provincial government might well exacerbate violence against women – for example, cuts to unemployment benefits or lack of social housing – others in White Ribbon might disagree with us and support that government; we simply agree to disagree. Each of us finds ways outside White Ribbon to express views on other issues.

Where there is no confusion is on the core issues concerning men's violence against women: we are united against wife assault, against sexual assault, against sexual harassment, against men's controlling behaviour in relationships. We are united in support of increased funding for women's programmes, including women's shelters and rape crisis centres. We are united in support for equality and equity between the sexes. We are united in supporting men playing a greater role as nurturers and care-givers. All that is a lot to agree on and to work towards.

Such an approach not only gives us the potential to create unity among quite a range of men and boys working to end men's violence against women; it also allows men to redefine traditional ways of working together. By building unity, not only do we better address our issues, but men can find ways to work together in a co-operative and positive environment. Although we have our differences and occasional conflicts, we have managed to create an environment largely free of the nasty competition and back-biting that has typified most organizations dominated by men, including many of those that deem themselves as progressive or pro-feminist.

For me one symbol of this type of approach was the launching of the Swedish WRC in the autumn of 1998. On a public stage, a group of men stood side-by-side to put on white ribbons and to commit themselves to working to end violence against women. There was a former social democratic prime minister standing next to the head of a right-wing taxpayers coalition, there were corporate leaders and trade unionists and standing next to each other were the leaders of the Swedish Turkish Association and the Swedish Kurdish Association. Whatever their many areas of conflict, these men stood together, as a unitary voice of men speaking to, and challenging, their brothers.

Areas and type of work One area of focus for the WRC is in the school system. We do so to reach boys whose ideas about the other sex and about themselves as men are still forming. White Ribbon has produced a series of education kits for teenagers that are now used in over a thousand junior highs and high schools across Canada, representing one million students. Many more schools hold annual White Ribbon activities during which they do educational work and raise money for local women's programmes.

We also want to reach men where they work, and men and women where they shop. So a second and rapidly growing area of our work has been with corporations and trade unions. We have worked hard to develop these partnerships for several important reasons: most adult Canadians spend a good part of each day at work. A trade union or corporation can act as a transmission belt, bringing the ideas of White Ribbon to a large audience in offices and on the shop floor. The corporate partnerships also allow us to reach people as consumers.

The support of corporations and unions is also important because the WRC in Canada has chosen not to accept government funding (so as not to take money from women's programmes). We rely entirely on support from these groups, foundations and many concerned individuals.

We also work in that most nebulous of areas, the public arena. This has a number of components:

- We work with women's organizations to respond to current events, court decisions and government policy concerning violence against women. This work includes lobbying, public demonstrations, press conferences and letter-writing.
- Each year public relations firms donate resources to produce radio, television and print advertisements that the media broadcast or print for free.
- For several years we have produced a large poster with a headline 'These men want to end violence against women' followed by a hundred empty lines. The posters are displayed in schools, workplaces, places of worship, union halls and shops for men and boys to sign.
- One version of the poster (which is also produced as a magazine-sized advertisement) has signatures by a wide range of well-known Canadian men from the arts, sports, business, various ethnic communities, labour and so forth.
- We distribute press releases, hold occasional press conferences, write articles for newspapers on the issues of the day.
- We maintain a web page and distribute a newsletter to our members and supporters.
- We have a relationship with several programmes that work with men who use violence.

White Ribbon Week The focus and signature event of the WRC in

Canada is our annual White Ribbon Week – a slight misnomer as it now runs from 25 November (the International Day for the Eradication of Violence Against Women) until 6 December. The latter is the anniversary of what we in Canada call 'the Montreal Massacre', the day in 1989 when a man murdered fourteen women engineering students. That day was a catalyst not only for the White Ribbon Campaign, but for national soul-searching and action that continues to this day.

Around that time, our public service ads are broadcast on television and radio, and are printed in newspapers and magazines. We distribute white ribbons in schools, universities, places of worship, workplaces, on the street and in selected shops. Our posters are displayed in many locations for men and boys to sign.

Although White Ribbon Week is our signature event, our office and volunteers are busy year round responding daily to requests for information, ideas and resources; organizing other activities; responding to the issues of the day; organizing the fund-raising events that sustain the WRC and draw in new groups of men.

One newer area of work is on fatherhood issues, raising awareness and a sense of collective purpose in redefining fatherhood and manhood as embracing nurturing and care-giving. This, as we have seen in the analysis above, is part of the long-term solution to the problem of men's violence.

Supporting women's efforts and women's groups I have already mentioned several ways we work in support of women's groups. From the outset, White Ribbon has viewed women's organizations as the experts on these issues and looks towards them for leadership in the field. This does not mean that the WRC operates as a subcommittee of women's groups. Indeed, if our agenda is to address and involve men, we feel that we have a particular expertise and insights that may or may not be shared by women's organizations. As well, we know there is a diversity of views in the women's community and the approach of White Ribbon will not please everyone.

At the same time, we know that these organizations have far more knowledge of the dimensions of the problem, of legislative and judicial issues, of issues concerning programming. We know both our volunteers and staff have a tremendous amount to learn. In a similar vein, we believe in the importance of men listening to the voices of women. This, indeed, is the lead point on our flyer 'What Everyman Can Do to End Violence Against Women'.

As noted above, our joint efforts with women's groups include co-sponsoring vigils or rallies, appearing together at press conferences, exchanging policy ideas and lobbying in support of women's programmes.

We also see it as part of our mandate to carry out fund-raising for women's programmes. During our annual White Ribbon Week, we encourage local WRC efforts across the country to raise money not for the WRC but for local women's shelters, rape crisis centres and other programmes. This local fund-raising has both a financial and an educational aspect. The small amount boys and girls in a school raise for a women's shelter has little financial impact. However, students will identify with this service, girls learn about resources should they need them in the future, youth learn about them for a mother in need, and boys support an effort rather than feel pointed to as the problem.

At a national level, we have a formal partnership with the Canadian Women's Foundation and make a major contribution each year to support their grants to women's projects across Canada.

But Based on Love?

I would like to end with a suggestion which space does not allow me to explore, but which is part of the ongoing discussions of White Ribbon.

I believe that most versions of feminism are based on the possibility of men's participation in a radically different gender order, that is, on men's ability to change. This in turn presupposes some inherent goodness of males, or at least an inherent capacity to relate to women as equals and as leaders worthy of love and respect. Such an approach hinges on the distinction between males (as a biological entity) and men/masculinity as a gender order that is predicated on men's domination, on men's practices of domination, and on the whole contradictory experiences of that power.

What this (and the whole preceding analysis) suggests to me, is that the approach of efforts such as White Ribbon must be based on respect for males (while showing no respect for harmful behaviours or attitudes). It must be based on an appeal to goodness, not simply excoriating faults, crimes and problems. While the latter might make some of us feel superior, self-righteous or different from men who use violence, it will do little or nothing actually to reach those men who do use violence and draw them into a process of change. It also sets up a false dichotomy between those men who actively use violence and those of us who do not (but certainly engage in various dominating and negative practices, however subtle or accepted these might at times be).

The whole analysis of the seven 'Ps' suggests that it is the crippling process inherent in the development of 'normal' hegemonic forms of manhood that is at the root of the problem of men's violence (or, at least, activates biological potentials). Part of ending the violence is urging, pressuring and encouraging men to heal so that they will not continue to inflict their own pain on women, children and other men. I say all this not simply in a feel-good, 'let's all love each other' sense, but from the entirely practical viewpoint of how change might actually happen.

I believe this is true whether it applies to working with abusive men who use violence, or for general public education and awareness to reach men. It is this, a message of change that invites men into a dialogue with women to end the violence, to redefine relations between the sexes and, ultimately, to redefine what it means to be a man, that ultimately will play a role in ending the longest epidemic the people of our planet have known.

White Ribbon Campaign: www.whiteribbon.com
365 Bloor St East, Suite 201, Toronto, Canada M4W 3L4
tel: 1–416–920–6684
fax:1–416–920–1678
whiterib@idirect.com

References

Burstyn, V. (1999) *The Rites of Men: Manhood, Politics and the Culture of Sport*, Toronto: University of Toronto Press.

Kaufman, M. (1985) 'The Construction of Masculinity and the Triad of Men's Violence', in M. Kaufman (ed.), *Beyond Patriarchy: Essays by Men on Pleasure, Power and Change*, Toronto: Oxford University Press; Reprinted in Laura L. O'Toole and Jessica R. Schiffman (eds) (1997) *Gender Violence*, New York: New York University Press.

— (1993) *Cracking the Armour: Power, Pain and the Lives of Men*, Toronto: Viking Canada.

— (1994) 'Men, Feminism, and Men's Contradictory Experiences of Power', in H. Brod and M. Kaufman (eds.), *Theorizing Masculinities*, Thousand Oaks, CA: Sage.

— (1999) 'The seven Ps of men's violence': www.michaelkaufman.com

Kimmel, M. (1996) *Manhood in America*, New York: Free Press.

Maté, G. (2000) 'A Solution to Violence is in Our Hands', *Globe and Mail*, 2 August.

4

Adopting a Global Perspective on Fatherhood

Graeme Russell

In the past twenty years, the practice of fatherhood has come under increasing scrutiny from researchers, policy-makers, practitioners and the media. Similar to the focus on questions of boys and men (see Connell 2000), this interest appears to transcend geography and culture (see Engle and Breaux 1998; Hewlett 1992; Lamb 1987). There are now international conferences (for example, the International Fatherhood Conference 2000 in the USA), forums on the practice of fatherhood and many websites. Interest also continues on the links between fatherhood research and social and organizational policies (for example, Lamb and Sagi 1983; Engle and Breaux 1998; Tamis-LeMonda and Cabrera 1999; Haas et al. 2000; Russell et al. 1999; Burghes et al. 1997; Burgess and Ruxton 1996; Warin et al. 1999; Levine and Pittinsky 1997).

It also seems that many societies now have several definitive texts, writings or authors on fatherhood, for example, Australia (Lupton and Barclay 1997; McMahon 1999; Russell 1983; Russell et al. 1999; Dye 1998); USA (for example, Blankenhorn 1995; Hawkins and Dollahite 1997; Levine 1977; LaRossa 1997; Lamb 1997; Parke 1996; Snarey 1993); UK (Burghes et al. 1997; Burgess 1997; Lewis 1986; McKee and O'Brien 1982); New Zealand (Pudney and Cottrell 1998); Ireland (McKeown et al. 1999).

Importantly, too, there have been several national analyses of fatherhood that have focused on reviews of research, policies and practices, and have also attempted to provide direction for future work and practice (for example, in Australia: Russell et al. 1999; in the UK: Burgess and Ruxton 1996; Burghes, Clarke and Cronin 1997; USA: Federal Interagency Forum on Child and Family Statistics 1998; Tamis-LeMonda and Cabrera 1999).

These analyses, however, have mostly been restricted to a particular culture and internal subcultures, and the discourse has tended to be dominated by USA data and commentaries. With the changing dynamics of globalization, however, there seems good reason to expand these analyses. With the rapid transfer of information and travel, fatherhood is now emerging as an issue of global concern – in much the same way as the women's movement has become international. It is timely to begin both (1) a process of global analysis and (2) to turn our attention to the impact that globalization is having on emerging fatherhood. These are the issues that provide the focus for this chapter, albeit for a restricted set of fatherhood commentaries.

Several themes appear to be common in the approaches being taken in the analysis of fatherhood. The aim of this chapter is (1) to identify and describe these common themes; and (2) to highlight issues related to the workplace and to the impact of globalization on the practice of fatherhood.

Common Themes

Broadly, the common themes can be categorized as:

1. A focus on fatherhood.
2. The practice of fatherhood. (What do fathers do?)
3. Explanations for the current emphasis on fathers.
4. Policies to support fatherhood.

A focus on fatherhood There is little question that, compared with twenty years ago, there is a greater focus on fathers in a wide range of cultures and countries. This interest is reflected in academic research, social commentaries and in popular culture (see also Marsiglio et al. 2000). As Michael Lamb commented in 1981 and in 1997:

> Although the spate of activity appears to have died down, the contemporary literature reveals a new maturity: Fathers are now accorded serious attention in textbooks and treatises on socialization; theorists and researchers ponder the patterns of influence within the family rather than independent maternal and paternal 'effects'; and parenting manuals are directed to a mixed readership of mothers and fathers. (Lamb 1981: 1)

Perhaps the biggest difference between the first and third editions of Lamb's collection (*The Role of the Father in Child Development*) is reflected in the consistent attempts by all contributors to view fathers in a broader social context. In addition, there is widespread recognition of the fact that fathers play a variety of roles in the family, with the relative salience of these roles varying across time and subcultural context.

Although these comments have been made by US investigators, they reflect the situation in most other western countries. For example: McKeown et al. (1999: xiv) noted that in Irish society: 'We live, then, at a time when issues surrounding men are now subjects for debate in the media, academia, and everyday life.'

In Britain: 'Now they are prominent on television, in films and advertising and are of apparent interest to the public in general and central to the concerns of policy makers in particular. Indeed, what fathers do – and do not do – is frequently a matter of public and political debate and analysis' (Burghes et al. 1997: 9).

Increased interest is also being shown in several Asian countries, for example, the Centre for Fathering in Singapore, and in Japan: 'Over the past few years Japanese men ... have gone through a sharp awakening as to the nature of fatherhood ... more fathers nowadays turn up at elementary school, nursery school and on day-care center activity days' (Mutsumi 1999: 87).

Whether this heightened focus on fatherhood is directly related to a fundamental change in the level of involvement of fathers and the emergence of a 'New Father' who is highly involved in the day-to-day care of children is also debated in many countries. In a comprehensive review of fatherhood in the USA, Cabrera et al. (2000: 128) argue that 'paternal involvement, responsibility, and care have increased over the past three decades'. Evidence cited to support this comes from Pleck's (1997) comprehensive review as well as the findings from Yeung et al. (1998).

Time-use findings from Australia provide a slightly different perspective. Russsell and Bowman (2000) reported that there is very little evidence that a gender redistribution of family work has occurred (Bittman and Pixley 1997). Findings indicated that, overall, fathers are not spending any more time than they always have on family and child activities. Mothers reported spending, on average, 6 hours 46 minutes a day on child-care activities in 1992 and 6 hours 7 minutes in 1997. Fathers reported spending 2 hours 31 minutes on child-care activities in 1992, and 2 hours 24 minutes in 1997. Nevertheless, in their study of a national random sample of 1,000 fathers, Russell et al. (1999) found that in comparison with fifteen years earlier, fathers were spending more time *alone* with their children. This study also found that fathers, their spouses and family workers had the perception that the current generation of fathers are closer to and spend more time with their children than the previous generation of fathers did.

McMahon (1999) and LaRossa (1997) present alternative views on the 'New Father' debate. Based on an analysis of a mixture of mainly Australian, UK and US data on men's involvement in child-rearing and household chores, McMahon concluded that little has changed and that researchers and social commentators have been overly optimistic about the extent of change. Further, he argues that discussions about these issues have avoided the political point that men's material interests provide a major motivation for resistance to pro-equity change and, indeed, that men are in fact 'caring for themselves' by ignoring this.

LaRossa, in examining US data on the changing nature of fatherhood argued: 'Thus, while it may be gratifying for men in the late twentieth century to believe that they are the first generation to change a diaper or give a baby a bath, the simple truth is that they are not' (LaRossa, 1997: 3). This is a view supported by the analysis of Burgess who argued: 'From every historical period fathers are revealed as being deeply attached to their children, and struggling with many of the same issues which worry fathers today' (Burgess 1997: 38).

Providing a definitive answer to the question of whether there has been a significant shift in the level of involvement within any culture or sub-culture will remain difficult given the paucity of data and the lack of consensus about what the appropriate measures of father-involvement should be. We can, however, be certain that there has been an increased scholarly and social interest in what men do and feel as fathers.

The practice of fatherhood A common thread in studies of fathering is an attempt to clarify what is meant by father involvement and how to measure it. Pleck (1997) distinguished three components: (1) paternal engagement – direct interaction with the child in terms of care-taking, play or leisure; (2) accessibility or availability to the child; and (3) responsibility for the care of the child, as distinct from the performance of care.

Russell (1999) broadened the conceptualization of paternal involvement in two ways. First, by including measures of involvement in decision-making and responsibility (e.g. monitoring) as well as task performance. Second, by identifying six core domains of fathering: (1) employment and family financial support; (2) day-to-day care of and interaction with children; (3) child management and socialization; (4) household work; (5) maintaining relationships between care-givers; and (6) parental commitment/investment.

Taking a broad-brush approach, studies over the last fifteen years are consistent in showing both that there is significant diversity in the practice of fatherhood and that there are still quite marked gender differences in patterns of involvement in family life (Bittman and Pixley 1997; Dempsey 1997; McKeown et al. 1999; McMahon 1999; Pleck 1997; Russell et al. 1999). For example, time-use data indicate that fathers spend approximately 30 per cent of the time mothers do on child-care tasks. Nevertheless, in contrast to figures often quoted in the media, fathers report spending significant amounts of time either engaged with children (especially young children) or available to them. Pleck (1997) in his comprehensive review reports that for younger children, estimates of engagement range from 2.0 to 2.8 hours/day and for availability they range from 2.8 to 4.9 hours/day. In the recent Australian study (Russell et al. 1999), the average available time was 4.2 hours/day and the average time fathers reported they spent taking sole responsibility for their children was 1.5 hours/day.

An essential ingredient of the description of fathering is the need to recognize the diversity of involvement, from the highly nurturant (for example, Pruett 1987; Russell 1983; 1999), to the more traditional (for example, the breadwinner, the head of the house and family protector, the disciplinarian and masculine model – especially for sons), to fathers who are disengaged and fathers who are physically and sexually abusive.

For example, a recent study by Jain et al. (1996) with sixty-nine intact middle-class Caucasian families in North America, raising their infant first-born male child, identified four 'types' of fathers: the 'Disciplinarian' who engages mainly in controlling and socializing and/or the 'Disengaged' father who remains aloof. Two-thirds of the sample fitted these descriptions. However, the study also found a significant number of two other types of fathers: the 'Caretaker' who engaged mainly in basic care activities and the 'Play-mate/Teacher' who appeared more versatile and spent most time engaged in play and demonstrating things to the child.

Marsiglio et al. (2000) also highlighted the diversity of fatherhood contexts included in research studies: divorced, non-resident or 'absent' fathers, resident single-father families, stepfathers, young fathers of children born to teenage mothers, gay fathers and fathers from different racial and ethnic backgrounds. Relatively little cross-national comparative research has been conducted (most compares USA, Japanese and German fathers).

Discussions of diversity also need to include families in which both parents are employed and share child-care, and those in which fathers are unemployed and at home caring for their children full-time – commonly termed 'shared' or father-primary care-giving families (Pruett 1987; Russell 1999). Findings also show that divisions of labour for family work are potentially problematic in dual-worker families (Dempsey 1997; Russell 1983). Employed mothers adjust their jobs and personal lives to accommodate family commitments more than employed fathers do. Mothers are less likely to work overtime and are more likely to take time off work to attend to children's needs. Mothers spend less time on personal leisure activities than their partners, a factor that often leads to resentment.

Family therapists and social workers are increasingly defining family problems in terms of a lack of involvement and support from fathers, and are concerned with difficulties involved in having fathers take responsibility for the solution of family and child-behaviour problems (Heubeck et al. 1986). The need for a change in divisions of responsibilities for family work has also been raised by those concerned about incest and domestic violence. A consistent theme has been the relationship between incest and domestic violence, and a lack of responsibility taken by men for family work and nurturance. The need to focus on shared responsibility rather than 'helping out' has been emphasized in this debate. At least one study from North America supports the global concern that fathers are not willing to educate themselves or their children about sexual abuse (Elrod and Rubin 1993). The social facts of sexual abuse demand closer scrutiny by researchers to examine those paternal factors that lead to this outcome.

Finally, it is worth noting that little research has been conducted into the subjective experiences or *feelings* of fathers – how men in diverse contexts perceive and construct both their identities as fathers and the nature of their involvement with their children. Marsiglio et al. (2000) drew attention to the growing body of recent research that has used either symbolic interactionism or identity theory to address this aspect of fathering. What this research shows is that for fathers 'there are competing discourses and desires that can never be fully and neatly shaped into a single identity' (Lupton and Barclay 1997: 16). Knowledge of the subjective experiences of fathers is critical for our understanding of both the nature and diversity of father involvement, the effects fathers have on other family members and the effect fathering has on the development of men themselves (see Heath 1978; Russell 1983; Snarey 1993).

Explanations for the current emphasis on fathers Reasons for an increased emphasis on fathers will obviously differ from one culture to another, as well as within a particular culture. There do, however, appear to be some recurring themes. The most common is that both the interest in the practice of fatherhood, as well as explanations for changing fathering patterns (within personal relationships), are direct responses to changes in the behaviour and expectations of women.

Many commentators view broader social changes (e.g. feminism, changing maternal employment patterns) as being *the* major or a major driver of the current focus on the practice of fatherhood. For example, Lupton and Barclay (1997: 1) argued that the major drivers of the fatherhood debate in Australia are 'the second-wave feminist movement, the entry of larger numbers of women into the workforce, their continuing participation in paid employment after having children and a decrease in the size of families'. Segal (1993) argued that most change in men's lives occurs when '*women's power to demand change in men* has been greatest'. Mutsumi (1999: 88) also commented that in Japan his experience was that most men who take child-care leave to look after their children are 'married to women earning as much or nearly as much as they are'.

White (1994) argued that the fatherhood debate is associated with the 'politicization and theorization of gender relations'. White also argued that higher divorce rates with more men living apart as single parents, with compulsory child support payments and the availability of paternity leave, added to men finding themselves unemployed because of retrenchment or depressed job opportunities in today's economic climate, provide opportunities and pressures more than ever before to be available for child-care.

Other analyses (for example, Haas et al. 2000; Russell 2000) indicate that the pattern of increased female participation in the paid workforce is widespread across a range of western and Asian societies. To cite three examples:

- In Australia, the proportion of couple families with dependent children where both parents are in the paid workforce increased from 50 per cent in 1988 to 56 per cent in 1998 (Russell and Bowman 2000).
- In the UK, mothers' employment increased dramatically from 49 per cent in 1984 to 59 per cent in 1994 (Brannen 2000).
- In Japan, in 1997 60 per cent of women who were married were in the paid workforce, compared with 38.6 per cent in 1965 (Russell 2000).

Tamis–LeMonda and Carbrera (1999: 2) also argued that in the USA, 'as more and more women enter the workforce, often with non-standard work schedules, a lack of affordable and accessible child care is causing fathers to take on increasing responsibility in the care of their children'. Cabrera et al. (2000) highlighted additional changes in the USA context that have had an impact on fatherhood. These include: a decline in the proportion of two-parent families in which fathers are the sole breadwinners; the increase in the number of families in which fathers do not live with their children; an increase in the number of families in which children live alone with their fathers (associated with an increased acceptance of paternal custody by courts and society, and an increased tendency by fathers to seek custody); changing conceptions of fatherhood; and marked changes in the racial and ethnic composition of the USA population resulting in a greater diversity in views of the appropriate attitudes and behaviours of both mothers and fathers.

McKeown et al. (1999) argued that four factors can explain the increased emphasis on fathers in Ireland. First, the growth in maternal employment. This increased from 28 per cent to 36 per cent from 1971 to 1996 (with a corresponding decrease in labour force participation by men: from 81 per cent to 69 per cent). The second factor is the reduction in the breadwinning role because of the high levels of male unemployment. Third is the increased number of single parent households, and therefore, the number of households where children are growing up without the daily presence of their father. Fourth is the identified change in expectations about fathers. It is argued that there has been a shift from viewing the role of fathers as mainly that of provider (the investment role) to an increased expectation that fathers be more involved in caring (the involvement role). Further, they argue that this shift has created confusion about the role of fathers in Ireland, for example, 'For men in employment, there is a growing expectation that they will become more involved with their children, even if the demands of work can make that difficult' (McKeown et al. 1999: 28–9).

There can be little question that changes in economic and social (for example, changes in family law) circumstances and the nature of work (for example, changes in family and employment patterns), the feminist debate and changed expectations of women regarding gender equity are common themes in explanations for an increased interest in fatherhood. What is not clear is the extent to which fathers themselves have been active in the process of change. Much of the discussion concerning the active involvement of men in changing the perspective of fatherhood comes from social movements associated with men's rights, especially in relation to custody and access. Yet, Russell (1999) in a review of families in which fathers are primary care-givers indicated that recent findings suggest that fathers have become more active participants in advocating and supporting this family pattern. Connell (2000) also highlights the active involvement of men themselves in addressing gender issues and in advocating change.

Policies to support fatherhood Fatherhood and social policy has been a topic of concern for academics, policy-makers and practitioners for quite some time (for example, Levine 1977; Levine et al. 1993; Levine and Pitt 1995; Levine and Pittinsky 1997; Russell 1983), as it has been in Scandinavian countries (for example, Haas 1992; Haas and Hwang 2000). What has changed in recent years, however, has been the increased involvement of governments and employers, as well as the consideration of the diversity of the needs of fathers.

Tamis-LeMonda and Cabrera (1999) provide a useful beginning framework for an analysis of approaches to the support of fathers. They identified two key areas of public policies: (1) *legislative policies* which include paternity establishment and child support, custody laws, welfare reform and parental leave; and (2) *public education and programmes* which include public education and intervention programmes funded by state and federal governments. What needs to be added to this is privately funded (for example, Ford Foundation in the USA, Bernard Van Leer Foundation, Joseph Rowntree Foundation in the UK) and workplace supported programmes (see Levine and Pittinsky 1997; Russell 1998).

Social policy and community-based support for fathers Scandinavian countries have a long history of government interest in supporting the active involvement of fathers in family life and in recognizing the positive contribution they can make to child outcomes (see Haas 1992; Haas and Hwang 2000). Many other national governments have begun to show an interest in evaluating their approach to fathering and have become more active in influencing practice by developing support programmes. The Japanese government in its review of the issues associated with declining birth rates (Prime Minister's Task Force 1977) considered factors that might lead to a greater involvement by men in parenting. In the USA, there is the Fatherhood Initiative, the purpose of which is to 'examine how fathers are conceptualized in social policies and how research and policy can jointly strengthen the father's role in the family'. As part of this, President Clinton in 1995 issued a one-page memorandum requesting that federal agencies provide greater leadership in promoting father involvement (Tamis-LeMonda and Carera 1999: 5).

This concern for fathers has been the impetus for thousands of state and federally-funded programmes in the USA (Tamis-LeMonda and Carera 1999: 13). The major intention of these is to help fathers, 'especially unmarried and adolescent males, through job training/search and employment, parent training, and school involvement. A key theme in the programme development is encouraging "responsible fatherhood"', a theme that is also reflected in aspects of social debate in the USA (for example, Promise Keepers; Million Man March).

In Australia, the federal government has implemented the 'Men and Family Relationships Initiative' to fund a range of family relationship support services through community-based organizations. A major goal is to assist men to deal with the emotional effects associated with marriage relationship breakdown, so that they can manage relationship difficulties (e.g. with children and ex-partners), and re-establish positive relationships. The initiative also funds service organizations to develop more sensitive and responsive approaches to working with men both in the community and the workplace – to be attractive to men and to take men's particular help-seeking strategies into account.

In the UK, the government has recently funded several fatherhood initiatives. Fathers Direct, for example, has been given two grants by the Home Office to raise public awareness about fathering and to develop a family services network. Fathers Direct has also been highly successful in obtaining private sector support (e.g. the Bernard van Leer Foundation – public awareness work; the Tudor Trust – family services network).

While most reviews of national initiatives observe that fathers have been largely ignored in policy deliberations and in social support services, or that the emphasis has been on fathers as breadwinners and ensuring that they fulfil their financial responsibilities in the context of family separation, it is clear that this is in the process of rapid change in many countries. This is also true of workplace initiatives.

Paternity leave While mandatory unpaid paternity leave is now widely available in many countries (see Burghes et al. 1997; Haas et al. 2000; Wilkinson et al. 1997), mandatory paid paternity leave is much less common. Further, in countries where it is not mandated, very few organizations offer paid paternity leave. In the USA only 1 per cent of fathers in either the public or private sector are eligible for at least some paid paternity leave (Tamis-LeMonda and Cabrera 1999). In a 1995 survey of 2,700 workplaces in Australia (Morehead et al. 1997) 34 per cent of organizations reported that they offered paid maternity leave (23 per cent private and 59 per cent public sector) while only 18 per cent offered paid paternity leave (13 per cent private and 31 per cent public sector). Findings from another study of 154 private sector organizations are broadly consistent with this: 14 per cent were found to offer paid paternity leave (Mulvena 1998).

The situation is very different in Sweden where paid parental leave is mandated. Since the 1960s the Swedish government has been the major force in helping parents combine paid employment with raising children by ensuring equal employment opportunity for women, subsidizing child-care and mandating paid parental leave for both fathers and mothers (funded by employers' payroll taxes). It was also declared that women and men should have equal rights, responsibilities and opportunities in the areas of breadwinning, child-care, household work and participation in public life (Haas 1992; Haas and Hwang 2000). The intention was for fathers to share parental leave with mothers, and one month was reserved for each parent (the remaining ten months could be taken by either parent). As a way of encouraging more fathers to take parental leave, as from 1994 it was not possible to allocate the reserved months to the other parent. If fathers did not use their month, couples lost it.

The rate of Swedish fathers taking parental leave is much higher than in any other country that offers men this option (Haas and Hwang 2000). But not all fathers take leave, and it seems that the uptake rate for fathers has reached a plateau The percentage of fathers who took regular parental leave was 3 per cent in 1974 and it reached 55 per cent for children born in 1990; however, this figure dropped to 51 per cent in 1994.

Haas and Hwang (2000) argue that Sweden is more 'advanced' than other countries in the extent to which the government has mandated family-friendly policies programmes. Another characteristic of Sweden is the emphasis placed on changing men's roles to facilitate gender equity in both breadwinning and care-giving responsibilities. While many countries emphasize gender equity in paid work, there are few that emphasize men being equal partners at home (Haas and Hwang 2000).

Fatherhood: An Item on the Corporate Agenda?

In the recent study of 1,000 Australian fathers (Russell et al. 1999), participants were asked what they thought were the major barriers to men becoming involved as fathers. Of the responses given, 57 per cent were workplace factors (for example, work demands, hours). Further, when asked what support and information they needed as fathers, the two most common responses were: 'greater workplace flexibility and support' and 'better access to advice and education'. While the most commonly thought-of workplace initiative to support fathers is parental leave, there is a range of other possibilities.

Workplace support programmes for fathers Supporting men in their roles as fathers is now quite clearly positioned in the corporate arena. The book by Levine and Pittinsky (1997) is based on twenty years of research and consulting on fatherhood in the corporate world. It covers topics such as 'DaddyStress'; 'DaddySuccess – the payoff for fathers, mothers, companies and kids'; 'Creating a father-friendly culture'; 'Managing paternity leave'; 'Staying connected when travelling'. Levine and Pittinsky define father-friendliness in the following way: 'The father-friendly company is one that maintains a culture and programmatic mix that supports working fathers in both responsive and proactive ways ... Even more, they foster an understanding that it makes good business sense to enable men to be good fathers ... and that helping employees be good parents helps them be better workers' (Levine and Pittinsky 1997: 62).

Russell (1998) has described both the pathways to getting fatherhood on to the corporate agenda and the different contexts in which fatherhood issues can be addressed. These pathways include: (1) conducting fatherhood workshops as part of a broader and more inclusive approach to advancing equal employment opportunity and diversity agendas; (2) developing fatherhood education programmes in response to needs identified either as part of counselling conducted by an employee assistance programme or findings from employee surveys; and (3) addressing the work/life balance issues for senior managers and their partners/spouses – a focus on parenting and fatherhood will be an inevitable outcome of this process. Russell provides several examples of the nature of his corporate work with fathers (for example, workshops for fathers; workshops for senior managers and their partners/spouses).

Globalization: a conflict for fatherhood? The globalization process has resulted in increased and intense competition for talented employees and for market share based on higher product quality and lower prices. A consequence has also been significant changes in the job demands experienced by many employees and especially managers – most of whom are fathers. Demands have increased for employees to travel and to be accessible during twenty-four hours of operations (either in person, or via video links, telephone or email). In a recent study conducted by the author, senior managers in a global organization said they worked an average of sixty-six hours a week, and that in the past three months they had spent an average of thirty days away from their home base, ten of which were spent overseas. Of the fathers in this corporation, only 52 per cent said it was possible to have a good family life and still get ahead, and only 30 per cent were satisfied with the degree of balance they had between their work and family/personal life.

Globalization has also meant that organizations have a greater need to ensure higher levels of productivity and expanded market share by having flexible workforces able to relocate quickly in response to changing market and business demands.

To ensure competitive levels of productivity and business success, organizations have found that it is essential that work practices and policies be implemented that take account of the diversity of employees' needs and values, as well as the cultural influences in the areas in which companies operate (Russell 1999b). Global organizations have found it necessary to understand variations in work/family issues from one country or region to another, and what the key drivers of these variations are. This enables human resource staff and managers to (1) respond appropriately to the work and family needs of expatriates; (2) enable employees to make more informed decisions about relocating; and (3) importantly, develop effective local policies to become employers of choice. Yet, few organizations have conducted an analysis of the impact of expectations associated with globalization on the practice of fatherhood.

Organizational factors that potentially could impact on a man's ability to be an involved father include:

1. The structure of the organization, especially reporting systems. In many global organizations it is common to report to more than one person – and these people are often at different locations.
2. Career path expectations. This includes expectations about the nature of work experiences (for example, in different parts of the business), and the location of assignments. The timing of these (for example, in early versus mid-career phases) will also have an impact on fatherhood opportunities (including whether or not to become a father!).

3. Expectations about overseas assignments, including the specific location and for how long. How a company plans for this and supports an employee and his/her spouse/partner and children will have a major impact on employee well-being and organizational outcomes.
4. Expectations about access or availability. Many organizations now require people to be available outside local business times. For some, access is expected in their family homes by telephone and computer. This can also have an impact on fatherhood opportunities.

These globalization expectations could have an impact on fathers by limiting their psychological and physical availability to their children; limiting their opportunities to be available at critical and salient times (e.g. when a child has an accident, when a child has an important school function); reducing a man's positive self-image as a father and reducing his sense of efficacy as a parent; and it could impact on the quality of his relationships with his children by reducing his opportunities to spend focused and 'hanging out' time with them. With men themselves, their partners, their children and the community expecting more of fathers, increased work demands within a global environment will necessarily lead to higher levels of conflict and provide new challenges for men seeking to establish an identity as an involved and committed father.

'Thinking globally and acting locally' is even more relevant when considering work and family, and especially fatherhood issues. Indeed, the long-term success of a global organization in a particular product or workforce market will depend to a large degree on the extent to which policies, practices and marketing are sensitive to localized family issues – issues both for the local community and for expatriate families living and working in these communities. Understanding the work and family interface provides a way for an organization to demonstrate corporate responsibility and community commitment. Organizations need to be responsive to the family and community values that sustain a society. This understanding is also critical both to ensure effective working relationships between local and expatriate staff, and for expatriate managers and supervisors who need to be responsive to a different set of work and family needs. Western-based or global work and family policies (and management skills in implementing these) might also need to be revised. Accepted western responsiveness to work and family needs may not in fact drive loyalty and commitment in other cultures in the way we expect.

Conclusion

This brief review highlights several key points. First, that the academic, social and policy interest in fatherhood is widespread. Further, because of the increased opportunities for scholars and commentators to communicate in a global context, our level of understanding of the nature, antecedents and consequences of fatherhood should be enhanced. Second, while we can be certain that there is a greater focus on fathers, we cannot be certain of the extent to which there has been an increase in the level of involvement of fathers in family life. Third, much greater attention has been paid to what fathers do, with little attention being paid to the feelings of fathers. Yet, understanding better the subjective experiences of fathers in a range of social and cultural contexts is critical to inform both our theoretical conceptualizations of fatherhood and our approaches to policies directed at fathers. Fourth there is a high degree of commonality across different contexts in the social, economic and relationship factors that are influencing the increased attention being given to fathers. Fifth, it is now much more common for public policies and public funding (for example, for community programmes). Sixth, for a small but significant group of fathers, changed work demands and expectations in the global marketplace are likely to have an impact on their opportunities to be involved as fathers. Seventh, in contrast to earlier perspectives on fathers, there is now a growing literature that recognizes the diversity of fatherhood both across and within cultures. One of the challenges for scholars, policy-makers and practitioners is to recognize, understand, value and work with this diversity. LaRossa (1997) and Lamb (1997) both draw attention to this issue:

> I strongly recommend that fatherhood scholars do some serious sitting down in the years ahead in order to develop *histories of fatherhoods* that are empirically valid and ultimately usable (it is time to return to the plural). (LaRossa 1997: 201)

> Influence patterns also vary substantially depending on social factors that define the meaning of father involvement for children in particular families in particular social milieus. More generally, this underscores the variation in the relative importance of different paternal functions or roles across familial, subcultural, cultural and historical contexts. (Lamb 1997: 14)

References

Bittman, M. and J. Pixley (1997) *The Double Life of the Family: Myth, Hope and Experience*, Sydney: Allen and Unwin.

Blankenhorn, D. (1995) *Fatherless America*, New York: Basic Books.

Brannen, J. (2000) 'Mothers and Fathers in the Workplace: The United Kingdom', in Haas et al. (eds), *Organizational Change and Gender Equity*.

Burgess, A. (1997) *Fatherhood Reclaimed: The Making of the Modern Father*, London: Vermilion.

Burgess, A. and S. Ruxton (1996) *Men and Their Children: Proposals for Public Policy*, London: Institute for Public Policy Research.

Burghes, L., L. Clarke and N. Cronin (1997). 'Fathers and Fatherhood in Britain', Occasional Paper No. 23, London: Family Policies Centre.

Cabrera, N. J., C. S. Tamis-LeMonda, R. H. Bradley, S. Hofferth and M. E. Lamb (2000) 'Fatherhood in the Twenty-First Century', *Child Development*, Vol. 71, No. 1: 127–36.

Connell, R. W. (2000) *The Men and the Boys*, Sydney: Allen and Unwin.

Dempsey, K. (1997) *Inequalities in Marriage: Australia and Beyond*, Melbourne: Oxford University Press.

Dye, P. (1998) *The Father Lode: A New Look at Becoming and Being a Dad*, Sydney: Allen and Unwin.

Elrod, J. M. and R. H. Rubin (1993) 'Parental Involvement in Sexual Abuse Prevention Education', *Child Abuse and Neglect*, Vol. 17: 527–38.

Engle, P. L. and C. Breaux (1998) 'Fathers' Involvement with Children: Perspectives from Developing Countries', *Social Policy Report: Society for Research in Child Development*, No. XX: 1–23.

Haas, L. (1992) *Equal Parenthood and Social Policy: A Study of Parental Leave in Sweden*, New York: State University of New York Press.

Haas, L. and P. Hwang (2000) 'Programs and Policies Promoting Women's Economic Equality and Men's Sharing of Child Care in Sweden', in Haas et al. (eds), *Organizational Change and Gender Equity*.

Haas, L., P. Hwang and G. Russell (eds) (2000) *Organizational Change and Gender Equity: International Perspectives on Fathers and Mothers at the Workplace*, Thousand Oaks, CA: Sage.

Hawkins, A. J. and D. C. Dollahite (1997) *Generative Fathering: Beyond Deficit Perspectives*, Thousand Oaks, CA: Sage.

Heath, D. H. (1978) 'What Meaning and Effect Does Fatherhood Have for the Maturing of Professional Men?', *Merrill-Palmer Quarterly*, Vol. 24, No. 4: 265–78.

Heubeck, B., J. Watson and G. Russell (1986) 'Father Involvement and Responsibility in Family Therapy', in Lamb (ed.), *The Father's Role*.

Hewlett, B. S. (ed.) (1992) *Father–Child Relations: Cultural and Biosocial Contexts*, New York: de Gruyter.

Jain, A., J. Belsky and K. Crnic (1996) 'Beyond Fathering Behaviours: Types of Dads', *Journal of Family Psychology*, Vol. 10, No. 4: 431–42.

Lamb, M. E. (1987) *Fatherhood: A Cross-Cultural Perspective*, Hillsdale, NJ: Lawrence Erlbaum.

— (1981) *The Role of the Father in Child Development*, 2nd edn, New York: Wiley; 3rd edn, 1997.

— (ed.) (1986) *The Father's Role: Applied Perspectives*, New York: Wiley.

Lamb, M. E. and A. Sagi (1983) *Fatherhood and Social Policy*, Hillsdale, NJ: Lawrence Erlbaum.

LaRossa, R. (1997) *The Modernization of Fatherhood: A Social and Political History*, Chicago, IL: University of Chicago Press.

Levine, J. A. (1977) *Who Will Raise the Children? New Options for Fathers (and Mothers)*, New York: Bantam.

Levine, J. A. and E. W. Pitt (1995) *New Expectations: Community Strategies for Responsible Fatherhood*, New York: Families and Work Institute.

Levine, J. A. and T. Pittinsky (1997) *Working Fathers: New Strategies for Balancing Work and Family*, San Diego, CA: Harvest Books.

Levine, J. A., D. T. Murphey and S. Wilson (1993) *Getting Men Involved: Strategies for Early Childhood Programmes*, New York: Scholastic.

Lewis, C. (1986) *Becoming a Father*, Milton Keynes: Open University Press.

Lupton, D. and L. Barclay (1997) *Constructing Fatherhood: Discourses and Experiences*, London: Sage.

McKee, L. and M. O'Brien (eds) (1982) *The Father Figure*, London: Tavistock.

McKeown, K., H. Ferguson and D. Rooney (1999) *Changing Fathers? Fatherhood and Family Life in Modern Ireland*, Dublin: Collins.

McMahon, A. (1999) *Taking Care of Men: Sexual Politics in the Public Mind*, Cambridge: Cambridge University Press.

Marsiglio, W., P. Amato, R. D. Day and M. E. Lamb (2000) 'Scholarship on Fatherhood in the 1990s and Beyond', *Journal of Marriage and the Family*, Vol. 62: 114–32.

Morehead, A., M. Steele, M. Alexander, K. Stephen and L. Duffin (1977) *Changes at Work: The 1995 Australian Workplace Industrial Relations Survey*, Canberra: Department of Industrial Relations and Small Business.

Mulvena, L. (1998) 'Characteristics of Organizations with Family Friendly Policies and Practices', Masters of Organizational Psychology Thesis, Macquarie University.

Mutsumi, O. (1999) 'Dad Takes Child-care Leave', *Japan Quarterly*, January–March: 83–9.

Parke, R. D. (1996) *Fatherhood*, Cambridge, MA: Harvard University Press.

Pleck, J. H. (1997) 'Paternal Involvement: Levels, Sources, and Consequences', in Lamb (ed.), *The Role of the Father in Child Development*, 3rd edn.

Prime Minister's Task Force on Declining Birth Rates (1997) *On the Basic Viewpoint Regarding the Trend Towards Fewer Children – A Society of Decreasing Population Responsibilities and Choices for the Future*, Tokyo: Planning and Evaluation Division, Ministry of Health and Welfare.

Pruett, K. (1987) *The Nurturing Father*, New York: Warner Books.

Pudney, W. and J. Cottrell (1998) *Beginning Fatherhood: A Guide for Expectant Fathers*, Sydney: Finch.

Russell, G. (1983) *The Changing Role of Fathers?*, St Lucia, Queensland: University of Queensland Press.

— (1998) 'Reaching Fathers in the Corporate World', paper presented to the conference on 'Men and Family Relationships', Canberra.

— (1999) 'Primary Caregiving Fathers', in M. E. Lamb (ed.), *Nontraditional Families*, 2nd edn, Hillsdale, NJ: Lawrence Erlbaum.

— (2000) *Work and Family Issues in Japan and the Republic of Korea*, Work–Family Policy Paper Series. Boston: Center for Work and Family, Boston College.

Russell, G. and L. Bowman (2000) *Work and Family: Current Thinking, Research and Practice*, Canberra: Department of Family and Community Services.

Russell, G., L. Barclay, G. Edgecombe, J. Donovan, G. Habib, H. Callaghan and Q. Pawson (1999) *Fitting Fathers into Families*, Canberra: Department of Family and Community Services.

Segal, L. (1993), 'Changing Men: Masculinities in Context', *Theory and Society*, Vol. 22: 625–41.

Snarey, J. (1993) *How Fathers Care for the Next Generation: A Four-Decade Study*, Cambridge, MA: Harvard University Press.

Tamis-LeMonda, C. S. and N. Cabrera (1999) *Perspectives on Father Involvement: Research and Policy. Social Policy Report*, Society for Research in Child Development Monograph, XIII (2): 1–26.

Warin, J., Y. Solomon, C. Lewis and W. Langford (1999) *Fathers, Work and Family Life*, London: Family Policy Studies Centre.

White, N. R. (1994) 'About Fathers: Masculinity and the Social Construction of Fatherhood', *Australian and New Zealand Journal of Sociology*, Vol. 30, No. 2: 119–31.

Wilkinson, H., S. Radley, I. Christie, G. Lawson and J. Sainsbury (1997) *Time Out: The Costs and Benefits of Paid Parental Leave*, London: Demos.

Yeung, W. J., J. F. Sandberg, P. Davis-Kearn and S. L. Hofferth (1998) 'Children's Time with Fathers in Intact Families', paper presented at the annual meeting of the Population Association of America, April.

5

Global Men's Health and the Crisis of Western Masculinity

Ben Wadham

In the last thirty or so years the notion of Men's Health[1] has emerged as a social issue within a number of western liberal democratic countries. In America, with the turn of second-wave feminism came a wave of public opinion that saw the effects of patriarchy as harmful for men as well as for women. Harrison (1978), for example, wrote that masculinity was a health hazard. In 1986, a South Australian community health service commissioned a report into men's health which focused on the ways that being male can have detrimental effects on men's health. Today, in western countries including Australia, America, Canada, New Zealand and England, the social issue of Men's Health has become a community issue as well as a concern of governments, even if tentative at times. Interestingly, Men's Health does not have a public face and name in other parts of the world, that is Men's Health does not appear as a specific marking within public discourse, nor within government policy. But at the same time the health of men is an issue that constitutes many local and global health activities.

Men's Health is a term that acknowledges a 'new and legitimate concern'. Richard Fletcher, an Australian health researcher, names this issue the New Men's Health and develops a working definition of what this might mean: 'A men's health issue is a disease or condition unique to men, more prevalent in men, more serious among men, for which risk factors are different for men or for which interventions are different for men' (Fletcher 1996: 1). Fletcher brings Men's Health to life in his definition, broadening men's health issues from the specific, i.e. prostate or testicular cancer, to the general, i.e. sporting injuries, accidents, suicide, lung cancer, heart disease or detrimental lifestyle practices such as smoking. Interestingly, Fletcher uses what has now become a central strategy of legitimizing Men's Health; he adopts an American women's health definition and transposes it to focus on men. This, it seems to me, is a central point of contention within the discourses of Men's Health. Men's Health, although articulated as a legitimate issue of concern, and as a seemingly obvious humanitarian issue, relies heavily upon its relationship with Women's Health to achieve its legitimacy. The first part of this chapter is dedicated to outlining this and related practices.

Outside this naming practice in the west[2] the 'unmarked *men's health*' also exists. This is not the Men's Health of explicit public policy attention, of media representation or even of unquestioned legitimacy. Rather, this men's health sits unnamed and unmarked within the health policies and practices of national health systems and global aid organizations, or within the problems of structural adjustment that face the World Bank Group (WBG), or the World Health Organization (WHO). Men's health constitutes problems of development, globalization and their constitutive concerns of poverty and population. This men's health is the implicit marker of difference from which Women's Health in global development has emerged. In this chapter I will outline how this men's health is situated within the global context, undertaking some comparative analysis between the priorities of Men's Health and men's health.

Finally, it is important to note that I write this chapter as a western scholar located in Australia, so I come to Men's Health with considerable experience of western men, western institutions and the western men's movement. I have little explicit experience of these issues outside the western context.

The New Men's Health

Nancy Fraser (1989), an American feminist scholar, uses the notion of 'need claims' to articulate the western liberal-democratic practice of lobbying for one's needs to be met. Women's health in the west and across the globe emerged from women's capacity to have their claims about patriarchy, male dominance and women's subjection to masculinist culture heard and addressed. Michel Foucault (1979: 26) perspicuously notes that 'need is a political instrument, meticulously prepared, calculated and used'. Thus, beyond any questioning of the legitimacy of a 'need claim' is the understanding that 'need' is something that is used and manipulated within particular economies of power with the intent of challenging or maintaining that power. For example, as I have already suggested, feminism articulated its needs in relation to male dominance. A subsequent logical question is: 'How does Men's Health articulate its need claims and in what context?'

The articulation of need is a window into the experience of the claimant and a representation of contemporary power and gender relations. For example, there is something to be understood by the different contexts in which Men's Health and Women's Health have emerged. Women's Health emerged in a time of progressive politics, the challenging of the monolith of the nation-state, of protests against conscription to Vietnam, of the war itself, of labour conditions, of heterosexual dominance (see Butler 1995) and discrimination against diverse sexualities, and of protest against the white racial supremacy of the western nation-state (i.e. the Black Panthers). Men's Health in its contemporary expression has emerged in a time of broad cultural reaction to the liberation struggles and achievements of the 1960s and '70s. Economic rationalism, privatization, cutbacks to health and welfare services, the growth of the very small, but not inconsequential, men's movement and its claims of a crisis in masculinity, globalization and disputes over national identity and territories are all issues that embody a conservative ethic that appears to have political and social dominance within the contemporary west.

Need claims also exist within particular economies of knowledge and power. In those western countries already mentioned, Men's Health is articulated within a liberal democratic framework where claims are heard, listened to and addressed in quite culturally specific ways. Anna Yeatman (1994), a feminist political theorist, explains that the liberal practice of hearing need claims can be quite illiberal. Yeatman (1994: 81) explains that for a group or an issue to be heard it has to be represented within a fictional headship. In other words, Men's Health, in order to be heard, needs to generate leaders within the field, it needs to draw upon a range of knowledges, it has to find strategies of representing itself as more impending and important than other issues and it has to be represented within a totalizing concept in order to have itself recognized. Thus, the diversity of views that constitute Men's Health become located within a hierarchical and competitive environment. One might also note that these attributes also help to constitute Men's Health as a commodity within the western market, something that can be bought, sold and used as capital.

Before trying to map and comment on global men's health, there is a set of distinctions about the representation of men's and women's health that needs to be discussed. Within the western Men's Health discourse there is a common claim that men's health has been neglected by the domination of the health-care system by Women's Health. I find this a difficult notion to accept, primarily because of its myopic perspective. Western feminism marks the successful (but by no means complete) struggle for women's health needs to be met by health systems that are male dominated. Feminist knowledge has demonstrated how the male body is represented as the generic body within medical knowledge and the female body has been considered an aberration (Dresser 1992: 24). Many public health campaigns, for example, drink driving, vehicle speeding or occupational health and safety, create a 'gender vacuum' when they approach these issues without considering who the *subjects* of their campaigns are. It is fair to say that these general population campaigns, which have no explicit subject for their concerns, are implicitly focusing on men. For example, it is men who predominantly have motor vehicle accidents, who smoke and drink excessively and who work in occupations that are dangerous to their health (Mathers 1994).

When Men's Health commentators claim that men's health is neglected and women's health is privileged, they are engaging the traditional masculine practice of universalizing their claims and speaking for others (Seidler 1989: 2). In this sense the privilege of being male is demonstrated in its implicit representation within particular health issues. This arises from an environment that privileges male sovereignty. Men's presence exists in an environment in which 'masculine bodies (particularly if they are heterosexual) are represented as signifying the "body politic" that public health agencies and activities are designed to protect' (Petersen and Lupton 1996: 85). The effect at one level is a kind of disadvantage, but one firmly grounded in a legacy of masculine privilege. In other words, men pay a price for privilege. This privilege takes many forms: men being the generic body for health research, men allowing women to take responsibility for their health-care, or men experiencing health concerns because of their occupational habits – after-work beers, long lunches, long working hours (with significant financial rewards). However, this privilege is neither universal nor seamless. Within the universal claim of male neglect there lies significant disadvantage that is subsequently trivialized by these universal claims. Men experience poverty, exclusion, oppression, violence and subjugation at the hands of other men and those women that share their status and power. John Pilger, an expatriate Australian, demonstrated in *South Africa: Apartheid Did Not Die* (1998), how the abolition of the apartheid system of law has not stopped unacceptable levels of black male workers dying in white-operated goldmines across the South African continent each year. These men's health concerns are silenced.

Four Sites for Men's Health

Men's Health in Australia and those other countries of focus has emerged within a number of locations; nursing, medicine, the media, community health services, governments and community groups. Subsequently, it is useful to think of Men's Health as operating within four arbitrary contexts: the men's movement, the health sector, the government and the media.

A number of social theorists have articulated the relationship between the medical profession and the state (Foucault 1979; Willis 1990; Friedson 1984). Foucault's work on the birth of the prison and the origins of mental health demonstrate how bodies of knowledge and systems of authority interact to generate environments of power and knowledge. The nation-state is the dominant system of governance within the west and it operates, among many other things, to maintain a healthy population. Subsequently, there are many professional bodies drawing upon, and generating, different professional knowledges to establish strategies for achieving this goal. Moreover, these professional bodies of knowledge are constituted by, and constitutive of, broader social conceptions of gender, race, the body and lifestyle.

Evan Willis (1990) and Eric Friedson (1984), both health sociologists, have demonstrated how medicine[3] shares a common aspiration with the state, namely that they both operate within a corporatist management model aimed at maintaining a population of healthy and increasingly self-regulating citizens (see Petersen and Lupton 1996). Existing within a context of capitalist production and consumption these ideas and structures work towards generating a healthy and self-regulating labour force.[4] In the medical community, prostate cancer, stress, obesity, testicular cancer, sexual dysfunction, heart disease and sporting injuries have attracted a good deal of attention in medical journals and in workshops and discussions. This medical and allied health-care model fits neatly with contemporary state health ideologies, focusing on the epidemiological profiles of different groups, their relationship of need to other groups and the development of strategies that are evidence-based and outcome-focused. It is within this environment that Men's Health has found a home.

The state health systems of the above-mentioned countries all adopt population health strategies that are generated and legitimized through the use of these knowledges. Government health systems rely upon medical expertise and epidemiological profiles to understand how different populations of people 'live and do' health. Petersen and Lupton (1996: ix) demonstrate how the New Public Health takes the focus of 'population [and] environment ... conceived of in their widest sense to include psychological, social and physical elements' in order to achieve the goal of health for all. Within this framework the notion of 'risk' figures prominently, used as a way of understanding who is at risk, from what, where, why and how. The point is that, as Giddens (1991) among others (see Petersen and Lupton 1996) has expressed, the 'public health gaze' has become ubiquitous and seeks to regulate everybody in relation to norms and benchmarks constructed by the public health system. Thus, Men's Health becomes a new category of population that can become entangled in the visions and practices of a removed and objectifying state health system.

Although significantly removed from the state health system and its determination of health, the men's movement in these western countries all have some interaction with the state-sanctioned Men's Health. In a recent study in South Australia (Wadham 1998), the notion of health and men's health was explored within metropolitan men's groups. Questions of gender and identity were also asked. The notion of health these men expressed was one that mirrored the state-sanctioned notion of health. Furthermore, these groups and their men were representative of broader men's movement claims. Good health-care was the basis for raising a number of concerns that were not directly related to men's health (that is, they were not articulated in an epidemiological/medical/state framework) but were used in directly supporting the claims of those making men's health need claims. For example, issues of female violence towards men, resistance against feminism, gender equity issues in boys' education, and fathers' rights and child custody/residence issues all contributed to a general notion of a 'male crisis'. Community health, and subsequently men's health, provided an environment where men came together to discuss these issues. These claims demonstrate the reliance that Men's Health has upon Women's Health (or that man has upon woman), in order to justify this need claim. This relationship manifests in two key strategies for justifying Men's Health: the strategies of equivalence and comparison.

Warren Farrell (1998), an American men's rights commentator, writes in an American government-related website that Men's Health has been neglected at the hands of Women's Health: 'We justify an Office for Research on Women's Health – but no office on men's health – because we claim women's health research is neglected. But Medline computer searches have always found more articles on women's health research than men's' (Farrell 1998: 1). Similar claims mark the interest in men's health across England, Australia and New Zealand also. One common claim in Australia and the USA focuses on a perceived disparity between prostate cancer and breast cancer funding. This strategy of comparison is used to claim that men's health has been neglected at the expense of women's health. Moreover, this comparison uses the strategy of equivalence to buttress its claims. The equivalence argument suggests that men and women should be receiving equal funding and equal attention. The problem with such logic is, of course, that men and women's health issues become decontextualized – gender analysis becomes inarticulate and power relations become obsolete. (For a discussion of these strategies see Wadham 1997.)

Two social theorists who studied the operation of power and the relations of dominance in post-war Germany made the following appraisal of the strategy of equivalence: 'Bourgeois society is ruled by equivalence. It makes the dissimilar comparable by reducing it to abstract quantities' (Adorno and Horkheimer 1973: 7). It seems clear that this is the strategy employed in Men's Health when one begins making claims that Men's and

Women's Health should receive equal funding.[5] Moreover, this strategy is also employed in a different fashion when Men's Health is continually compared with Women's Health.

Men's Health is constructed through and on Women's Health; for example, policy documents, discussion papers, community health reports and strategic direction papers, men's groups discussions, workshops and papers, medical and allied health-care articles and reports and media representations justify their subject area through comparisons between men's health and women's health status. For example, an English Community Health publication entitled *The Crisis in Men's Health* begins its exposé with the facts:[7] 'Men die seven years younger than women. Young men are twice as likely than young women to die from violence and accidents, and unemployed men are even more at risk. Three times as many men kill themselves as women' (Bruckenwell et al. 1995: 1).[6]

The problem with this widespread need to justify Men's Health through Women's Health via the strategies of comparison and equivalence is that it reduces the 'dissimilar to abstractions' that offer fallacious representations of men's and women's health issues as comparable. It is not that many of women's and men's health issues are not comparable, but that this comparison is used in a zero-sum fashion promoting the needs of men above and beyond the needs of women. Lost within the abstractions of epidemiological statistical analysis are the contexts in which men and women's health issues arise. Using the breast/prostate issue as an example, we can see that there is little use for comparative analysis: breast cancer is more virulent than prostate cancer, women are diagnosed with breast cancer earlier than men, more men die with prostate cancer than from it, the methods of diagnosis are extremely different (breast cancer diagnostics are more effective than the digital rectal examination or the prostate specific antigen blood test).

Finally, the media assist in exacerbating this desire for equivalence. Over a period of two years, media articles addressing men's health in Australia more often than not explicitly generated their news from the men v. women logic. For example, Ferrari (1994) in *The Australian* states, 'although both men and women live longer, men still die earlier and in greater numbers'. An article in *The Advertiser* by Williams (1996) entitled 'The Weaker Sex' also constructs men's health in relationship to women's health status and the *Sydney Morning Herald* in 1995 asks, 'What's Killing Men more than Women?' Furthermore, an article by Maslen (1995) in *The Bulletin* is indicative of the logic underlying the men's health and men's issues discourse. Emblazoned in sensational style across the front cover of the magazine are the words: 'Superior Sex – Women are smarter, healthier, more honest and live longer. These days it's the men who need help.'

From Woman to Gender: Bringing Men into Focus

A clear strategy for justifying Men's Health in the west involves the understanding of man through the notion of woman. Although Men's Health is described and articulated as a discrete issue it clearly has less potency without its use of the technology that 'woman' provides. This technology provides the basis for Men's Health to emerge and find legitimacy in a state health arena where finding support and voice is highly competitive. Within the global context, however, this process of articulating population health concerns takes on a different character within a significantly different context. There are several key issues that need to be addressed in understanding this context: globalization and its relationship with global health concerns, the health focus of the supra-national organizations, WHO, WBG and the UN; and the relationship between global Women's Health and global men's health.[7]

The position of women in development and world politics emerged as a significant social and political issue in the late 1960s. Feminist researchers established and have continued to maintain that women 'were either ignored by the development process, or assigned roles which did not allow them to benefit from development as much as men' (Schech and Haggis 2000: 12). In 1975 the United Nations declared International Women's Year, initiating a decade devoted to women's needs. Development thinking has adopted this strategy of addressing Women's Health as one way of closing the gap between the 'First World' and the 'Third World'. However, as Caroline Moser explains, although a significant amount of positive work has been done within this focus on women, there is also significant lip-service being paid to 'women and development at international, governmental and non-governmental levels' (Moser 1993: 84; see Cornwall and White 2000). For example, Garcia-Moreno (1998: 2) explains: 'little [has been done] to alter women's basic position in society. Women's economic, social and political status has remained largely unchanged and in some communities has actually deteriorated.'

Moreover, data from the International Parliamentary Union (2000) show that the current representation of women in parliaments across the globe currently stands at about 13.8 per cent. This has declined by about 1.2 per cent over the past decade. Clearly, the message here, in the context of western Men's Health, is that the introduction of a specific Men's Health focus, unless done critically and thoughtfully, would contribute to the subversion of 'woman' in the international health field.

This is borne out in contemporary critiques of gender analysis within the international health field. Moser (1993: 84) also explains that while Women in Development (WID) organizations have proliferated in countries such as Japan, Belize and Zimbabwe, these organizations operate within authorities that remain male-dominated and often gender-blind. Currently, a 'woman focus' tends to be 'added and stirred' to an environment where the generic health body, and health interest, is male-centred. Subsequently, women's health and development, in many situations, remain marginalized (Moser 1993: 84–5). More recently, there has been a shift to establish a gender planning approach that supersedes the singularly woman-focused approach (Moser 1993; Garcia-Moreno 1998; Kabeer 1994). A gender planning approach may in some circumstances remain loyal to antiquated ideas about the practice and power of gender itself. For example, gender may be another word for a woman-focused approach or gender may be conceived in terms of an individual attribute (Connell 1995: 1–2). A gender planning approach to health-care needs to move beyond these now relatively antiquated approaches to health-care and begin to define health *relationally*.

A Relational Notion of Health

Within the context of global development and health it would be possible for some to suggest that men's health has been neglected. Although Women's Health has been the specific subject of United Nation and WHO policies for around twenty-five years, this has not meant that men's health has been neglected. Moreover, the fact that men's health has not been explicit in the policies of global aid organizations is demonstrative of the operation of power within this context. To a large extent men have been the subject of those global and regional programmes that have not targeted women specifically (WHO 1994). However, this invisibility of men's health issues needs to be uncovered, not through comparisons with women's health, but through a relational understanding of their health issues and the global and cultural contexts in which men and women live their lives.

The first step in developing a relational notion of health is to understand the contexts of advantage and disadvantage that shape men's and women's lives. We live in a male-dominated world. Feminism marks this in terms of disadvantage, in the ways that femininity as a form of cultural capital is devalued in relation to masculinity. Connell (1995) suggests that we also turn this understanding on its head and consider the privilege of men in terms of a patriarchal dividend – the privilege that most men have in any given context relative to their cultural female counterparts. It has been the intent of feminism to challenge this dividend and to (re)assert the prominence of women in social affairs. This focus needs to become established within gender planning approaches in order to address men and women's relative disadvantage.

Probably the most theorized axis of men's and women's relationship is the notion of the split between the public and private spheres. Across the globe, the public/private split within different cultures tends to manifest itself in major inequalities between men and women: women constitute about 70 per cent of those in poverty around the world, many receive no independent income and those who do receive, on average, around three-quarters of the comparable male salary (UNDP 1999). Moreover, inequities exist beyond material considerations, as the critical notion of masculinities that I outlined earlier suggests. Being female, or not matching up to the various dominant notions of masculinity throughout the world, results in the devaluation of women (and femininity). Working from home, raising children, the practices of caring, compassion and community-building are given less value than the practices of production, trade and planning and decision-making. For example, according to Garcia-Moreno (1998), women continue to outnumber men by two to one among the world's illiterate and girls constitute most of the 130 million children without access to primary school. Therefore, it is important to recognize that when we talk of men's health in this context, we still live in a world where men, even those men who are disadvantaged, have relative privilege when compared with the women of their communities.

Moser (1993) moves on from this point to suggest a general global context of men's and women's lives that ultimately affect their health. Women experience a triple lifestyle burden: they are the prime agents of reproductive work (work that extends to the reproduction of the labour force), they also engage in productive work like men, mainly as secondary-income workers, and they are the prime agents within the informal sector, volunteering, community-building and engaging with local-level issues and politics (Barnett and Marshall 1991). Men, on the other hand, generally have the primary role of being 'the breadwinner'. Their work means they are often absent from the domestic scene for significant periods of time during the day and over longer periods. Even when men are unemployed, there is little evidence to suggest that women's triple burden diminishes (Moser 1993). Men's role in community work tends to be paid work; organizations and authorities are usually established upon men's work and men's interests, for example, national politics, planning agencies and the establishment of regional authorities. Subsequently, the tendency to represent men and women's health needs as similar or in comparison is uncovered as a misrepresentation.

Martin Foreman implicitly adopts a relational approach to health when he illuminates the different influences that gender relations have on HIV/AIDS. Foreman writes in his book (1999), 'women are vulnerable to HIV, men are at risk'. This point asserts that HIV is a disease that affects men and women in different ways. Women's vulnerability arises from the ways they engage in sexual activity, as does men's risk. Foreman (1999: ix) suggests that many women contract HIV through faithfulness to male partners who are not faithful to them. Men from many cultures are more likely to have a number of partners, often concurrently, while women are often in the position of experiencing sex with their partner as part of their duty within a relationship; or women are kept ignorant of their male partner's promiscuity. Culturally, it is often considered a sign of potency and sexual prowess for men to have numerous sexual partners, while women are considered negatively if they engage in similar practices. Foreman lists other reasons why men and women contract HIV that illuminate the complex relationships between men and women's health: in many societies women are expected to comply with men's sexual demands; condoms are often experienced as emasculating for men or diminishing their sexual pleasure; although men are more at risk of contracting HIV because of their sexual practices, women are more vulnerable because of their contact with HIV-positive men.

Globalization has had its effects on the health of men and women also. Technological growth from the period of industrialization to the practices of Development today have seen men in different countries take on new risks as the labour force changes and expands. Bob Connell (1995: 87) describes these changes as 'crisis tendencies'. Crisis tendencies is a term used to explain the way that gender relations shift in relation to broader social changes. For example, changes in the relations of production, in the demands of capitalism and in mass communications, things that development discourses have been intent on in the past, have implications for the way that gender is practised and understood. Thus, the health risks to men within the labour force have changed significantly since industrialization and will continue to change as globalization affects more people and cultures. One such example, a result of multinational corporations setting up operations in 'Third World' regions, is the increase in the use of women (and men to some extent) in 'sweated labour'. To take another example, occupational risks are higher for men than for women (Mathers 1994; Moller and Lumb 1996), and some groups of men are significantly harmed by their working conditions (e.g. miners, transport workers).

In a broader sense, globalization can affect men's and women's health in several ways such as enhancing the spread of diseases and by reducing public health funding. Diana Smith (1999) shows how the association of globalization with economic rationalism, and the practices of reduced public spending and privatization, have had a detrimental impact upon those people living in and with poverty around the globe. In Australia, an initial connection has been demonstrated between white, privately educated, bourgeois males dominating management positions within the federal bureaucracy and this economic ideology (see Pusey 1991). Moreover, if we consider globalization as the application of western cultures upon other cultures, then part of this cultural transmission is gendered. For example, the application of the structural adjustment programmes of the World Bank Group, whose intention is to assist regions to develop sufficiently to produce, trade and consume within the global market, results in the making and remaking of global masculinities. One could speak of a corporate masculinity that focuses on a form of colonization of 'underdeveloped' nations. The desire to open up a global market relies upon the application of particular capitalist ideas and practices upon 'Third World' nations effecting changes to the roles of men and women within regional contexts.

Conclusion

Men's Health is named and marked within the west, within the health sector, in public policy, through the media and in the politics that constitutes the men's movement. Just as feminism has not touched countries across the globe in the same way as it has touched many western countries, the men's movement is an explicitly western phenomenon. Men's Health has emerged in relation to women's health in the west, as well as in a context of proliferating health discourses and the increase in health messages. These factors – a sense of crisis in masculinity and resistance to feminism, and a highly competitive health service environment – have encouraged an already competitive and adversarial Men's Health discourse. Within the global context, Women's Health has struggled to be heard in a global context of male dominance. When Women's Health needs have been heard, the tendency has been to see women as the 'problem' or to see gender as an attribute of the individual, or gender as merely a category of analysis. A relational approach to men's and women's health suggests that the local, regional and global contexts of people's lives need to be considered in order to avoid an adversarial and insular approach to men's and women's health. The positions of men and women within their communities and cultures, the economies of gender, power and authority and the influence of global change all need to be considered as ways of improving the health, and lives, of men and women across the world.

Notes

1. I refer to two notions of men's health in this opening section of the chapter. I have marked Men's Health as a proper name, an appellation, with capital letters, for the form it takes as an explicit health issue in the anglophone western context. I have marked men's health without capital letters, as a description, of that set of interests that implicitly constitute some areas of health concern in other parts of the world.

2. I have chosen to represent the west without the use of capitals as a gesture of resisting the taken-for-granted dominance of this geo-political notion.

3. For brevity's sake I consider medicine to include allied health-care professionals as well.

4. That is, 'reduce overheads and increase productivity'.

5. For example, arguments of equivalence are often made between research and screening resource allocation for breast cancer and prostate cancer. The suggestion is that these forms of cancer are somehow equivalent for men and women across gender – if women receive funding for breast cancer then men should receive equal funding for prostate cancer (see Dow 1995). This argument is also articulated within the field of domestic violence, that men and women are equally perpetrators and victims of domestic violence (see Coochey 1995a; 1995b).

6. Other documents that adopt this strategy of justification are the Australian Draft National Men's Health Policy, the South Australian Men's Health Discussion Paper, Richard Fletcher's *A Picture of Boys' and Men's Health in Australia*, numerous global websites from the USA, Australia, UK and New Zealand.

7. Women's Health is an issue that has global importance and acknowledgement, whereas men's health remains a silent partner, not being discretely named and targeted.

References

Adorno, T. and M. Horkheimer (1973) *The Dialectic of Enlightenment*, London: Verso.

Barnett, R. and N. Marshall (1991) 'The Relationship Between Women's Work and Family Roles and Their Subjective Well-being and Psychological Distress', in M. Frankenhaeuser, U. Lundberg and M. Chesney (eds), *Women, Work and Health: Stress and Opportunities*, New York: Plenum Press.

Bruckenwell, P., D. Jackson, M. Luck, J. Wallace and J. Watts (1995) *The Crisis in Men's Health*, Bath: Community Health UK.

Butler, J. (1995) 'Melancholy Gender/refused Identification', in M. Berger, B. Wallis and S. Watson (eds), *Constructing Masculinity*, New York: Routledge.

Connell, R. W. (1995) *Masculinities*, Sydney: Allen and Unwin.

Coochey, J. (1995a) 'Domestic Violence Survey Provokes a Row', *IPA Review*, Vol. 48, No. 1: 18–20.

— (1995b) 'All Men are Bastards', *Independent Monthly*, November: 48–51.

Cornwall, A. and S. C. White (2000) 'Men, Masculinities and Development: Politics, Policies and Practice', *IDS Bulletin*, Sussex: Institute of Development Studies.

Dow, S. (1995) 'Man's Unholy Trinity: Diet, Habits, Cancer', *The Age*, 8 July.

Dresser, R. (1992) 'Wanted: Single White Male for Medical Research', *Hastings Centre Report*, January–February: 24–8.

Farrell, B. (1998) 'Do We Care More About Saving Whales Than Saving Males?' MenWeb: http://www.vix.com/menmag/farrheal.htm

Ferrari, J. (1994) 'Men Fail the Health Test', *The Australian*, 19 November.

Fletcher, R. (1996) *Testosterone Poisoning or Terminal Neglect: The Men's Health Issue*, Research Paper No. 22, Canberra: Parliamentary Research Service.

Foreman, M. (1999) *AIDS and Men: Taking Risks or Taking Responsibility*, London: Zed Books.

Foucault, M. (1979) *Discipline and Punish: The Birth of the Prison*, New York: Penguin.

Fraser, N. (1989) *Unruly Practices: Power, Discourse and Gender in Contemporary Social Theory*, New York: Polity Press.

Friedson, E. (1984) 'The Changing Nature of Professional Control', *Annual Review of Sociology*, Vol. 10: 1–20.

Garcia-Moreno, C. (1998) 'Gender and Health: A Technical Paper', Gender Working Group, Geneva: World Health Organization.

Giddens, A. (1991) *Modernity and Self Identity*, Cambridge: Polity Press.

Harrison, J. (1978) 'Warning: The Male Sex Role May be Dangerous to Your Health', *Journal of Social Issues*, Vol. 34: 65–86.

International Parliamentary Union (2000) *Women in Parliaments*, http://www.ipu.org/wmn-e/world.htm

Kabeer, N. (1994) *Reversed Realities: Gender Hierarchies in Development Thought*, London: Verso.

Maslen, G. (1995) 'Boy, You're in Big Trouble', *The Bulletin*, April: 28–30.

Mathers, C. (1994) *Health Differentials Among Adult Australians Aged 25–64 Years*, Canberra: Australian Government Publishing Services.

Moller, G. and P. Lumb (1996) *Men and Injuries*, Men's Health Reference Paper No. 7, Adelaide: South Australian Health Commission.

Moser, C. (1993) *Gender Planning and Development: Theory, Practice and Training*, London: Routledge.

Petersen, A. and D. Lupton (1996) *The New Public Health: Health and Self in the Age of Risk*, Sydney: Allen and Unwin.

Pilger, J. (1998) *South Africa: Apartheid Did Not Die*, Melbourne: Carlton International Media.

Pusey, M. (1991) *Economic Rationalism in Canberra*, Melbourne: Cambridge University Press.

Schech, S. and J. Haggis (2000) *Culture and Development: A Critical Introduction*, London: Routledge.

Seidler, V. (1989) *Rediscovering Masculinity: Reason, Language and Sexuality*, London: Routledge.

Smith, D. (1999) 'What Does Globalization Mean for Health?' Third World Network: http://www.twnside.org.sg/title/1905-cn.htm.

UNDP (United Nations Development Program) (1999) *Human Development Report*, New York: United Nations.

Wadham, B. (1997) 'The New Men's Health: A Media Marvel', *Social Alternatives*, Vol. 16, No. 3: 19–22.

— (1998) 'The Politics of Men's Health: Contesting Masculinities and Strategies of Change', unpublished Honours Thesis, Flinders University of South Australia, Adelaide.

Williams. N. (1996) 'The Weaker Sex?', *The Advertiser*, 23 April: 20.

Willis, E. (1990) *Medical Dominance*, 2nd edn, Sydney: Allen and Unwin.

World Health Organization (1994) *Women's Health: Towards a Better World*, Report of the First Meeting of the Global Commission on Women's Health, New York: WHO.

Yeatman, A. (1994) *Postmodern Revisionings of the Political*, London: Routledge.

Part II

National Contexts

6

Nation, State and Welfare: The Cases of Finland and the UK

Jeff Hearn

Introducing the 'Comparative' Dimension on Men

In both recent scholarship and popular discussion about men and men's practices there has been a growing emphasis on difference, diversity, even fragmentation and fracturing. Sometimes, though sadly rather rarely, these themes have been connected back to the long-running question of unities and commonalities among men (Hearn and Collinson 1993). The question of men's collective situation and collective power is most easily located within debates on patriarchy (Walby 1986; 1990; Hearn 1987) and patriarchies (Hearn 1992). However, most, even critical, commentaries on these issues have taken the nation–state as taken-for-granted, as the context and culture of, in this case, men (Hearn 1996; 1997). In such national or cultural individualism, treating each society, nation or culture as a given 'individual', 'men' may be assumed to be constructed differently, especially those appearing to correspond to the nation–state or substantial parts with strong ethnic solidarities. There are at least two significant, interrelated questions around this perspective. First, there is the historically specific and problematic nature of the nation–state, in, for example, assuming homogeneity within any one nation or state. Second, there is the impact of globalization. While globalization theory attempts to look beyond the confines of the nation–state, the nation–state has rarely been theorized in terms of the intersection of class, race and gender (Yuval-Davis 1997). Instead, we might attend to the historical construction of masculinities in the context of globalization (Connell 1998). From this we can attempt to retheorize world patriarchy or global patriarchy (Mies 1986; 1998), with necessary attention to difference, diversity, fragmentation and fracturing. Men are thus understood here in relation to broad debates that problematize the nation and the state, and understand national citizenship, men's relation to the state, and changing global conditions as distinctly historical and changing phenomena.

Two Nations, Two States

Men's relations to the nation, the state and welfare are not uniform; they vary according to the specific histories of particular parts of the world, including the intersections of welfare and warfare. The nation-state constructs men, and powerful men have historically constructed the nation-state. The specifics of 'the British case' need to be understood in relation to its former power in the world, the empire, the English language, social class, migration, racialization and of course gender, along with many other associated features, such as the specific construction of citizenship, age, generation and sexuality. Such contextualizations are demanded more routinely when analysing small and marginalized countries; but the general methodological and political point should be taken up by all, especially those in larger, 'more central', more dominant societies that take themselves for granted much more easily and powerfully. This specificity becomes more apparent when we compare the UK with another country. However, I focus here on Finland not simply for 'cultural comparison', not least because of the problematic status of 'culture' (Hearn 1998), but because I live there, so that trying to understand the place and its very different history becomes necessary. Equally this unsettles my understandings of the UK.

The UK is a post-imperial nation at the west of Europe, with a cool temperate climate. It industrialized and urbanized early, is relatively densely populated (59 million people), and is ethnically and culturally diverse, especially in the larger towns and cities. Finland is a newly established nation, formed out of the experience of imperialism at the north of Europe, with a relatively harsh winter climate. By European standards, it industrialized and urbanized late, first in the 1870s, then in the 1950s, is relatively lightly populated and is ethnically relatively homogenous, especially in the rural regions. The very peculiar nature of British nation-state and 'welfare state', and men's relations thereto, derives from its very peculiar cultural history. 'Great Britain' has grown, formerly at the 'centre' of an empire, with the strange persistence of the Irish Question on Britain's doorstep, itself a spur to the development of 'political policing' (Bunyan 1977). The state has been dominated by patriarchal, white ethnic, class interests with an associated distrust of the state by the working classes, and broad antagonisms between the state and the individual. At the same time the demands for welfare reforms were made very much through women's political pressure and the labour movement, itself traditionally male-dominated. These histories intersect with those of 'race' and ethnicity, through imperialism and the politics of race, with control of post-war immigrations of black and ethnic minority people, many from former Commonwealth countries.

The British state welfare system has been notable for its imperialist, patriarchal family, class-based and moralistic forms, especially in an assumed relation between the male breadwinner family and the state. It has been widely assumed that it is sensible to deliver state welfare through the heterosexual family rather than to individual citizens. The post-war British welfare state model was based on contributions from what was assumed to be lifelong employment for men (Wilson 1977). Those not able to achieve this, often women with family responsibilities, received reduced benefits and provisions. This family–state settlement has been challenged, by the welfare cuts following the 1973 oil crisis, the break in welfare consensus under Thatcherism, and the welfare selectivity of New Labour. The British welfare state has shifted from a neo-Keynesian to a neo-liberal model (Pringle 1998).

This specificity of the UK is made clear when it is contrasted with Finland, a much less densely populated country (5.1 million), with a very different history, positioned between Sweden and Russia, and previously ruled by Sweden then Russia. From 1155 to 1809 Finland was part of Sweden; then it became a Grand Duchy, an internally separate part of the Russian Empire. This was seen in Russia as a 'punishment' to Sweden, Great Britain's ally. It paradoxically guaranteed a qualified autonomy, as well as the continuation of the Swedish social order, including the Lutheran Church, Swedish law, its own currency and constitutional system, and government by Finns. From the 1860s Finland had a four-estate parliament, and a strongly cultural form of nationalism was growing more generally, to the extent that it suffused political debate by the 1880s. By the late nineteenth century, Finnish opposition to Russian rule was expressed in demands for greater human rights. General (including women's) suffrage was introduced in 1906. By 1916 the socialists won the majority in parliament. The process of independence from Russia culminated in 1917. In January 1918 the socialists created a 'Red' administration in Helsinki, leading to the Civil War or the War of Independence (depending on one's perspective), won by the 'White' (right-wing) forces the following May (Alapuro 1988). The Finnish constitution dates from 1919. The antagonism between the two political sectors of Finnish society – the left and the right – continued long after the Civil War into the 1920s and 1930s.

While Finland is a 'young' nation-state, it can be argued that it maintains much longer established traditions from its Swedish, Russian and rural pasts. The Swedish-speaking minority, making up 6 per cent of the population, has full language rights (MacRae 1997). As with other Nordic nations with their small, culturally relatively homogenous populations, Finland developed a form of democracy involving a specific, positive relation of the citizen and the state. Finnish industrialization was late, initially from the 1870s, not long before Britain began relative industrial decline. The 1950s and 1960s brought rapid industrialization, especially with electronic industries, and movement from rural to urban areas. This meant that 'Finland went almost directly from an agricultural to a modern service' (Rantalaiho 1996: 22) or 'postindustrial society' (Husu and Niemelä 1993: 60). The modernization of welfare in Finland has been through a more social democratic (Esping-Andersen 1990) form than the British case. In gender terms, it has developed as a 'partly egalitarian patriarchy' (Schunter-Kleeman 1992: 145), on the basis of a 'dual role contract' rather than an 'equality contract' (Hirdman 1990; Duncan 1994). Following the depression and high unemployment of the early 1990s, the Finnish state welfare model has been somewhat in retreat and faced with the greater impact of neo-liberal ideas and policies; this occurred shortly after the post-war 'welfare consensus' was broken in the UK. Globalizing conditions may produce more similar welfare, state and trans-state interventions and services, including those that affect men, fathers and fatherhood.

Two Issues: Men's Violence and Fatherhood

Taken-for-granted similarities In the remainder of this chapter I focus on the two issues of men's violence and fatherhood, along with their interconnections. Why these two? This is for two main reasons: because of the way they have both been taken-for-granted; and because of their significance as sources of power for men, both particular men and men more generally. Fathers are virtually always gendered as men; many, but clearly not all, men are fathers. There is no pre-given reason why a man should have automatic rights in law 'as a father' over children and indeed women, by virtue of having passed some fluid into the woman's body and regardless of what he does later. Historical constructions of conception, birth, sexuality and marriage lie at the heart of the politics of fatherhood and violence, taking us to the base of private patriarchy. Religious, community and state debates around fatherhood have usually historically taken paternity and heterosexuality for granted. The state, often in collaboration with religious institutions, has characteristically reinforced the rule of the father, for example, through the acceptance of the male line, property inheritance and heads of household. Fatherhood has historically often been given special treatment so that the state has not intervened against father's (men's) violence to children and women. Legal, religious and state constructions of violence have generally served to play down its significance and to limit its definition. Violence has historically been an arena of neglect. Interestingly, biological notions have suffused dominant understandings of both fatherhood and men's violence, in both societies.

Religion, state, law and constructions of biology have intersected closely with each other.

These taken-for-granted similarities are overlain by very different histories of fatherhood and men's violence over the last 250 years, with the differential impacts of industrialization, nation-building and welfare development. These represent sedimented constructions of fatherhood and violence. Earlier taken-for-granted conceptions from biology, religion and law do not vanish but continue as bedrocks of more recent historical change. The social and political practice of men, men's violence, fathers and fatherhood has been constructed in recent centuries through historical change in state law and legal practice. In critically assessing the impact of the state, there has been and often still is an implicit coalition between the state and fathers, particularly respectable fathers. A particular challenge is to bring together the broad analysis of different kinds of violence, such as military violence and violence to women in the home, in debates on fatherhood, nation and citizenship.

Two different histories Following early industrialization in Britain, state powers accumulated in the 1830s. The 1833 Factory Act regulated child labour and was thus an early state intervention in fathers' authority; the 1833 Education Act began government grants for education; the Poor Law Amendment Act enabled family break-up in the workhouse. From 1839 fathers' rights over legitimate children were formally no longer absolute in law, though women and children were property of the husband/father until 1857. Despite moves to legal equalization of women's and men's marital property rights, by the end of the nineteenth century in practice little had shifted in men's authority over women and children in marriage. While mixed in content, nineteenth-century reforms clarified criminal law and shifted the father into the state's purview.

Around the turn of the twentieth century, men were constructed more explicitly as workers and soldiers, and rather implicitly as fathers or disposable (in war). The relationship of men and nation derived from the move to modern welfare and national mass male armies in the Boer War and the First World War. Recruitment campaigns appealed to men's responsibilities to defend Queen/King and Country, and 'their' women, children and families. They also revealed the parlous state of British men's health. Response to this concern contributed to the strong historical associations of manhood and the modern nation-state at the turn of the century, involving, for some men at least, forms of imperialist manhood/nationhood, mediated by age, class, ethnicity and sexuality (Mangan and Walvin 1986). Throughout the twentieth century the norm of the 'working man', the so-called 'family wage' and the 'family man' (Collier 1995; Rose 1996) has continued, often through alliances between government and organized trade unionism. The Second World War impacted strongly on national citizenship, state planning, welfare priorities and gender relations (Thane 1982). Gendered wartime processes included British soldiers often being away from home, new patterns of gender-mixing and sexual relations, women's work in munitions, engineering and similar industries and later loss of such employment, and the evacuation of women and children and subsequent return. The post-war period brought national welfare reform. Compulsory national service was abolished in 1957, but continues for men in Finland, along with 'community service'.

More recently, the British state, as many others, has been challenged in its responses to second-wave feminism. With men's, often husbands' and fathers', violence to women and children, the state has been urged to increase its powers and involvement against husbands and fathers. Increasing recognition of the problem by state agencies followed the actions of Women's Aid. Despite reforms in the 1960s and 1970s, no fundamental state action occurred freeing women from violence (Freeman 1987). The 1970s and 1980s saw heightened awareness and intervention around child abuse, leading to 'scientific' risk assessment and proceduralized state responses. Though clearly relevant to the power and violence of fathers, this was rarely presented as such. There has been increased concern for child sexual abuse, informed by increased awareness of sexuality, survivors' accounts, and feminist theory and practice. The 1989 Children Act, and its nine supplementary volumes of guidance, gave local authorities a duty to safeguard and promote the welfare of children in their area, and emphasized the desirability of maintaining social and emotional ties with both parents after separation and divorce. In the 1990s, gradually, the private violence of men, husbands and fathers, has been brought more fully into the view, sometimes control, of the state. There is gradually increased recognition of the problem in law and policy, and to an extent implementation by police, prosecution and probation services.

In Finland, nation-state development is more recent; regulation of fatherhood has been less intense and less complex. Recent rural traditions and lesser industrialization and urbanization made for a somewhat less interventionist state in the nineteenth century. Since 1866, parental punishment of children has been considered a legal violation, within the terms of the criminal law on assault, if severe bodily harm has been caused. This has meant that corporal punishment was considered acceptable only if it caused mild bodily harm (Pösö 1997: 144–5). From the late nineteenth century women have had relatively high participation in the labour market and trade unions, and strong educational traditions. Governmental welfare intervention dates from the early twentieth century, with financial support to child-care centres beginning in 1913, and state legislation on financial support to kindergartens or child-care centres in 1923 (Tyyskä 1995: 31). The position of the father as breadwinner was reinforced in the 1920s, with greater emphasis on the woman as the manager of the household responsible for raising the next generation (Lähteenmäki 1997: 340). The husband's formal guardianship over his wife continued until 1930 (Bradley 1998: 199). In the 1930s, the father as breadwinner was increasingly challenged, with working-class women's claims for the right to work made more loudly. This right-to-work debate borrowed from the Swedish magazine *Morgonbris*, and the British magazine *The Labour Woman*. The Finnish trade union movement took a more supportive position on women's employment than many comparable national movements, though it supported a family wage system (Lähteenmäki 1997: 341). In the 1936 Child Welfare Act, the state assumed the right to intervene in the family and suspend parental rights. Children became entitled to state protection (Pösö 1997: 145). Those under sixteen years could be taken into the custody of the state, and the parents' right to raise and educate their children passed to local municipal authorities.

In the Second World War, while British men/fathers/soldiers were away from 'home', their Finnish counterparts were more occupied with fighting on the home front, first against the Russians then the Germans. Finnish men and women lost much: they lost the battle but won the war against rejoining the Russian Empire, though large border areas were ceded to the Soviet Union. Significantly, these areas were in the Karelian region, which is recognized as the cradle of Finnish cultural nationalism in the late nineteenth century. Peacetime often brought a return of the father in more senses than one. Jaana Kuusipalo (1990: 16) reports: 'During the war women took the main responsibility for farming and the production of industry as well as for the continuity of civil life and thus they were breaking the division of labour between the sexes. At the end of World War II more than one half of the Finnish industrial labour force consisted of women.' After the war Finnish women kept these jobs and did not 'return to the home' (Rantalaiho 1997: 26), as in some European countries including the UK.

As in the UK, the basis of the Finnish welfare system was laid in the 1940s, 'the decade of family policy' (Simonen 1990: 62). This established the framework of the modern welfare state. With a coalition government of the Agrarian and Social Democratic parties, welfare state construction was part of a national consensus during and after the war. Maternity benefit, family allowances, free school lunches, child health centres, loans for newly married couples, child benefit and housing benefit for families with several children were introduced in the 1940s. Acts on municipal health visitors and midwives, school transport, health-care of school children, housing production, and clothing for children in low-income families were passed between 1944 and 1958. While the British welfare state was an outgrowth of wartime and subsequent concessions by the state, the Finnish welfare state can be seen as part of the merging of state and civil society in much closer ways (Anttonen 1997): '[p]eople are used to organizing but their ideal is to act on behalf of their issues through the state, to pressure "the state to do something"' (Rantalaiho 1997: 23). There has been much greater development of a preventive, institutional, 'consensual' welfare state than in the UK. These contexts have presented the conditions for fatherhood and men's violence. In the Finnish case, the supposedly (and compared with the British) 'woman-friendly' welfare state has been developed around employment, family, education and care, much less against violence and abuse. In the 1970s the so-called 'child package', including the Paternity Act and the Child Maintenance Act, was enacted. The starting point of the former is the child's 'right to have father'. A married man automatically becomes the father to a child born to a woman to whom he is married (Committee on Fatherhood 1999: 5). An unmarried man can become a child's father in the eyes of the law through voluntary recognition or through establishment of paternity by the court. The 1983 Finnish Child Welfare Act embodied the principle of children's welfare as paramount, in social work, education, health, environmental planning, and other state functions. 'Family support' has been the focus rather than 'child protection'.

The state welfare contexts of policy on fatherhood and men's violence in the UK and Finland are thus distinct. In the UK, it follows from its class-divided, imperial and multicultural history; the Finnish stems from the creation of a Nordic welfare nation-state for a relatively homogenous population. The level of basic welfare provision is one contrast. Provision of publicly-funded child-care in the UK remains derisory, only 2 per cent of children up to three, and one of the lowest rates in Europe. This lack of funding is a governmental underwriting of the dominant system of unpaid care, largely by women. The UK can be characterized in terms of a strong patriarchal welfare state tradition, with systems of surveillance of class-defined 'deviant' men/fathers; greater antagonism of a patriarchal state and recalcitrant individual fathers; the relative absence of state welfare support, within a broadly neo-liberal welfare regime; remedial rather than preventative family policy, separating child protection from general child welfare; family- and individual child-orientated rather than community-orientated intervention; law-led 'legalism' rather than discretion-based intervention; family policy separated from income maintenance.

In some senses the welfare base in the Nordic countries may be more conducive to more progressive social change around fatherhood. Finland can be characterized in terms of a more egalitarian welfare tradition; greater taken-for-grantedness in and sympathy for the positive benefits of father-hood; greater public welfare provision; preventative rather than remedial family policy; family- and community-orientated rather than individual child-orientated intervention; discretion-based intervention rather than law-led 'legalism'; family policy integrated with income maintenance. The Nordic equality model has simultaneously provided relatively stronger support for family life, greater public participation by women, and a much more child-centred model of welfare (for example, 21 per cent of children up to three years are in publicly-funded daycare) than the British (Millar and Warman 1996; Rubery et al. 1996). However, while there has been less structural inequality between women and men, even compared to other Nordic countries, Erik Allardt (1985: 71) has argued that 'there is much to suggest that attitudes in Finland are more patriarchal and more indifferent to the emancipation of women than in the other [Nordic] countries'. Indeed, it might be argued that the public welfare system has been a means of protecting the father, spreading the load of caring work *among women*, and supporting taken-for-granted patriarchal fatherhood within heterosexual families.

Contemporary convergences? In recent years, fathers and fatherhood have become a *disputed terrain* across and between state and policy arenas. In the UK there has been a growing range of political and social com-mentators arguing that some, many or too many fathers are not behaving as they should; that they are too absent and/or too distant (Williams 1998). Much concern has focused on fathers/men who are long-term unemployed, defined within the 'underclass' and seen as neglecting fathering; described by Dench (1994: 10) as 'a core of irresponsible and purposeless men at the centre of our social malaise ... unattached and unlovable ... linked ... to the erosion of the male breadwinner vocation'. An important aspect of the debate, especially under the 1979–97 Conservative governments, has been the relation of lone mothers parenting sons; more or less absent fathers; and the assumed ineffectiveness of those sons becoming law-abiding young men and breadwinning fathers. Lone-mother families are accused, especially by the right wing, of producing sons and young criminal men rather than future fathers/husbands. The paradoxical relationship of the critique of 'feckless fathers' and the promotion of fatherhood rarely addresses taken-for-granted (hetero)sexuality, less still in a critical way. Such constructions contrast with the Finnish case where 'the problem of men' has been recognized much more in terms of isolated, alcoholic, depressed, unhealthy, older men – though they may of course also be fathers. This was highlighted in the so-called Finnish 'misery studies' of the 1980s. There is also growing public debate about what are the appropriate ways of being a father. As in the UK, this includes elements of nostalgia and tradition, more caring orientations, and uncertainties and worries about the future of fathering.

There is a growing array of state interventions in the 'rights' and 'responsibilities' of fathers and fatherhood, with the state becoming more fragmented rather than a single coherent institution. The state intervenes in complex ways in the construction of individual responsibility of fathers and the distribution of cash when parents separate or divorce. In the UK these impacts are seen most obviously in the Child Support Agency and the Children Act of 1989, but more subtly in state control of reproductive technology. Recent years have seen growing emphasis on the idea of the 'rights' of fathers, as in the assumption that such power and authority are 'natural' and 'normal'. There has been stress in both Finland and the UK on the positive benefits of heterosexual fatherhood and positive models thereof. In the UK there is less precise governmental support for fathers' caring, though even there the Labour government has initiated 'Fathers Direct', offering information, advice and support to fathers, through a telephone helpline, guidance to employers on working fathers, and internet information. This modest initiative may be a counter-balance to likely increased payments by absent fathers under child support regulations (Thomas 1999). Yet possible connections between violence, cash and care are rarely noticed in state policy. Fatherhood is a recurring, synthesizing theme throughout policy debates on the family. It is often assumed to be a fixed reference point within a world of rapid change. The ideological message from a broad political spectrum is that 'families do need (hetero-sexual) fathers'. There are current local initiatives in the UK around court-mandated parental education following children's offending, and the 'After Dark' police-enforced curfew scheme for under-sixteen-year-olds and linked parental advising. Thus, state surveillance extends into the hearts, minds and actions of parents – read often, fathers. There are indications here of some movement towards a greater assumption of consensus between state, citizenry and 'responsible fatherhood'.

In Finland there is rather more explicit, proactive governmental pro-motion of fatherhood and fathers' 'involvement'. *Equality: A Habit to Aim For* (Ministry of Social Affairs and Health 1996) makes three main references to fathers:

> Finnish fathers nowadays play their part in caring for their children and home. This significant change of attitude supports women caught between work and family and enriches men's lives. (p. 8)

> [C]linics train mothers and fathers for the birth and care of the baby, and for their role as parents. Finnish fathers often participate in the birth. (p. 8)

The father is entitled to 6–12 days of paternity leave at the child's birth and to an additional 6 days later on. About half of all fathers make use of this right. After the maternity leave, either parent is entitled to a parental leave of 158 days: the mother may return to work and the father stay at home. Only 3% of all fathers make use of this right. (p. 9)

In *From Beijing to Finland: The Plan of Action for the Promotion of Gender Equality of the Government of Finland* (Ministry of Social Affairs and Health 1997) the tone is much more proactive. Under 'Reinforcing men's role as fathers and grandfathers' (p. 40), we learn that:

While reinforcing the father's role helps reconcile family life with working life, fatherhood should be promoted in all phases of life and in different family situations. If fathers were to participate more actively in the care and upbringing of their children this would also be in the children's interest ... The majority of modern Finnish fathers attend childbirth, a practice that definitely reinforces fatherhood ... The Government recommends that fathers' rights and their possibility of experiencing fatherhood to the full in different stages of their lives be examined and promoted. (Ministry of Social Affairs and Health 1997: 40)

At the Nordic conference, 'New Ways with Dad', in Helsinki, August 1998, sponsored by the Finnish Council of Equality Between Women and Men, and the Nordic Council of Ministers, the Minister of Justice spoke in favour of policy 'to improve the status of fathers'. The ideology is clear (also see Committee on Fatherhood 1999).

Heterosexual hegemony in father–state relations is reaffirmed in the organization of the state, medicine, birth and conception. Childbirth is now a thoroughly medicalized process, but not in a simple technological way. Medical hegemony operates through responses to practices, such as the favouring of the presence and involvement of men/fathers at and around birth, whether 'being there' or more actively participating. 'Enlightened' shades of opinion, medical and non-medical, agree it is a 'good thing' for fathers to be present and 'more involved'. With new medical technology, such as ID and *in vitro* fertilization (IVF), the state takes a greater interest in and control of who accesses them and who becomes a father. This raises many new issues around fatherhood: new technologies may both subvert fatherhood and reinforce dominant constructions, by heterosexual imperatives rather than lesbian or gay parenting. At the Helsinki conference the Finnish Minister of Justice said his government policy was that wherever possible the father should be named even if conception had occurred using new technologies. The prospect of cloning, even the dispensability of the father, may bring a reassertion of 'normal, heterosexual fathering', underwritten by the state, medicine and those affirming the rule of the father. State sponsorship of fathers and individual patriarchal power may work together. Empirical research indicates no difference in the developmental progress of children in lesbian, gay and heterosexual households (Rights of Women 1984; Patterson 1992). Despite legal advances in lesbian and gay rights, as in the lowering of the age of consent for male homosexuals in the UK, lesbian and gay parents and gay fathers have few civil rights in many countries. In the UK, lesbian and gay couples cannot marry; there is extensive discrimination regarding parenting, with 'parenting rights' following from biological status or marriage (Lewis 1998). In Finland, adoption is possible for single people and married couples; while there are no reported cases of denial of parents' 'parenting rights' because of homosexuality, due to the lack of same-sex marriage, adoption is not an option for homosexual couples (Hiltunen 1998).

Another area of possible convergence concerns time. For some men, becoming fathers involves major changes in responsibilities and work in the home. Often fatherhood carries fewer obligations of care/work on men than motherhood does on women. Many studies report low amounts of time spent by fathers in personal family tasks and the relative rarity of fathers' *prime* responsibility for them, rather than 'helping out'. Clarke and Popay (1998: 200) conclude from the literature that '[d]epending on household type, women's employment status, age of children, men's con- tribution to parenting labour alternates between a quarter and a third', while '[t]heir contribution to overall responsibility has been reported as negligible'. There are national variations, with Nordic countries showing slightly more participation by fathers. While these 'contributions' are increasing, many fathers specialize in tasks such as doing the main shop- ping, washing up, taking the children out, putting them to bed, rather than the continual, everyday work/care that comprise family life. Fatherhood is not just social construction but sets of material practices whereby women generally do more work than men. Time-use is an increasing policy focus in EU debates, as in the 1993 European Directives on Working Time, calling for minimum daily rest periods, a maximum working week of forty- eight hours, a maximum average working day of eleven hours, minimum periods of annual leave, and restrictions on night and shift working. Government interest in controlling working time contradicts trends towards a culture of long hours, unlimited-hours contracts, performance-related and commission pay systems. Contradictions can be acute for men with younger children, especially where there are alliances between employers' pressure to extract full value from workers and male employees' apparent preference for the (male) world of work to that of the family. Some of the longest hours outside the home are worked by fathers with children under sixteen (Fagan 1996). The time young people spend with their families can have more impact on how they do at school and work than growing up with both natural parents (*The Relationship* ... 1996).

Under the 1996 parental-leave agreement of the Social Chapter, all EU countries had parental leave arrangements except the UK (Labour Research 1996). Parental leave of three months was introduced in December 1999 for women and men when they have a baby or adopt a child (HMSO 1998a). This should be contextualized by the UK government's greater orientation towards children and 'families', as in Working Families Tax Credit and the National Childcare Strategy (HMSO 1998b). This sets out good intentions but relatively little actual new child-care provision (Himmelweit and Perrons 1999). The broad contrasts between the Nordic and the British welfare models remain. In Finland where 'fathers ... are entitled to a separate allowance paid for a period of six workdays at some point during the maternity/parenthood period ... [and] Fathers can also get an allowance for 6–12 days in connection with the birth of a child' (Families and Children 1997: 2), there is still considerable non-take-up of their possible allowances after childbirth; similarly, about one-fifth of fathers look after children when they are ill (Kjellberg 1997; also see Lammi-Taskula forthcoming).

In both Finland and the UK, state procedures for (fathers') violence towards children and (husbands') violence towards women have developed separately: the former is located in social services child protection systems or child welfare services; the latter in the criminal justice system. Yet the latter often provide the context of the former. In Finland men's violence to women has not been seen as a high profile problem until relatively recently. There is no tradition of *autonomous* women's refuges, as in many countries. The Sub-committee on Violence Against Women in the Council for Equality Between Women and Men was created in 1990, and the national and regional Project on the Prevention of Violence Against Women was set up from 1998 to 2002 by the Ministry of Social Affairs and Health. An important recent study is *Faith, Hope, Battering. A Survey of Men's Violence Against Women in Finland* (Heiskanen and Piispa 1998), based on a postal survey to 7,100 women aged between eighteen and seventy-four. This highlights the frequency of men's/fathers' violence to women: '22% of all married and cohabiting women have been victims of physical or sexual violence or threats of violence by their present partner, 9% in the course of the past year'; and 'violence or threats by their ex-partner had been experienced by 50% of all women who had lived in a relationship which had already terminated' (p. 3). These are comparable to UK figures. Recent British research suggests that between 10 and 25 per cent of British women have been a victim of violence from a male partner (Dobash et al.

1996: 2). Mooney's (1993; 1994) survey in Islington, London, found 27 per cent of women reported physical abuse by a partner and 23 per cent reported sexual abuse. Even such estimates should be treated with caution, as they may not fully account for rape, sexual harassment, coercive sex, pressurized sex, and emotional, psychological and other abuses. Stanko et al.'s (1998) survey in Hackney, London, reports that more than one in two women had been in psychologically abusive relationships during their lives; one in four women had been in psychologically abusive relationships in the past year; one in three women had suffered physical and sexual abuse requiring medical attention in their lives; and one in nine women had suffered physical and sexual abuse requiring medical attention in the past year. It is absurd to develop policy or practice to change fathers and fatherhood without attending to men's violence. Worse still, it is *positively dangerous* to provide material and ideological support for fathers who have been violent, are violent or will be violent in the future. Changing fathers' violence involves general actions and campaigns against men's violence.

Conclusion

There are certainly strong similarities in the way both violence and fatherhood have been naturalized in the two countries. In both it has been taken-for-granted as patriarchal and heterosexual, been seen as linked to marriage, and generally underwritten by the state. Yet at the same time there are differences. The recently established Nordic welfare state has provided a much sounder base of welfare, particularly child-care provision, than the British. There has been a much greater trust and faith in the citizens' state, much more focus on prevention and 'family support', and much less concentration on differentiating surveillance by the state than is the case in Britain. This is partly because it is much more widely accepted that citizens inform the state where they are, something strongly resisted in the UK. There has also been less evidence of an independent women's movement, and thus no strong development of feminist or women-only refuges for women fleeing men's violence; instead these tend to be municipal or para-state organizations. In this context fatherhood is seen as a good thing and rarely is the connection with men's violence made. This is despite the fact that, even with the strong welfare provision, Finland has a high rate of murder of women by male partners and ex-partners, and rather similar rates of violence towards women as are found in the UK and USA. The welfare state has until recently not focused on matters of the body, sexuality, sexual abuse and violence, to the advantage of men and fathers.

In contrast, men, fatherhood and men's violence in the UK are more closely constructed through differentiation from the state and each other, by class, locality, ethnicity, racialization and sexuality. The British state does not have a social-democratic history or tradition, but one that can be characterized as post-imperial. The basic welfare provision is much less developed. There has also been a greater tradition of autonomous organizing outside the state, including by women's, black and gay organizations. The greater urbanization and greater inequalities mean that there are more obvious 'social problems' to be monitored and perhaps dealt with. Fathers are both naturalized and heterosexualized; yet at the same time there are complications in both the surveillance of problematic fathers, and a growing optimism about fatherhood, that is strangely removed from the extensive debates on men's violence that take place at other times. Meanwhile there are signs of growing convergence. Diverse policy and practical realities are sedimented upon each other, sometimes in abrupt contradiction; they rarely completely supersede their historical antecedents.

Finally, a further growing complication is the impact of changing global relations. While national state boundaries can be incredibly rigid for some movements of some people, especially according to wealth and 'race', there is the growing possibility of greater local access across those boundaries. The development of the EU and the breakdown of the Soviet bloc have in different ways facilitated greater population movements within Europe. The relative isolation and homogeneity of Finland is gradually being changed with more migrants from Estonia and Russia, and more contacts within the EU. While greater cultural contacts can have positive implications for both those concerned, transnational fatherhood can also bring major legal complications. Sometimes this involves legal disputes across and between different state, legal and cultural traditions, and, in the worst cases, violence and abduction. There is a slow development of transnational legal processes on fatherhood.

Note

I am grateful to many Finnish researchers, and in particular Tarja Pösö, for discussions on these issues. I would also like to thank Barbara Hobson, Trudie Knijn, David Morgan and other members of the Riksbanken Jubileumsfond 'Fatherhood and the State' Research Group, University of Stockholm, for the lively meetings and debates 1997–99.

References

Alapuro, R. (1988) State and Revolution in Finland, Berkeley, CA: University of California Press.
Allardt, E. (1985) Finnish Society, Helsinki: Research Group for Comparative Sociology, University of Helsinki.

Anttonen, A. (1997) *Feminismi ja Sosiaalipolitiikka. Miten sukupuolesta tehtiin yhteiskuntateoreettinen Ja Sosiaalipoliittinen Avainkäsite*, Tampere: Tampere University Press.

Bradley, D. (1998) 'Equality and Patriarchy: Family Law and State Feminism in Finland', *International Journal of the Sociology of Law*, Vol. 26: 197–216.

Bunyan, T. (1977) *The History and Practice of the Political Police in Britain*, London: Quartet.

Clarke, S. and J. Popay (1998) ' "I'm just a bloke who's had kids": Men and Women on Parenthood', in J. Popay, J. Hearn and J. Edwards (eds), *Men, Gender Divisions and Welfare*, London: Routledge.

Collier, R. (1995) *Masculinity, Law and the Family*, London: Routledge.

Committee on Fatherhood (1999) *In Search of a New Kind of Fatherhood*, Helsinki: Ministry of Social Affairs and Health.

Connell, R. W. (1998) 'Masculinities and Globalization', *Men and Masculinities*, Vol. 1, No. 1: 3–23.

Dench, G. (1994) *The Frog, the Prince and the Problem of Men*, London: Neanderthal Books.

Dobash, R., R. Dobash, K. Cavanagh and R. Lewis (1996) *Research Evaluation of Programmes for Violent Men*, Edinburgh: Scottish Office Central Research Unit.

Duncan, S. (1994) 'Theorizing Differences in Patriarchy', *Environment and Planning*, Vol. 26: 1177–94.

Esping-Andersen, G. (1990) *The Three Worlds of Welfare Capitalism*, Cambridge: Polity Press.

Fagan, C. (1996) 'Gendered Time Schedules: Paid Work in Great Britain', *Social Politics*, Vol. 3, No. 1: 72–106.

Families and Children (1997) http://www.kela.fi/english.family.htm#maternity

Freeman, M. D. A. (1987) *Dealing with Domestic Violence*, Bicester, Oxon: CCH Editions.

Hearn, J. (1987) *The Gender of Oppression: Men, Masculinity and the Critique of Marxism*, Brighton: Wheatsheaf.

— (1992) *Men in the Public Eye: The Construction and Deconstruction of Public Men and Public Patriarchies*, London: Routledge.

— (1996) 'Deconstructing the Dominant: Making the One(s) the Other(s)', *Organization*, Vol. 3, No. 4: 611–26.

— (1997) 'Searching for the Centre of Men and Men's Power?: Historical, Geographical and Theoretical Perspectives', paper presented at International Colloquium on Masculinities, University of Natal, South Africa, July.

— (1998) 'Context, Culture and Violence', in R. Kauranen, E. Oinas, S. Sundback and Ö. Wahlbeck (eds), *Sociologer om Sociologi och Metod: Festskrift till Kirsti Suolinna*, Åbo, Meddleanden Från Ekonomisk-Statsvetenkapliga Fakulteten Vid Åbo Akademi, Socialpolitiska institutionen Ser., pp. 1–22.

Hearn, J. and D. L. Collinson (1993) 'Theorizing Unities and Differences Between Men and Between Masculinities', in H. Brod and M. Kaufman (eds), *Theorizing Masculinities*, Thousand Oaks, CA: Sage.

Heiskanen, M. and M. Piispa (1998) *Faith, Hope, Battering. A Survey of Men's Violence Against Women in Finland*, Helsinki: Statistics Finland/Council for Equality Between Women and Men.

Hiltunen, R. (1998) 'Finland', in ILGA-Europe, *Equality for Lesbians and Gay Men*, Brussels: ILGA.

Himmelweit, S. and D. Perrons (1999) 'Gender Dimensions of Recent Labour Market Policies: Changing Patterns of Work and Care in the UK', paper presented at Nordic–UK Collaborative Seminar on Employment Policies and Gender Relations, Stockholm, June.

Hirdman, Y. (1990) 'Genussystemet', in *Demokrati och Makt i Sverige*, Stockholm: Statens Offentliga Utredningar.

HMSO (1998a) *Fairness at Work*, London: HMSO.

— (1998b) *Meeting the Child-care Challenge: A Framework and Consultation Document*, Cmnd 3959, London: HMSO.

Husu, L. and P. Niemelä (1993) 'Finland' in L. L. Adler (ed.) *International Handbook on Gender Roles*, Westport, CT: Greenwood Press, pp. 59–76.

Kjellberg, H. (1997) 'Joka viides isä jää kotiin hoitamaan sairasta lasta', *Helsingin Sanomat*, 24 October.

Kuusipalo, J. (1990) 'Finnish Women in Top-level Politics', in M. Keränen (ed.), *Finnish 'Undemocracy': Essays on Gender and Politics*, Jyväskylä: Finnish Political Science Association, pp. 13–36; trans. as *Gender and Politics in Finland*, Aldershot: Avebury, 1992.

Labour Research (1996) 'Opt-out Means UK Parents Lose Out', *Labour Research*, January: 15–17.

Lähteenmäki, M. (1997) *Mahdollisuuksien aika. Työläisnaiset ja yhteiskunnan muutos 1910-30-luvun Suomessa*, Helsinki: Suomen Historiallinen Seura; (English summary: The Time of Opportunities: Working-class Women and the Change in Finnish Society in the 1910s–1930s).

Lammi-Taskula, J. (2000) 'Combining Work and Fatherhood in Finland', in C. Harvey (ed.), *Walking a Tightrope: Balancing Work and Family*, Aldershot: Avebury.

Lewis, J. (1998) 'United Kingdom', in ILGA-Europe, *Equality for Lesbians and Gay Men*, Brussels: ILGA.

MacRae, K. D. with the assistance of M. Helander and S. Luoma (1997) *Conflict and Compromise in Multilingual Societies: Finland*, Waterloo, Ont: Wilfred Laurier University Press.

Mangan, J. A. and J. Walvin (eds) (1986) *Manliness and Morality: Middle-class Masculinity in Britain and America 1800–1940*, Manchester: Manchester University Press.

Mies, M. (1986) *Patriarchy and Accumulation on World Scale*, London: Zed Books.

— (1998) 'Globalization of the Economy and Woman's Work in a Sustainable Society', *Gender, Technology and Development*, Vol. 2, No. 1: 3–37.

Millar, J. and A. Warman (1996) *Family Obligations in Europe*, London: Family Policy Studies Centre.

Ministry of Social Affairs and Health (1996) *Equality: A Habit to Aim For*, Helsinki: Ministry of Social Affairs and Health Publications on Equality.

— (1997) *From Beijing to Finland: The Plan of Action for the Promotion of Gender Equality of the Government of Finland*, Helsinki: Publications of the Ministry of Social Affairs and Health, p. 20.

Mooncy, J. (1993) *The Hidden Figure: Domestic Violence in North London*, London: Islington Borough Council.

— (1994) 'The Prevalence and Social Distribution of Domestic Violence: An Analysis of Theory and Method', unpublished PhD thesis, Middlesex University.

Patterson, C. J. (1992) 'Children of Lesbian and Gay Parents', *Child Development*, Vol. 63: 1025–42.

Pösö, T. (1997) 'Finland: Child Abuse as a Problem', in N. Gilbert (ed.) *Combating Child Abuse: International Perspectives and Trends*, New York: Oxford University Press, pp. 143–63.

Pringle, K. (1998) *Children and Social Welfare in Europe*, Milton Keynes: Open University Press.

Rantalaiho, L. (1997) 'Contextualizing Gender', in L. Rantalaiho and T. Heiskanen (eds), *Gendered Practices in Working Life*, London: Macmillan.

The Relationship Between Family Life and Young People's Lifestyles (1996) Social Policy Research Findings No. 95, York: Joseph Rowntree Foundation.

Rights of Women (1984) *Lesbian Mothers on Trial: A Report on Lesbian Mothers & Child Custody*, London: Rights of Women.

Rose, N. (1996) 'The Death of the Social? Refiguring the Territory of Government', *Economy and Society*, Vol. 25, No. 3: 327–56.

Rubery, J., M. Smith and E. Turner (1996) *Bulletin on Women and Employment in the EU*, No. 9, October.

Schunter-Kleeman, S. (1992) 'Wohlfahrtsstaat und patriachat – ein verleich europäischer länder', in S. Schunter-Kleeeman (ed.) *Herrenhaus Europa – Geschlecterverhältnisse im Wohlfahrtsstaat*, Berlin: Edition Sigma.

Simonen, L. (1990) *Contradictions of the Welfare State, Women and Caring*, Acta Universitatis Tamperensis. Ser. A, Vol. 295, Tampere: University of Tampere.

Stanko, E. A., D. Crisp, C. Hale and H. Lucraft (1998) *Counting the Costs*, Swindon: Crime Concern.

Thane, P. (1982) *The Foundation of the Welfare State*, London: Longman.

Thomas, R. (1999) 'Fathers Must be More than "walking wallets"', *Observer*, 24 April, p. 5.

Tyyskä, V. (1995) *The Politics of Caring and the Welfare State: The Impact of the Women's Movement on Child-care Policy in Canada and Finland, 1960–1990*, Suomalainen Tiedeakatemia, Ser. B, tom. 277.

Walby, S. (1986) *Patriarchy at Work*, Cambridge: Polity Press.

— (1989) 'Theorising Patriarchy', *Sociology*, Vol. 23, No. 2: 213–34.

— (1990) *Theorizing Patriarchy*, Oxford: Basil Blackwell.

Williams, F. (1998) 'Troubled Masculinities in Social Solicy Discourses: Fatherhood', in J. Popay, J. Hearn and J. Edwards (eds) *Men, Gender Divisions and Welfare*, London: Routledge, pp. 63–97.

Wilson, E. (1977) *Women and the Welfare State*, London: Tavistock.

Yuval-Davis, N. (1997) *Gender and Nation*, London: Sage.

7

Men as Social Workers in the UK: Professional Locations and Gendering Global Discourses of Welfare

Alastair Christie

The social work profession provides a unique site for the study of 'men' and work. The position of men as social workers in the UK is contentious because of men's violence towards children, women and other men, as well as men's over-representation in the most senior levels of social work organizations and under-representation in other areas of the profession (Christie 1998a). The social work profession in the UK is changing rapidly with the abandonment of the Central Council for Education and Training in Social Work and the development of General Social Care Councils and Training Organizations for the Personal Social Services, in England, Northern Ireland, Scotland and Wales (Jones 1999). The profession continues to receive generally negative media coverage (Franklin 1998), with one senior commentator arguing that by 'redefining and renaming the role, the profession [social work] could make a fresh start' (Brindle 2000: 10). Alongside national debates and developments, supra-national bodies and global trends are increasingly influencing the social work profession. While social policy in the EU remains under-developed, legislation on the training of professions (Directives 89/48/EEC and 92/51/EEC) and employment conditions is less and less defined within national boundaries and increasingly structured by EU policy initiatives. Social work, therefore, can be viewed as a set of ever-changing policies and practices framed by a variety of discourses including transnational discourses of welfare and social work.

In this chapter, I use the concept of discourse to describe a 'framework of meanings which are historically produced within a particular culture at a particular time' (Watson 2000: 70). Discourses of welfare frame gendered subject positions for men and women as social workers and as service users. Social workers and their clients are constantly involved in the production of welfare discourses as well as being constituted by them.

Discourses of welfare constitute 'appropriate' and 'acceptable' gendered practices for men and women, linking what is considered 'normal', 'natural' and 'common sense' to social policies, institutional practices and the professional practices of individual social workers. Discourses of welfare provide frameworks of meaning for social workers' practices and produce subject positions for men (and women) as social workers. Men's professional identities comprise a variety of subject positions and these subject positions may be fragmented and contradictory (Jackson 1990). As Pease (2000) argues, the multiplicity of discourses and subject positions produce internal conflicts and contradictions which provide men with starting points to both understand the patriarchal social world and to generate alternative discourses of welfare. In this chapter, I consider how men social workers'[1] often contradictory and fragmented subject positions in the UK are produced through global discourses of welfare.

While this book provides examples of how 'men' can be analysed at local, national and global levels, this chapter describes the organizational positions of men within the social work profession in the UK and considers the discursive production of the category 'men social workers'. The gendered discourses of the post-Second World War welfare state in the UK and recent developments in the construction of welfare are discussed. It is argued that the 'crisis'/'restructuring' of the welfare state in the late twentieth century has brought about new gendered discourses of welfare. Because the provision of welfare has to be understood as the product of local as well as supra-national and international developments, in the final section of this chapter, global discourses of 'risk' and 'professional expertise' are considered in relation to how they impact on men social workers' practices and professional identities in the UK.

Organizational Locations of Men Social Workers in the UK

While men are numerically under-represented in the social work profession in the UK, men social workers are over-represented in particular areas of the profession. Gendered horizontal and vertical patterns of occupational segregation have been identified by a number of authors (Lyons et al. 1995; Pringle 1995; Christie 1998b). In England, the number of social workers employed by social service departments has increased from 30,400 in 1994 to 33,900 in 1999 (Department of Health 2000b). In 1999, 27 per cent of social workers were men. The highest percentage of men worked in generic teams (30 per cent) and health settings and specialist teams (29 per cent). Men were least likely to be found working in day-centres (22 per cent) and equally likely to work in child-care services (24 per cent) and with the elderly (24 per cent). While these figures do not show marked differences in horizontal gender occupational segregation, they do suggest that men are over-represented in higher status, special posts. Men are also over-represented in generic posts in which social workers provide services to a variety of clients and often develop community-based as well individually focused approaches. Men social workers are under-represented in daycare where more direct care is provided to clients. Despite these differences, these figures also suggest that men are present across the professional areas of social work practice.

Another area of social work in which men tend to be over-represented is the probation service. For more than twenty years, until the mid-1990s, both probation officers and social workers gained their professional qualification by completing generic social work training. However, in 1996, the Home Office decided that the social work qualification was no longer required for employment as a probation officer. Sponsorship of students on social work programmes was stopped and nine regional consortia were established to provide qualifying probation training. From 1993 the number of men probation officers started to decline and for the first time more women than men were employed as probation officers. The slow-down and decline in the number of men probation officers may be partly explained by the general decline in the number of men social workers (Annison 2001). The introduction of specialist training might have been expected to reverse this trend; however, as yet, the decline in the number of men probation officers continues.

There are very clear patterns of vertical gender occupational segregation in the social work profession in the UK. In 1971, 90 per cent of directors of social service departments in England and Wales were men; twenty-six years later in 1997, the percentage had only reduced to 82 per cent of directors being men (Social Services Inspectorate 1997). When this change was analysed in more detail, Foster (1999) found that women have been particularly successful in gaining directorships in the relatively small, new unitary authorities. However, between 1992 and 1997, there was an increase in the percentage of men directors in the larger London and metropolitan boroughs. It is perhaps surprising to note that as recently as 1997, 18 per cent of social services departments in England and Wales employed only men as senior managers (Social Services Inspectorate 1997).

The gender occupational segregation within the profession is clearly related to the number of men and women applying for social work training. In the 1990s, the overall number of men and women applying to social work courses declined rapidly. Since 1995, the number of applications to social work courses has halved (Sanders 2000). While there has been a general decline in the overall number of applicants for social work training, there has been a particularly marked decline in the number of men applying for places on social work courses. In 1995, 3,264 men applied for places on social work qualifying courses through the Social Work Admissions System.[2] By 1999, the number of applications from men had reduced by 35 per cent to 1,142. This decline in the number of men applying for social work courses may be partly explained by the ending of the Residential Child Care Initiative which sponsored the training of mostly residential child-care managers and the ending of sponsorships by the probation service. However, other factors such as media coverage of men social workers' violence to children in residential settings (see discussion later in this chapter) may have reduced men's interest in the profession. The recent review of social work education (Department of Health 1998) argued that social work has a low status in comparison to other professions. The report suggests that social work is a 'low-tech' occupation dealing with the more vulnerable in society with a relatively low academic threshold for qualification. It noted that the social work profession lacks an established research base and that there is a lack of high-profile professional leadership. These factors may discourage applicants, particularly men applicants who are interested in professional status, from applying for social work training.

Another factor affecting the drop in applications is the replacement of third-level student grants with a system of loans. Social work courses often attract men as mature students and/or men from working-class communities and both groups will have been affected by reductions in financial support for students. Individual men's choices to train as social workers are clearly related to available choices in the labour market as well as numerous other factors. The motivations of individual students are often complex and sometimes contradictory (Christie and Kruk 1998). Particular life experiences of students are also significant in choosing to become social workers (Christie and Weeks 1998), and men social work students often have had experiences of caring for adults and/or children before entering social work training (Cree 1996).

The organizational locations of men social workers and their numbers suggest that the profession in the UK is gendered in particular ways. Men are present in all areas of practice; however, they are over-represented in senior management positions. With the current changes in the definitions and status of the profession, it is likely that the locations of men in social work will not fluctuate greatly in the short term. It has yet to be seen how the professional realignment of the probation service and the establishment of community care managers will influence the numbers of men and their specific locations within the profession in the UK.

National and Global Discourses of Welfare

In this section I discuss how the identities of men in the UK are (re)produced within national and global discourses of the welfare. The post-Second World War Keynesian welfare state in the UK was based on two assumptions: that the national government could manage the national economy which would provide full, male, lifelong employment; and that the patriarchal nuclear family would continue to be the basic unit of society (O'Brien and Penna 1998). The welfare state promoted the division of men into the public sphere of paid work and women into the private sphere of unpaid domestic and caring work in the home. The family was the basic unit of a nationally bounded society, the welfare of which was a state concern in the 'national interests'. In the UK, the Keynesian welfare state constructed men as 'breadwinners', 'family-men', 'nation-builders' and 'soldier heroes' (Christie 2000). Beveridge, in producing the blueprint for the welfare state in the UK, privileged a particular family form, described by Pascall (1997) as the 'Beveridge family' in which men were positioned as breadwinners assuming financial responsibility for the family, earning the 'family wage' as well as exercising control over family members. Discourses of welfare legitimated men's patriarchal position within the 'Beveridge family' to exercise control over women and children. While the 'Beveridge family' may now be less common in the UK, with women's increasing participation in the labour market, men often continue to have disproportionate control over how the combined income of the family is spent and retain part of the 'family wage' for personal spending money (Millar 1996).

The Keynesian welfare state also positioned men as 'nation-builders' and 'soldier heroes'. 'Race', 'nation' and 'empire' are deeply embedded in the Beveridge view of the welfare state (Lewis 1997). The welfare state was expected to produce British men who could defend the 'empire'. Black workers, who were invited to the UK in the 1940s and 1950s to augment the labour force, were denied or restricted access to welfare services. Social work, as one of the professions within the welfare state, was required to prepare future generations of men to drive the British economy and maintain its colonial position. The discourse of welfare and social work, therefore, even in a context of immigration, was firmly located within national borders and in the 'best interests' of the 'nation'.

During the 1990s, a 'crisis' or restructuring of welfare has occurred in most welfare states. The Keynesian welfare state was based on individual nation-states controlling their economies and developing their own social policies. This relationship has broken down under the impact of globalization (Penna et al. 2000). Globalization is usually understood as a predominantly economic process in which new centres of production and consumption emerge alongside new technologies of transport and communication and changes in the division of labour. However, social, economic and political arenas are not easily separated and along with the integration of international economies, goods, services and finance, new forms of regional, national, supra-national and global social regulation have emerged. These global social and economic structures and discourses have become increasingly important in how welfare services are gendered and the professional identities of social workers are produced.

Before discussing the emergence of global discourses of welfare, I want to highlight the contested nature of 'globalization' as a social phenomenon. Dearlove (2000) argues that nation-states, including Britain, still maintain considerable power and that the British did not have as much economic control, in the immediate post-Second World War period, as is suggested by many advocates of globalization. The uncritical use of globalization 'robs politicians of control and responsibility at the same time as it minimizes the importance of the domestic story' (Dearlove 2000: 111). National politicians still maintain powerful positions in determining national policies. Instead of playing a diminishing role, the nation-state has growing significance in such areas as the mediation between local and regional/global levels of governance. A further danger with the uncritical use of globalization is that a circular argument can develop in which the same social phenomena that define globalization are used to point to its existence. Pugh and Gould (2000) argue that attributing all social change to globalization may lead to a de-politicization of social work and to underplaying the possibilities of resistance.

While the concept of globalization may be used uncritically, there is evidence of the development of transnational, if not global, discourses of welfare. While the European Union has had a limited role in developing social policy, there has often been a 'spillover' from the development of the economic system into other areas of activity (Leibfried 2000). European social policy has followed market integration, often to encourage economic competitiveness. Even at the inception of the European Union in 1957, the French parliament almost failed to ratify the Treaty of Rome because of disagreement over the disparity between social entitlements in France and Germany. The Social Charter (the Charter of the Fundamental Rights of Workers of the European Union) and more recently the Social Chapter included in the Maastricht Treaty (1991) have been adopted to avoid 'social dumping' and individual member countries gaining competitive advantages by reducing social costs and lowering employment protection. The European Union provides an example of how supra-national economic and social policies impact on the national context and locate British social work within broad structures that regulate a more globalized, transnational market economy.

Gender equality and mobility legislation have been encouraged by EU initiatives to facilitate the flows of migrant labour and the pool of labour available. This has involved a consideration of family/workplace relationships. Under Directive 96/34/EC, which came into force in the UK on 16 December 1999, parents of children under the age of five years are entitled to up to thirteen weeks' unpaid leave from their employment. The British government is currently considering whether parents should be entitled to paid rather than unpaid parental leave. The government estimates that only 2 per cent of men and 35 per cent of women will take parental leave if it remains unpaid. The reconstruction of relationships between the home and the workplace has considerable implications for how men are positioned within the family and within the workplace. Prime Minister Tony Blair's public decision to take time off work on the birth of his son, Leo, produced much public discussion about men as fathers. The idea that the role of father can interfere with men's roles as workers suggests an increasing blurring of the clear public/private dichotomy of the post-Second World War welfare state. Equally, the focus on men in families has become an increasingly critical feature of public discourse that has implications for the expectations of men social workers and men social service users. In a globalized context, in which the workplace is becoming feminized, the family seems to be becoming a more publicly invoked site of masculinity, mainly through discourses of paternity and fatherhood.

Yet the power of the economic sphere to impact on family welfare has not gone away. Economic institutions such as the IMF, World Bank and NAFTA in the latter part of the twentieth century, present themselves as technically, rationally and economically driven. However, it can be argued that there is an underlying neo-liberal political agenda which promotes liberalization, deregulation and privatization leading to the further accumulation of capital. It is clear that the 'neo-liberal restructuring of the labour market results in the redistribution of income and power upwards' (Mishra 1999: 96). In the UK, neo-liberal policies on welfare provision have resulted in ever-increasing health and income disparities (Pugh and Gould 2000). The restructuring of the labour market has resulted in particular groups of men being almost permanently excluded from the labour market and/ or suffering from ill health. There are no obvious channels by which these men are being supported by the social work profession or, indeed, by which they might gain access to social work as a career option.

While there has been a growth of neo-liberal global economies in the UK during the 1980s and 1990s, in response to feminism and anti-racist movements, anti-oppressive practice was established as a central tenet of social work practice (Penna et al. 2000). Since the 1980s the anti-oppressive agenda has broadened to include other critiques of inequality. Professional social work training in the UK requires social workers to be able 'to identify, analyze and take action to counter discrimination, racism, disadvantage, inequality and injustice' (CCETSW 1995: 4). Dominelli and McLeod (1989) argue that social work is a unique occupation for men because they are expected to use feminist theories to analyse their work. While men social work students who successfully complete their professional qualifying training have to demonstrate competence in anti-oppressive practice, there has been little research on how this training has transferred to the work-place (Christie 1998a). There is also evidence that the changing structure of local and national economies in a context of globalization may produce a backlash against such anti-oppressive initiatives.

The development of neo-liberal global economies has prompted the demand for global social policy, including the setting of global social standards that can be universally applied, but determined differentially depending on the level of economic prosperity in particular countries (Mishra 1999). To parallel this development, there has been a call for social work to develop transnational links and develop as an international lobby. Penna et al. (2000: 120) argue that international links have become increasingly important in the formation of professional social work identity and that international linkages between social workers might provide oppor-tunities to 'advance an alternative to neo-liberal, global social and economic governance'. In a similar vein, Otto and Lorenz (1998) argue that there is a global crisis of identity for social workers and that social workers can maintain a degree of professional autonomy only by developing inter-professional and international co-operation. They argue that social work should focus on the promotion of social citizenship and social justice for disadvantaged groups. Although there is evidence of international co-operation in the social work profession through such groups as the Inter-national Federation of Social Workers and the European Association of Schools of Social Work, as well as through educational networks (e.g. ERASMUS and SOCRATES), these have relatively little impact on public representations of the profession. Demonstrators at the 1999 World Trade Organization conference in Seattle proved the potential for globally organ-ized protest (Pugh and Gould 2000), but, at this point, it is not clear where the source of cohesion and politics for the social work profession may emerge from.

Global Discourses of 'Risk', Professional 'Expertise' and Men Social Workers

The post-Second World War Keynesian welfare state was expected to produce a society in which social responsibility was fostered and risk was shared. Social workers were to be equipped with new social and psychological knowledge and were expected to intervene in the lives of individuals and families in order to create a more cohesive and stable society. The creation of the social services departments in 1968 was founded on the belief that 'social problems could be overcome via state intervention by professional social workers with scientific knowledge and skills in the use of relationships' (Parton et al. 1997: 21). During the 1980s and 1990s, social workers increasingly realized the limitations of their professional practices in 'solving' social problems and started to recognize that some of their practices, although well intentioned, might create new risks (for example, the institutionalization of children and adults). Beck (1996: 38) has suggested that scientific knowledge (including psychological and social scientific knowledge) may provide solutions, but will also cause new sets of risk, as 'all attempts at solutions bear in themselves the seeds of new and more difficult problems'. In the UK, the provision of residential care for children has created a new set of risks, particularly involving violence from men workers. Although probably a necessary component of overall care services for children, it is now recognized that these services can never be risk free.

By the late 1990s, one-third of all police forces in the UK were involved in major investigations into child abuse within residential settings (Woffinden and Webster 1998). Frank Beck, a former manager in Leicestershire's children's homes, was given five life sentences for abusing approximately two hundred children over thirteen years (D'Arcy and Gosling 1998). The Warner Report (Department of Health 1992), produced after the Frank Beck case, focused specifically on the selection and management of staff in children's residential homes, but did not address the fact that the majority of the abusers of children are men. The report recommended such strategies as the psychological profiling of staff, but did not consider any gendered patterns of professional practice that could be modified.

The government report, *Lost in Care* (Department of Health 2000a), was published after a three-year enquiry into abuse of mostly boys in children's homes in North Wales. About 140 residents in one children's home had made allegations of physical and sexual abuse between 1974 and 1984, mostly against one man social worker. While *Lost in Care* made seventy-two recommendations to improve the quality of care provided in children's residential homes, the report failed to recognize the gendered nature of the abuse committed largely by one man social worker against mostly boys. Sexual abuse by men who work with children needs to be analysed within the context of a patriarchal society in which hegemonic discourses of masculinity frame men's sexual exploitation of women and children as trivial, or deny it, or claim it as the exception (Colton and Vanstone 1998). In addition to violence against children, violence by men social workers against adult clients has also been identified. For example, Brown and Turk (1994) describe violence by men workers and volunteers towards adults with learning disabilities, and Holt (1993) argues that older people are abused in residential settings and in their own homes by men professionals. While research is now highlighting men's violence across many areas of social work, research also needs to identify good practice by men in the professions so that we do not exclude the possibility of men doing social work well.

Trevillion (1999) has described the global shift from older technologies of institutional care to new technologies of community care. In some areas of social work in the UK, social workers have been redefined as 'community care managers', shifting their designation from workers in the field of the social to managers in the provision of community-based care. De-institutionalization provided opportunities for discussion on the quality of care provided in various institutions, which in turn encouraged the exposure of child abuse by men social workers in many of the institutions. The introduction of community care and the replacement of children's homes with fostering schemes does not guarantee the safety of social work clients. Indeed, community and family-based care may be even more difficult to monitor. If the end of the twentieth century exposed the limits of social work in managing risk in institutional care, it is the very expertise on which the profession is based that is being questioned in the UK and globally at the millennium.

Social work in the UK went through processes of professionalization, which Hearn (1992) describes as masculinization. Caring work undertaken by women in the private domain was transformed into an occupation in the public domain with associated bodies of knowledge and codes of ethics. The process of masculinization not only redefined and changed particular caring activities but also men were encouraged to take part in these activities as paid workers. In the 1950s, men were encouraged into the profession to raise the public status of social work (Younghusband 1951). The development of the Central Council for Education and Training for Social Work, university-based qualifying training, the British Association of Social Work, as well as social work agencies gaining specific legal powers, suggests that social work in the UK at least gained the status of a semi-profession. The status of social work as a profession in the UK has none the less always been ambiguous, with individual social workers and social work agencies questioning what the 'social' means as well as the parameters of the profession. Dominelli (1996) argues that the globalization of the economy and the internationalization of the nation-state have led to a deprofessionalization of social work in the UK. Social workers have lost their professional autonomy, carrying out increasingly technical activities tightly prescribed by legal requirements, government guidance/procedures and agency policies. These technical activities have led to a commodification of inter-personal relationships between social workers and service users. Professional expertise has been limited to a list of competences and the management of social workers has progressively become a bureaucratic exercise in which competition between service providers determines the quality of services provided (Dominelli 1999).

Postmodern writers have also challenged the status of professions and professional knowledge. Fook (2000) argues that central to the existence of a profession is its claim to a particular body of knowledge. This knowledge is challenged on epistemological grounds, with postmodern theorists questioning what types of knowledge become legitimated, how knowledge becomes legitimated and whose knowledge becomes accepted as the 'truth'. The 'mastery' of knowledge in which men's knowledge is privileged has been thoroughly critiqued by feminist writers (e.g. Stanley and Wise 1993). The 'grand narratives' that were once accepted are now increasingly being questioned. Second, Fook (2000) argues that the legitimacy of professional knowledge is being questioned in relation to the knowledges of service users who are being recognized as experts in their own problems. Globalization has led to both the dominance of neo-liberal politics and to the proliferation of interest groups that have used new global technologies to establish new local and international lobbies and knowledges (Lorenz 1998). It has encouraged both market-driven competition and increased accountability for social workers as their 'expertise' and the basis for its use are brought into question in discourses of 'risk'.

Social work in the UK has entered a period when global discourses of 'risk' and professional 'expertise' are positioning men social workers as both 'risky' and 'special'. Public discussion of men social workers' violence, particularly against children, has demonstrated that some men may be attracted to social work because it provides opportunities for them to abuse children. At the same time, men social workers are considered 'special' because they are under-represented as basic grade workers and their practices as social workers have the potential to challenge hegemonic constructions of masculinity. This process of polarization seems to prevent discussion of men's everyday practices as social workers. Globalization processes, such as the diminished significance of 'the national' and dominance of neo–liberal global markets, are undermining and destabilizing a profession that arose primarily in the interests of the nation-state as national economy and men's roles as 'breadwinners' and 'heroes' in maintaining that national economy.

Concluding Comments

Global discourses of 'risk' and deprofessionalization have positioned men in an uneasy relationship to social work in the UK. They can no longer assume professional status in a profession in which expertise is constantly questioned and reviewed by the state, legal profession and service users. Also their gender is often interpreted as representing a 'risk' in an occupation that works primarily with the vulnerable. Discourses of 'risk' and deprofessionalization increasingly represent the workplace, particularly within social work, as a contested site of masculinity. The public/private gendered divide, which was at the centre of Beveridge's welfare state, is becoming undone. Men's identities as 'breadwinners' and/or 'family men' have been undermined by a global labour market that is increasingly feminized. The private, as well as the public, has become a significant site for the discursive production of masculinity, with paternity and fatherhood endlessly contested in the British media. The decline of the British Empire, the rationalization of the British army, the recruitment of women in the army, increased reliance on technologies in warfare, and the expansion of transnational military institutions and alliances, mean that British men are no longer required to occupy the positions of 'soldier heroes' or 'nation-builders' that were the basis of Beveridge's welfare state. UK-based social workers working for local government social services departments are now encouraged to undertake Voluntary Service Overseas in such countries as Kenya, Uganda and Russia (Stark 2000), representing a concern with global rather than national welfare and governance.

Perhaps new possibilities for rehabilitating the 'man social worker' may emerge from the processes of supra-national and international solidarity building advocated by Otto and Lorenz (1998). Although ridiculed as 'unmanly', the focus on 'men' as 'men' seems to have shifted to the sphere of the family and fatherhood. It is not clear where this will lead in relation to the social work profession and perceptions of men in the profession as well as men clients. There is no doubt, however, that the home/workplace relationship is an increasingly significant site for the negotiation of gender identities in 'developed' countries, in EU and UK social policy. Men in social work, like the nation-state, seem, at present, to be unstably located somewhere between the domestic sphere and the transnational or global.

Notes

1. I use the term 'men social workers' rather than 'male social workers' to emphasize the variety of subject positions, including gendered subject positions, that men occupy while working as social workers.

2. The Social Work Admissions System is a 'clearing house' that processes 60 per cent of all applications to social work courses in the UK.

References

Annison, J. (2001) 'Men Probation Officers: Gender and Change in the Probation Service', in A. Christie (ed.), *Men and Social Work: Theories and Practices*, Basingstoke: Macmillan.

Beck, U. (1996) 'Risk Society and the Provident State', in S. Lash, B. Szerszynski and B. Wynne (eds), *Risk, Environment and Modernity*, London: Sage.

Brindle, D. (2000) 'Social Care: Rescuing a Tainted Service', *Guardian*, 22 May: 10.

Brown, H. and V. Turk (1994) 'Sexual Abuse in Adulthood: Ongoing Risks for People with Learning Disabilities', *Child Abuse Review*, Vol. 3: 26–35.

CCETSW (1995) *Rules and Requirements for the Diploma in Social Work*, Paper No. 30, London: CCETSW.

Christie, A. (1998a) 'Is Social Work a Non-traditional Occupation for Men?', *British Journal of Social Work*, Vol. 28, No. 4: 491–510.

— (1998b) 'A Comparison of Arguments for Employing Men as Child Care Workers and Social Workers in Denmark and the UK', *Social Work in Europe*, Vol. 5, No. 1: 2–17.

— (2000) 'Gendered Discourses of Welfare, Men and Social Work', in A. Christie (ed.), *Men and Social Work: Theories and Practices*, Basingstoke: Macmillan.

Christie, A. and E. Kruk (1998) 'Choosing to Become a Social Worker: Motives, Incentives, Concerns and Disincentives', *Social Work Education*, Vol. 7, No. 1: 21–34.

Christie, A. and J. Weeks (1998) 'Life Experience: A Neglected Form of Knowledge in Social Work Education and Practice', *Practice*, Vol. 10, No. 1: 55–68.

Colton, M. and M. Vanstone (1998) 'Sexual Abuse by Men Who Work with Children: An Exploratory Study', *British Journal of Social Work*, Vol. 28, No. 4: 511–23.

Cree, V. (1996) 'Why Do Men Care?', in K. Cavanagh and V. E. Cree (eds), *Working with Men: Feminism and Social Work*, London: Routledge.

D'Arcy, M. and P. Gosling (1998) *Abuse of Trust: Frank Beck and the Leicestershire Children's Home Scandal*, London: Bowerdean.

Dearlove, J. (2000) 'Globalization and the Study of British Politics', *Politics*, Vol. 20, No. 2: 111–18.

Department of Health (1992) *Choosing with Care: The Report of the Committee of Inquiry into the Selection, Development and Management of Staff in Children's Homes (Warner Report)*, London: HMSO.

— (1998) *Review of Central Council for Education and Training in Social Work*, London: Stationery Office.

— (2000a) *Lost in Care: Report of the Tribunal of Inquiry into the Abuse of Children in Care in the Former County Council Areas of Gwynedd and Clwyd since 1974 (Waterhouse Report)*, London: Stationery Office.

— (2000b) *Personal Social Services Staff of Social Services Departments at 30 September 1990 (England)*, London: Stationery Office.

Dominelli, L. (1996) 'Deprofessionalizing Social Work: Anti-oppressive Practice, Competencies and Postmodernism', *British Journal of Social Work*, Vol. 26, No. 2: 153–75.

— (1999) 'Neo-liberalism, Social Exclusion and Welfare Clients in a Global Economy', *International Journal of Social Welfare*, Vol. 8, No. 1: 14–22.

Dominelli, L. and E. McLeod (1989) *Feminist Social Work*, Basingtoke: Macmillan.

Fook, J. (2000) 'Deconstructing and Deconstructing Professional Expertise', in B. Fawcett, B. Featherstone, J. Fook and A. Rossiter (eds), *Practice and Research in Social Work: Postmodern Feminist Perspectives*, London: Sage.

Foster, J. (1999) *Women's Progress: Women Directors of Social Services 1997*, London: Stationery Office.

Franklin, B. (1998) *Hard Pressed: National Newspaper Reporting of Social Work Structures and Social Work*, London: Reed.

Hearn, J. (1992) *Men in the Public Eye: The Construction of and Deconstruction of Public Men and Public Patriarchies*, London: Routledge.

Holt, M. (1993) 'Elder Sexual Abuse in Britain: Preliminary Findings', *Journal of Elder Abuse and Neglect*, Vol. 5: 63–71.

Jackson, D. (1990) *Unmasking Masculinity: A Critical Autobiography*, London: Unwin Hyman.

Jones, D. (1999) 'Regulating Social Work: Key Questions', *Practice*, Vol. 11, No. 3: 55–63.

Leibfried, S. (2000) 'National Welfare States, European Integration and Globalization: A Perspective for the Next Century', *Social Policy and Administration*, Vol. 34, No. 1: 44–63.

Lewis, G. (1997) 'Welfare Settlements and Racialising Practices', *Soundings*, Vol. 4: 109–19.

Lorenz, W. (1998) 'The ECSPRESS Approach: The Social Professions Between National and Global Perspectives', *Social Work in Europe*, Vol. 5, No. 3: 1–8.

Lyons, K., I. La Valle and C. Grimwood (1995) 'Career Patterns of Qualified Social Workers: Discussion of a Recent Survey', *British Journal of Social Work*, Vol. 25, No. 2: 173–90.

Millar, J. (1996) 'Women, Poverty and Social Security', in C. Hallett (ed.), *Women and Social Policy: An Introduction*, London: Prentice Hall/Harvester Wheatsheaf.

Mishra, R. (1999) *Globalization and the Welfare State*, Cheltenham: Edward Elgar.

O'Brien, M. and S. Penna (1998) *Theorising Welfare: Enlightenment and Modern Society*, London: Sage.

Otto, H. and W. Lorenz (1998) 'The New Journal for the Social Professions in Europe', *European Journal of Social Work*, Vol. 1, No. 1: 1–4.

Parton, N., D. Thorpe and C. Wattam (1997) *Child Protection: Risk and the Moral Order*, Basingstoke: Macmillan.

Pascall, G. (1997) 'Women and the Family in the British Welfare State: The Thatcher/Major Legacy', *Social Policy and Administration*, Vol. 31, No. 3: 290–305.

Pease, B. (2000) *Recreating Men: Postmodern Masculinity Politics*, London: Sage.

Penna, S., I. Paylor and J. Washington (2000) 'Globalization, Social Exclusion and the Possibilities for Global Social Work and Welfare', *European Journal of Social Work*, Vol. 3, No. 2: 109–22.

Pringle, K. (1995) *Men, Masculinities and Social Welfare*, London: UCL Press.

Pugh, R. and N. Gould (2000) 'Globalization, Social Work, and Social Welfare', *European Journal of Social Work*, Vol. 3, No. 2: 123–38.

Sanders, C. (2000) 'Is Social Work Becoming an Outcast?', *The Times Higher Educational Supplement*, 21 April: 6–7.

Social Services Inspectorate (1997) *Women in Social Services: Maximising the Potential of the Workforce*, London: HMSO.

Stanley, L. and S. Wise (1993) *Breaking Out Again: Feminist Ontology and Epistemology*, London: Routledge.

Stark, R. (2000) 'A Global Resource', *Professional Social Worker*, April: 15.

Trevillion, S. (1999) 'On being a Social Worker: Globalization and the New Subjectivities', in P. Chamberlayne, A. Cooper, R. Freeman and M. Rustin (eds), *Welfare and Culture in Europe: Towards a New Paradigm in Social Policy*, London: Jessica Kingsley, pp. 63–80.

Watson, S. (2000) 'Foucault and the Study of Social Policy', in G. Lewis, S. Gewirtz and J. Clarke (eds), *Rethinking Social Policy*, London: Sage

Wothnden, B. and R. Webster (1998) 'Abuse in the Balance', *Guardian*, 9 May: 35.

Younghusband, E. (1951) *Social Work in Britain. A Supplementary Report on the Employment and Training of Social Workers*, Edinburgh: Constable.

Men and Masculinities in Late-modern Ireland

Harry Ferguson

When asked by a journalist in 2000 'What is a real man?', the Irish Taoiseach (Prime Minister), Bertie Ahern, replied through a spokesman, 'This wouldn't be high on his list of priorities at the moment' (Holmquist 2000). This sums up pretty well the position of men in power in Ireland with regard to critical reflection on men and masculinities: there is always something more important to do. Running the country obviously brings real demands that have a major impact on people's lives, but the crucial point is that reflection on gender, at least in terms of masculinity, is not seen as part of what governance is about.

In Ireland explicit attention to gender has invariably been considered as a women's issue. There are signs that this is just beginning to change, with growing attention paid to the notion that masculinity is 'in crisis' (Clare 2000). Irish history and social science have until recently been all about men, who have literally dominated Irish history and society, in the state, Church and civil society. The election for the first time of twenty women to the Dail Eireann (Irish parliament) in 1992 (out of a total of 166 seats) was heralded as a major breakthrough for women, and a tribute to thirty years of second-wave feminism and the efforts of the women's movement (Beale 1986; O'Connor 1998; Mahon 1995; Second Commission on the Status of Women 1993). However, while men are everywhere in Irish society, relatively little critical attention has been given to them *as men*. As Maria Lohan (2000) has argued, scholarship in Ireland has been slower than in other countries to incorporate the study of men and masculinities into gender studies. Men as gendered subjects have remained largely outside the gaze of critical enquiry.

My aim in this chapter is to begin to fill this gap by examining some of the forms that masculinities are taking in Ireland and providing an overview of what is known about men's lives, in terms of such core issues as work, sexuality, fatherhood, social exclusion and marginalization. I will argue that the Irish case exemplifies dramatic changes in how masculinities are configured in the western world. This is both in terms of a reconfiguration of power relations and hegemonic masculinity (Connell 1995; 1998), and the counter trend whereby processes of individualization (Beck 1992; Giddens 1991) are enabling men more actively to shape the construction of their identities as gender and the self take more fluid and reflexive late-modern forms.

Traditional Masculinity, Irish Style

It is important to be clear at the outset what is meant here by 'masculinity' and the kind of analytical framework that is required to examine masculinities and the gender order in particular times and places. As Connell (1995) shows, masculinities are 'configurations of practice', that is to say, ways of being men are constructed in relation to one another and the broad gender order. Just as there is no single femininity or womanhood, ways of being men are socially and historically variable. But while there is diversity in men's practices, each era has a hegemonic form of masculinity that dominates what manhood is meant to be. 'Masculinity' is 'a place in gender relations, the practices through which men and women engage that place in gender, and the effects of these practices in bodily experience, personality and culture' (Connell 1995: 71). Thus the study of masculinity as configurations of practice does not mean focusing in any simple sense on issues of character or men's personalities. It requires us to examine the shifting nature of power relations within the gender order and the processes and relationships through which men and women conduct gendered lives. Gender is a way of structuring social practice in general, not a special type of practice, which means that it is inherently involved with other social structures. Gender interacts with class and race as well as with nationality or position in the world order (Connell 1995: 75). Within this analytical framework, then, the study of masculinity needs to be historical, as well as alert to social relations with respect to ethnicity and class and the global order.

The island of Ireland is made up of thirty-two counties, twenty-six of which comprise the Republic of Ireland as constituted by the formation of the Irish Free State in 1922 – hereafter referred to as 'Ireland'. The other six counties remained under British rule in the United Kingdom and are not featured in any substantive way in this analysis. Some mention of the northern six counties is inevitable, however, as it is impossible to consider Ireland without reference to the thirty years of conflict in the North. Ireland is, by global standards, a small country, with a population of 3. 7 million. Yet its true 'size' and impact as a nation has to be seen globally in terms of the huge Irish diaspora, 'wherever green is worn'. Across the globe an estimated 70 million people have the right to call themselves Irish (Coogan 2000). Around the time of the great famine (c.1845–50) alone, at least a million of the then population of 8 million perished, while another 1.5 million, at least, emigrated. Because of the profound historical significance of emigration and the impact of colonization within the British Empire, identity in Ireland has always been constructed on a global stage, although the terms of that engagement have shifted over time, not least today with the emergence of globalization processes.

Traditional masculinity in Ireland was essentially rural, based heavily around the family, marriage and celibacy. Since the formation of the Irish state and for most of the twentieth century, it was the Catholic Church, with its monopoly over morality, which held the balance of power in the governance of society (Inglis 1998a). Ireland was 98 per cent Catholic and the extraordinary hold of the Church on people's everyday lives was such that, as recently as 1973, weekly mass attendance was 91 per cent. Today it is around 60–70 per cent and this decline causes alarm in some circles. The Irish state was made up of 'good-living' Catholic men whose deference to the Catholic hierarchy meant that the 1937 Constitution of Ireland and all other aspects of governance were heavily imbued with Catholic social teaching (Whyte 1980). The celibate priest was the role model for Irish masculinity. Having a son a priest was a status symbol and it was common for the first born to enter the priesthood. As a forty-five-year-old priest interviewed as part of a research project into Irish men's lives reflected upon it, 'You really had it made in society in our country if you had a well in the yard, a bull in the field and a son a priest' (Ferguson and Reynolds 2001).

The Catholic hierarchy in Ireland expected strict adherence to the compulsory celibacy rule and the form of hegemonic masculinity was cast around celibacy. At the core of this social order was the private family and heterosexual marriage whose sole purpose was procreation, rather than pleasure. Contraception was banned and the birth rate remained extremely high until the 1970s. Even within marriage the Irish man and woman were meant to be chaste. Sex was for procreation. Celibate men helped to create a silence, awkwardness and embarrassment about sexuality and intimate emotional relationships (Inglis 1998b). This does not mean that Irish men and women never had sexual pleasure. Rather, if they did it was a transgressive act within a dominant discourse which induced shame about the body and 'unruly passions'. Allied to this, sport played a key role in the production of the disciplined, Catholic, self-reliant Irish male body. The Gaelic Athletic Association (GAA), with 750,000 members and 360,000 registered players, is still the second largest organization in the country after the Catholic Church. Its attempts actively to create a national-minded manhood intensified after the creation of an independent Irish Free State in 1922 as part of an attempt to relieve Irish culture of an identity bequeathed by the colonizer (Doak 1998).

A further strand to the configuration of traditional hegemonic masculinity in Ireland was the hard-working man and the 'good provider' role. Men were the exclusive breadwinners, while women were constructed as the carers, the 'specialists in love and the emotions' (Giddens 1992). Irish men, married or single, have traditionally gone to extraordinary lengths to find work and make a living for themselves and their families. At times of economic recession and high emigration – such as the 1950s – many Irish men leave their families to travel the globe alone to find work and send home money to keep them. While often lampooned and the victim of anti-Irish racism in Britain and elsewhere (Foster 1993, Swift and Gilly 1989), the figure of the Irish labourer is part of a decent, deeply honourable male tradition which deserves great respect. The same can be said for those, like the 'bachelor farmer', who stayed at home (Curtin and Varley 1987). The assumption of the male breadwinner was so enshrined in Irish society that the 'marriage bar' legally required women, once married (and irrespective of whether or not they had children), to give up their jobs in public service employment, such as teaching and the civil service, a law that was repealed only in 1973. Underpinning such social policy is the pivotal position given to women – or, more accurately, mothers – as home-makers in the Irish constitution. Fathers, on the other hand, are not explicitly mentioned (McKeown et al. 1998).

Marriage and intimate relations were treated as 'fate' rather than as something based on negotiation and choices that had to be worked at (Giddens 1994). Similarly, relationships between adults and children were based on hierarchical authority relations, with little or no concept of children having rights to negotiate or to be heard in ways that were separate from their parents or other adults in authority, such as teachers. Child sexual abuse constituted fewer than 1 per cent of cases dealt with by agencies like the Society for the Prevention of Cruelty to Children prior to the 1980s (Ferguson 2001). The denial of sexual offences within the family was part of the broader repression of sexuality in intimate relations. (Hetero)sexuality was in itself regarded as fixed and treated as fate, and homosexuality was illegal. Homosexuality has, however, long been an integral, if silenced sexual practice in Irish society (Rose 1993), as 'gay men have engaged in same-sex sexual practices before they named themselves as "homosexual", "gay" or "queer"' (Ferguson and Reynolds 2001).

Those who transgressed the deeply moral norms of Irish society were severely punished. Women, and unmarried mothers in particular, suffered terribly as they were incarcerated in Magdalene Homes and their children routinely removed to the infamous Reformatory or Industrial Schools, where many were seriously abused (Raftery and O'Sullivan 1999). Boys were taught industriousness and taught the skills necessary to become labourers, while girls were prepared as future domestic servants and house-wives. While there was nothing unique to Ireland in having such beliefs about gender and sexual deviance, Irish cultural practices drew strongly on racial imagery in the context of building a post-independence nation. Church and state combined deliberately to construct masculinity and femininity to assert the difference between the Irish and the former British colonizers. This was especially expressed in terms of sexual purity and was demonstrated in clerical obsession with such things as 'evil literature', contraception and the unmarried mother (Leane 1999).

Men's sexuality and fatherhood did not escape being policed, but this occurred on different terms. If a man failed to be a good provider for his wife and children, agencies such as the Irish Society for the Prevention of Cruelty to Children stepped in to regulate 'defaulting fathers'. Typically, these men were among those who had emigrated to get work in England or the USA, leaving their families in Ireland, but who had failed to send money home. The Society would get its sister organization overseas to chase up the men and compel them to provide (see, for instance, Dublin and District Branch NSPCC *Annual Report*, 1953–54: 15). The disciplining of sexuality and class in the context of the construction of a particular view of nationhood was central to the attempts by the Church and state to produce their ideal configurations of masculinity and femininity in traditional Ireland: the well-trained domestic servant who would become the ideal of the virtuous Irish mother, 'the living embodiment of Our Lady – humble, pious, celibate and yet fecund' (Inglis, 1998a: 248–9); and the disciplined, chaste working man who would become the god-fearing priest or good breadwinning father.

Changing Men and Masculinities

At the beginning of a new millennium, the configuration of practices that constitute masculinity in Ireland is undergoing a process of change. Irish men's lives are being reconfigured around a number of social and economic processes, and with contradictory effects.

'Paedophile priests' and the decline in power of the Catholic Church Crucially, the bases for the dominance of celibate masculinity have been largely eroded as conditions for the defence of patriarchy have changed. Displacement of the traditional power of the Catholic Church has been a complex process that cannot be reduced to any single causative factor (Inglis 1998a). However, the social problem of child abuse is a key site around which the reconfiguration of gender and power relations and masculinities has occurred.

A series of clerical 'scandals' involving child abuse by priests, some of whom were known to the Church hierarchy but not reported or brought to justice by them and moved on to another parish, has dramatically weakened the Church's moral authority (Moore 1995). Men from a variety of social backgrounds have been disclosed as having perpetrated appalling child abuse, and in some cases women also. However, the ways in which men have gained prominence as offenders has been selective. The media focus has predominantly been on clerical sex offenders and the construction of the 'paedophile priest' (Ferguson 1995). This has involved explicit and crude links being made between compulsory celibacy and child sexual abuse. The clear implication is that men must have sex, and if they don't they will visit their irresistible urges on children, the most vulnerable in society. While, given the nature of Irish history, the symbolic significance of the priesthood is understandably high, the numbers of clerical offenders is statistically very small. The majority of offenders are in fact actively heterosexual men, many of whom are married. The selective focus on 'paedophile priests' has resulted in a playing down of the significance of the problem of active (married) heterosexual masculinity and a reluctance to problematize power, gender and age relations within the Irish family. Judges in historic cases have even characterized convicted married sex offenders as 'good family men' (Sheridan 1995). This is not to say that child abuse by fathers is not viewed as an abhorrent act in Irish society. The point is that active married heterosexuality has not of itself been treated as problematic, while celibate masculinity has been left to carry the weight of social disapproval and interrogation and has been marginalized. This is a legacy of how the construction of modern fatherhood involved rendering paternal masculinity 'safe' through the making of a distinction between the law's construction of the familial masculinity of the 'good father' and other 'dangerous masculinities' (Collier 1995). An assumption of compulsory heterosexuality is now at the core of how hegemonic masculinity is constructed. Irish men have been 'sexualized', but with ambiguous results (Ferguson 1995).

Economic change and the 'good family man' Ireland became set on a course of economic and social modernization in the 1960s. During the 1990s, the country experienced unprecedented economic growth and became known as the 'celtic tiger' (O'Hearn 1998). The locus of economic power has shifted from agriculture and the larger farmer to the institutions and executives of 'fast capitalism'. The 'globalization' of Ireland has seen the pattern of emigration shift to become much more fluid, with substantial return migration and people coming and going several times. Emigrants are now often highly educated – 30 per cent of all graduates emigrated in 1990 – and emigration is seen as a personal development opportunity as much as an economic or career necessity. If anything, the hegemonic construction of Irish masculinity emphasizes the 'good family man' as a hard-working man more intensely than ever. It excludes, for instance, a broader concept of men as nurturers as reflected in virtually non-existent paternity leave, and a very modest parental leave allowance (fourteen weeks to be taken before the child is five). The latter is unpaid and as men still earn on average 30 per cent more than women, not surprisingly has a low take-up.

Men in Ireland work an overall average of around forty-six hours per week, with fathers tending to work slightly longer hours than non-fathers (McKeown et al. 1998). Mothers, where they are employed, work an average of thirty-one or -two hours per week outside the home, fifteen hours less than the number of hours worked outside the home by fathers. While the father is the sole earner in about half of all households, fathers with dependent children (fifteen years and under) are more likely to be in full-time employment than any other category of men: 81 per cent compared with 60 per cent of fathers with older children and 55 per cent of non-fathers. There is clearly a connection between the financial respon-sibilities of younger fathers and their participation in employment. Younger families are twice as likely to have two earners compared with older families: one in three of younger families (36 per cent) are dual earners compared with one in six of older families (17 per cent). Two out of ten Irish families have no earners due to the effects of long-term unemploy-ment and the growth in one-parent families, the majority of which have no earners. Lone-parent families as a percentage of all families with children under fifteen years increased from 7 per cent in 1981 to 18 per cent in 1996. This is due mainly to marital breakdown and births outside marriage (McCashin 1996). Some 13 per cent of one-parent families in Ireland are headed by men.

A crucial change in the gender order is the growth in the number of women, especially married women, working outside the home. In the twenty-five years between 1971 and 1996, the proportion of women in the Irish labour force increased from 28 per cent to 36 per cent. In the same period, the labour force participation rate of men fell from 81 per cent to 69 per cent. In 1996, just under half (47 per cent) of all women in the labour force were married, compared with just over half (58 per cent) for men. Thus, by 1996 fathers were the exclusive breadwinners in only half of all families with dependent children, reflecting how the breadwinner role is increasingly shared by fathers and mothers as more women have entered the workforce (McKeown et al. 1998). This presents new challenges to men to share domestic responsibilities and be as committed to intimacy and household labour as to their work. While few empirical data are available on what men actually do 'at home' in Irish families, one study – based only on mothers' accounts of what fathers do – found that almost 70 per cent of the women interviewed said that their partners did participate in households as much as they (the mothers) would like. Despite this, considerable gender differences were apparent in child-care and domestic labour with women carrying the bulk of responsibility (Kiely 1996).

Against this background, it appears that the hegemonic form that masculinity is taking, at a policy level at least, approximates to what Connell (1998) characterizes as a 'transnational business masculinity'. This suggests 'a masculinity marked by increasing egocentrism, very conditional loyalties (even to the corporation), and a declining sense of responsibility for others (except for the purposes of image making)' (Connell 1998: 16). To argue this is not to suggest that it constitutes how most men live their lives. It refers rather to the dominant construction of masculinity which informs how the gender order is structured and is perhaps best illustrated in relation to men's relationship to children and care work.

In a context of economic growth and full employment, government policy has sought to attract mothers back into the workplace and begun to put more resources into the provision of public child care services. The entry of women into the workplace has not resulted in a corresponding reconfiguration of practices surrounding men, work and child-care. At a time when the absent 'deadbeat' dad is less culturally acceptable and fathers are generally expected to be more involved with their children, the pattern is for men in general to spend less time than ever with children. This is apparent when men's practices are examined across public and private spheres (Cameron et al. 1999). As increasing numbers of young children from dual-earner households are placed in daycare, it is women who are caring for them, at very low pay. Men are completely absent from public child-care provision and fewer and fewer are entering primary school teaching and other caring professions, such as social work and residential child-care work. The result is a feminization of childhood and shift from the private patriarchy of traditional Ireland that depended upon women's unpaid labour in the home, to a public patriarchy that exploits women's caring labour in the workplace. While the implications of performing love labour and such shifts for women and children have been quite extensively noted, the costs for men in terms of closing off opportunities to develop a generative, nurturing self have only begun to be recognized (Burgess 1997; McKeown et al. 1998). Many men resist these processes and manage to carve out meaningful caring and fatherhood roles. But they are having to do this in a culture which does little or nothing to support them as carers and which continues to regard parenting as synonymous with motherhood (Hawkins and Dollahite 1997). Yet men in general are complicit in this situation as a conspicuous public silence remains among men about their needs and desires with regard to such vital relationship issues. Nothing will change until men do.

Masculinity, individualization and the late-modern self One consequence of economic development and the decline in power of external authorities like the Church is increased individualization, processes which compel men and women to fashion their own biographies (Beck 1992). Men, women and children are required to make new kinds of decisions about how to live and who to be (Giddens 1991; 1994). There are clearly limits to the freedom people have to construct their lives, yet crucial new spaces have opened up within which men are having to make themselves the centre of their own life-planning and construct relationships and communities in historically unique ways. Because gender roles are no longer fixed in the traditional manner and heterosexual men and their partners are required to negotiate decisions concerning work and family commitments, late-modern 'intimacy' requires open emotional communication in the context of equal relationships (Giddens 1992). Irish men are experiencing these changes as a mixed blessing (Ferguson and Reynolds 2001). Some are deeply engaged in 'pure relationships' (Giddens 1992) where what matters is the quality of the relationship itself, rather than the power of tradition, the Church or family in keeping the couple together. Increasing numbers are having to endure the pain of relationship breakdown, and the introduction of divorce in Ireland in 1996 means that all men and women are having to live with the increased risk of relationship breakdown. While women still predominate in the use of therapeutic services, increasing numbers of men are turning to relationship counsellors and psychotherapists for help in planning their lives (Ferguson 1998).

After a lengthy campaign, the activism of the Irish gay rights movement eventually led to the decriminalization of homosexuality in 1993. While homophobia and violence against gay men remain painful realities and coming out is a process fraught with danger, many gay men have negotiated adversity, seized the opportunity freely to choose their sexuality and managed to build meaningful lives and communities (Rose 1993). Yet, culturally, extreme ambivalence continues to surround homosexuality and Irish identity, which is seen as an undesirable legacy of colonialism, an imported sexuality (Ferguson and Reynolds 2001). As Berriss (1996) puts it, 'If you're Irish and gay, your parents must be English.'

Masculinity Politics and the Welfare of Men

In this final section of the chapter, I shall focus on some further implications of changing configurations of masculinities for men's practices in Ireland. Ireland is no exception to the trend in late-modern societies for men to become increasingly well organized around particular issues and for intervention programmes to be targeted specifically at men (Pringle 1995; Pease 1999). Connell defines 'masculinity politics' as 'those mobilizations and struggles where the meaning of masculine gender is at issue, and, with it, men's position in gender relations. In such politics, masculinity is made a principal theme, not taken for granted as background' (Connell 1995: 205). Masculinity politics have become increasingly complex in Ireland, and it is within the scope of this discussion to refer only briefly to some of the forms they are taking, especially with respect to men and welfare.

As I have already argued, the central organizing ideology which dictates how men are governed in Ireland is the hard-working 'good family man'. When evidence emerges that not all men are in fact 'good', a deficit in governance and services arises. Violence against women by men is a major social problem in Ireland (Kelleher and Associates and O'Connor 1995). Between 1996 and 1999, fifty-five women were killed by men in Ireland. While, generally, the responses of social workers, police and the courts have improved, there is still a marked tendency to downgrade violence against women as a problem and place too much responsibility on abused women to protect themselves. Central to this is an absence of focus on the perpetrator (Ferguson and O'Reilly 2001). Intervention programmes based on group work with domestically violent men have been developing slowly in Ireland since the late 1980s and two programmes now exist. The Cork Domestic Violence Project operates in the Cork city region and adopts an accountability model of working which endeavours to have men referred to the programme by the courts as part of a sanction (O'Connor 1996). Men Overcoming Violence (MOVE), meanwhile, runs group work programmes in at least seven of the twenty-six counties of Ireland (Ferguson and Synott 1995). When it began in the late 1980s, it operated broadly on a self-help model, but has moved closer to an integrated approach based on court sanctions and accountability to abused women in terms of seeking partner contact to verify how effectively, or if, men are using the programme. Such shifts in policy and practice perspectives reflect a growing awareness of the complexities of such work with men. They have the capacity to manipulate programmes to become more skilled abusers and can further endanger women, who are prone to stay in the relationship in the hope that their partners will really change, and thus they lose the opportunity to reach true safety (Hearn 1998). A government task force has set out core principles for best practice, which must have the safety of abused women and children as its primary goal (Office of the Tánaiste 1997). Despite this, the Irish state provides little or no financial or institutional support for work with violent men, which is done by voluntary organizations.

Nor is much intervention work being done with men who abuse children. Around 90 per cent of child sexual abusers in Ireland are men, and as many as one-third of all offenders are adolescent males (McKeown and Gilligan 1991). The prosecution rate in child sexual abuse cases is very low, relative to the numbers being substantiated (McGrath 1996). Not only is justice often not served, but many sex offenders remain free and untouchable in the community. Few attempts are even being made to work with *known* offenders, especially those who have been imprisoned for such offences, as treatment programmes for sex offenders of all types are scandalously under-developed (Cotter 1999; Murphy 1998). While there are some 300 sex offenders in Irish prisons, just ten of these at any one time participate in a treatment programme (Geiran 1996). The situation with regard to physical abuse and neglect is quite different, with mothers being just as likely to be responsible as fathers (Ferguson and O'Reilly 2001). Again, however, men have tended to be systematically ignored and avoided by social workers and other child-care professionals (Buckley 1998; McKeown et al. 1998).

Masculinity politics with respect to violence are no longer confined to responses to 'dangerous men' and their victims. A self-help group for 'male victims of domestic violence', Abused Men [Amen], was established in Ireland in 1998. It has already held two international conferences and made a significant impact in terms of media coverage and placing the issue of domestic violence by women against men on the public agenda. Advocates for Amen, such as the journalist John Waters (2000), characterize supporters of the women's movement as 'feminazis' and accuse what they call the 'domestic violence industry' of having institutionalized the simplistic notion of man as perpetrator/woman as victim, and of being responsible for men being ignored as victims. They argue that domestic violence is perpetrated by women as much as by men. The value of public disclosure of men as victims is that it not only enables such men to get the help they need, it destabilizes the capacity of hegemonic masculinity to systematically expel all notions of men's vulnerability. However, the great injustice of the direction this is taking is that it undermines the legitimacy of responses to abused women and falls within a wider masculinity politics that advocates on behalf of men's rights at the expense of a broader equality agenda. Taking on the perceived excesses of feminism has become as, if not more, important than the substantive issues. All statements and initiatives connected with men are now being audited for their purity in terms of acknowledging men as victims. In 2000, for instance, an organized challenge was made by Amen and other men's rights advocates to the introduction by the Department of Education and Science (2000) of an *Exploring Masculinities* programme into the senior cycle of single-sex boys' schools. The programme has the aim of promoting the social and personal development of young men but was opposed on the grounds that it viewed masculinity as a 'social construct' and was based on allegedly feminist credentials (Waters 2000). It is too early as yet to be clear about the impact of such campaigns, which are being resisted (Lynch and Devine 2000).

A second area where men are featuring as victims is in fathers' rights to (joint) custody and access to their children in situations of relationship breakdown – a key site for men's rights politics across the western world (Clatterbaugh 1997: 70). In Ireland, Parental Equality: The Shared Parenting and Joint Custody Support Group was formed in 1993 in response to the problems experienced by fathers in obtaining shared custody of their children. Anecdotal evidence suggests that some men are given no parenting rights whatsoever. Yet due to a lack of hard statistical or research data it is unclear how many men actually apply to the courts for custody of their children, and if they do not this may reflect, at least in part, an implicit assumption that men are the secondary parents (Bertoia and Drakich 1995). The position of unmarried fathers is particularly problematic as they are not acknowledged as fathers under the Irish constitution (whereas mothers are given automatic rights by virtue of being mothers) and have to apply to the courts for guardianship of their children. While applications for guardianship are on the increase, the family courts in Ireland continue to be largely a resource used by women, not least to seek protection from domestic violence (Fahey and Lyons 1995).

The vulnerability of men in Ireland is most painfully apparent in quite dramatic increases in male suicide, especially in the eighteen-to-twenty-five-year-old bracket (Kelleher 1996). More generally, Irish men neglect their physical health – and die, on average, six years younger than women – and their mental health (Cleary 1997). The costs of traditional male socialization and of being a hard-working man are very high for men and their loved ones. This demonstrates the complexity of power relations and men's lives. Not all men are equally privileged by patriarchy, and some are marginalized due to inequalities connected to class, sexuality, ability and ethnicity. Configurations of practices which constitute masculinities involve not only relations of power between men and women but between men. For unemployed and socially excluded men, the old props of Church, work and community are largely gone. Some such men get stuck in grief for the old self, struggle to find a role for themselves, and tragically even kill themselves. Others survive through using supports like joining men's groups. At least some understanding of the vulnerability of marginalized men entered Irish government policy and practice in the mid-1990s when the then Department of Social Welfare began to provide funding to support men's groups in socially disadvantaged areas.

There is now more awareness in Ireland of the need to develop intervention work with men, and the big struggle surrounds developing an effective methodology for such work (Ferguson 1998; Hogan 1998; Hyde 1995; O'Neill 1998; Smith 1996). The validity of men's groups, or 'men's work', is conventionally evaluated in terms of its contribution to gender equality, the degree to which it challenges hegemonic masculinity, gets men to change, and be less sexist (Connell 1995; Kimmel 1995; Schwalbe 1996). This misses crucial dimensions of what men's work, especially with disadvantaged men, is all about. These are men who have lost the 'patriarchal dividend', who feel powerless, and essentially this is what they are. Such men's groups are best understood as a 'life-strategy', a resource which vulnerable men use to gain support and to engage in life-planning to help guide them in making crucial decisions about their lives (Ferguson and Reynolds 2001). They are a quintessentially late-modern practice in that they involve the construction by men of new kinds of relationships and communities in which self-conscious care for one another as men, self-identity and its reconstitution – rather than work, sport or some other external reason – are the reasons for the encounter. The first priority of such work, quite rightly, is to keep them alive, build self-esteem and help them to get and remain healthy. This may or may not eventually lead such men to pursue gender equality more actively, but it is much more likely to if men can first be helped to care for themselves (O'Neill 1998).

Conclusion

This chapter has examined the ways in which men and masculinities in Ireland have been constructed in 'modern' times. Traditional hegemonic masculinity was rural, dominated by the Church and privileged marriage, sexual purity and the celibate life. It has been replaced by a metropolitan business masculinity influenced socially and economically by global culture. Beyond this hegemonic form, men live out diverse lives and a plurality of masculinities co-exist. It has not been possible here to detail what those lives are like in anything other than a cursory way. Clearly, however, the local remains important. For instance, while under pressure from professionalization and the growing popular appeal of soccer and rugby, the GAA remains a very influential body in many Irish men's lives and communities. Pressures to position such 'traditional' nationalist cultural practices as anachronistic, as the despised 'other' to the idealized open state of modernity, need to be resisted if we are fully to understand the nature of Irish identities (Doak 1998).

The chapter has focused in particular on analysing the construction of masculinity that takes the dominant form in social policy, which I have argued today is the 'hard working good family man'. This way of seeing and governing men (and women and children) results in a marked tendency for the Irish state not to reflect the diversity that does exist in men's lives. It results in significant failures to address masculinity in terms of violence and the trauma it causes for women and children, and for men too. It leads to a repudiation of the nurturing capacities of men and a reluctance to intervene to support the creation of more opportunities for men to care for children, or others. Important beginnings have been made, however, to address these deficits, not least in intervening in the lives of vulnerable and marginalized men, types of 'men's work' that deserve global recognition.

Note

I am very grateful to Tom Inglis, Keith Pringle, Bob Pease and especially Sean Reynolds for their comments and support in the writing of this chapter.

References

Beale, J. (1986) *Women in Ireland*, Basingstoke: Macmillan

Beck, U. (1992) *Risk Society*, London: Sage.

Berriss, D. (1996) 'If You're Gay and Irish, Your Parents Must be English', *Identities – Global Studies in Culture and Power*, Vol. 2: 189–96.

Bertoia, C. E. and J. Drakich (1995) 'The Fathers' Rights Movement: Contradictions in Rhetoric and Practice', in W. Marsiglio (ed.), *Fatherhood: Contemporary Theory, Research, and Social Policy*, London: Sage.

Buckley, H. (1998) 'Filtering Out Fathers: The Gendered Nature of Social Work in Child Protection', *Irish Social Worker*, Vol. 16, No 3.

Burgess, A. (1997) *Fatherhood Reclaimed: The Making of the Modern Father*, London: Vermillion.

Cameron, C., P. Moss and C. Owen (1999) *Men in the Nursery: Gender and Caring Work*, London: Paul Chapman.

Clare, A. (2000) *On Men: Masculinity in Crisis*, London: Chatto and Windus.

Clatterbaugh, K. (1997) *Contemporary Perspectives on Masculinity: Men, Women and Politics in Modern Society*, Boulder, CO: Westview Press.

Cleary, A. (1997) 'Gender Differences in Mental Health in Ireland', in A. Cleary and M. P. Treacy (eds), *The Sociology of Health and Illness in Ireland*, Dublin: University College Dublin Press.

Collier, R. (1995) *Masculinity, Law and the Family*, London: Routledge.

Connell, R. W. (1995) *Masculinities*, Cambridge: Polity Press.

— (1998) 'Masculinities and Globalization', *Men and Masculinities*, Vol. 1, No 1: 3–23.

Coogan, T. P. (2000) *Whenever Green is Worn*, London: Hutchinson.

Cotter, A. (1999) 'The Criminal Justice System in Ireland: Towards Change and Transformation', in S. Quinn, P. Kennedy, A. O'Donnell and G. Kiely (eds), *Contemporary Irish Social Policy*, Dublin: University College Dublin Press.

Curtin, C. and A. Varley (1987) 'Marginal Men? Bachelor Farmers in a West of Ireland Community', in C. Curtin, P. Jackson, and B. O'Connor (eds), *Gender in Irish Society*, Galway: Galway University Press.

Department of Education and Science (2000) *Exploring Masculinities Programme*, Dublin: Department of Education and Science.

Doak, R. (1998) '(De)constructing Irishness in the 1990s: The Gaelic Athletic Association and the Cultural Nationalist Discourse Reconsidered', *Irish Journal of Sociology*, Vol. 8: 25–48.

Dublin and District Branch NSPCC (n.d.) *Annual Report*, 1953–54, London: NSPCC archives.

Fahey, T. and M. Lyons (1995) *Marital Breakdown and Family Law in Ireland*, Dublin Oak Tree Press in association with the Economic and Social Research Institute.

Ferguson, H. (1995) 'The Paedophile Priest: A Deconstruction', *Studies*, Vol. 84: 335.

— (1998) 'Working with Men and Masculinities', *Feedback: Journal of the Family Therapy Association of Ireland*, Vol. 8, No 1: 33–7.

— (2001) 'Ireland', in B. M. Schwartz-Kenney, M. McCauley and M. Epstein (eds), *Child Abuse: A Global View*, Westport, CT: Greenwood Publishing.

Ferguson, H. and M. O'Reilly (2001) *Keeping Children Safe: Child Abuse, Child Protection and the Promotion of Welfare*, Dublin: A. and A. Farmar.

Ferguson, H. and S. Reynolds (2001) *Gender and Identity in the Lives of Irish Men*, Research Report, Department of Social Policy and Social Work, University College Dublin.

Ferguson, H., and P. Synott (1995) 'Intervention into Domestic Violence in Ireland: Developing Policy and Practice with Men Who Batter', *Administration*, Vol. 43, No. 3: 57–81.

Foster, R. F. (1993) 'Marginal Men and Micks on the Make: The Uses of Irish Exile, c.1840–1922', in *Paddy and Mr Punch: Connections in Irish and English History*, London: Allen Lane.

Geiran, V. (1996) 'Treatment of Sex Offenders in Ireland: The Development of Policy and Practice', in H. Ferguson and T. McNamara (eds), *Protecting Irish Children: Investigation, Protection and Welfare*, special edition of *Administration*, Vol. 44, No. 2.

Giddens, A. (1991) *Modernity and Self-Identity*, Cambridge: Polity Press.

— (1992) *The Transformation of Intimacy*, Cambridge: Polity Press.

— (1994) *Beyond Left and Right*, Cambridge: Polity Press.

Hawkins, A. J. and D. C. Dollahite (eds) (1997) *Generative Fathering: Beyond Deficit Perspectives*, London: Sage.

Hearn, J. (1998) *The Violences of Men*, London: Sage.

Hogan, F. (1998) 'Soulful Storytelling with Men: An Invitation to Intimacy', *Feedback, Journal of the Family Therapy Association of Ireland*, Vol. 8, No. 1.

Holmquist, K. (2000) 'What is a Real Man?', *Irish Times*, 12 September.

Hyde, T. (ed.) (1995) *Fathers and Sons*, Dublin: Wolfhound.

Inglis, T. (1998a) *Moral Monopoly: The Rise and Fall of the Catholic Church in Modern Ireland*, Dublin: University College Dublin Press.

— (1998b) *Lessons in Irish Sexuality*, Dublin: University College Dublin Press.

Kelleher, M. (1996) *Suicide and the Irish*, Cork: Mercier Press.

Kelleher and Associates and M. O'Connor (1995) *Making the Links*, Dublin: Women's Aid.

Kiely, G. (1996) 'Fathers in Families', in C. McCarthy (ed.), *Irish Family Studies: Selected Papers*, Dublin University College Dublin Press.

Kimmel, M. (ed.) (1995) *The Politics of Manhood*, Philadelphia: Temple University Press.

Leane, M. (1999) 'Female Sexuality in Ireland 1920 to 1940: Construction and Regulation', unpublished PhD thesis, National University of Ireland, Cork.

Lohan, M. (2000) 'Extending Feminist Methodologies: Researching Masculinities and Technologies', in A. Byrne and R. Lentin (eds), *(Re)searching Women: Feminist Research Methodologies in the Social Sciences in Ireland*, Dublin: Institute of Public Administration.

Lynch, K. and D. Devine (2000) 'Factually Incorrect and Politically Mischievous', *Irish Times*, 7 November.

McCashin, A. (1996) *Lone Mothers in Ireland: A Local Study*, Dublin: Oak Tree Press in association with the Combat Poverty Agency.

McGrath, K. (1996) 'Intervening in Child Sexual Abuse in Ireland: Towards Victim-centred Policies and Practices', in H. Ferguson and T. McNamara (eds), *Protecting Irish Children: Investigation, Protection and Welfare*, special edition of *Administration*, Vol. 44, No 2.

McKeown, K. and R. Gilligan (1991) 'Child Sexual Abuse in the Eastern Health Board Region of Ireland in 1988: An Analysis of 512 Confirmed Cases', *Economic and Social Review*, Vol. 22, No. 2: 101–34.

McKeown, K., H. Ferguson and D. Rooney (1998) *Changing Fathers? Fatherhood and Family Life in Modern Ireland*, Cork: Collins Press.

Mahon, E. (1995) 'From Democracy to Femocracy: The Women's Movement in the Republic of Ireland', in P. Clancy et al. (eds), *Irish Society: Sociological Perspectives*, Dublin: Institute of Public Administration.

Moore, C. (1995) *Betrayal of Trust: The Father Brendan Smyth Affair and the Catholic Church*, Dublin: Marino.

Murphy, P. (1998), 'A Therapeutic Programme for Imprisoned Sex Offenders: Progress to Date and Issues for the Future', *Irish Journal of Psychology*, Vol. 19: 190–207.

O'Connor, C. (1996) 'Integrating Feminist and Psychological Systemic Approaches in Working with Men Who are Violent Towards Their Partners: The Cork Domestic Violence Project', *Feedback*, Vol. 7, No. 1: 2-8.

O'Connor, P. (1998) *Emerging Voices: Women in Contemporary Irish Society*, Dublin: Institute of Public Administration.

Office of the Tánaiste (1997) *Report of the Task Force on Violence Against Women*, Dublin: Stationery Office.

O'Hearn, D. (1998) *Inside the Celtic Tiger: The Irish Economy and the Asian Model*, London: Pluto Press.

O'Neill, A. (1998) 'The Men's Development Project: The Work of the South East Men's Network', *Irish Social Worker*, Vol. 16, No 3: 16.

Pease, B. (1999) 'Deconstructing Masculinity – Reconstructing Men', in B. Pease and J. Fook (eds), *Transforming Social Work Practice*, London: Routledge.

Pringle, K. (1995) *Men, Masculinities and Social Welfare*, London: UCL Press.

Raftery, M. and E. O'Sullivan (1999) *Suffer the Little Children: The Inside Story of Ireland's Industrial Schools*, Dublin: New Island Books.

Rose, K. (1993) *Diverse Communities: The Evolution of Gay and Lesbian Politics in Ireland*, Dublin: Gill and Macmillan.

Schwalbe, M. (1996) *Unlocking the Iron Cage: The Men's Movement, Gender Politics and American Culture*, New York: Oxford University Press.

Second Commission on the Status of Women (1993) *Report to Government*, Dublin: Stationery Office.

Sheridan, K. (1995) 'A Good Family Man', *Irish Times*, 18 March.

Smith, R. (1996) 'The Life of a Men's Group', in D. McCarthy and R. Lewis (eds), *Man and Now*, Cork: Togher Family Centre.

Swift, R. and S. Gilly (1989) *The Irish in Britain 1815–1939*, London: Routledge.

Waters, J. (2000) '"Big Mac Feminism" on the Education Menu', *Irish Times*, 24 October.

Whyte, J. (1980) *Church and State in Modern Ireland, 1923–1979*, Dublin: Gill and Macmillan.

9

Men's Practices in Prostitution: The Case of Sweden

Sven-Axel Månsson

Since 1999 there has been a new law in Sweden prohibiting the buying of sexual services.[1] Few if any changes in legislation have attracted so much attention and caused so much debate, both within and outside the country. There are many reasons for this, one of them being that this law cuts right into some of the most burning issues in the ongoing international debate on prostitution, issues that have to do with public control and regulation of prostitution. Sweden's attempt to do away with the 'world's oldest profession' through making criminal the buying of sexual services has been greeted with considerable ridicule and dismay from those who argue for the acceptance of prostitution as work and for commercial sex to be seen as a legitimate industrial sector of society. However, those who view prostitution as an expression of men's sexual exploitation of and violence against women, consider the law to be a major breakthrough and an important step towards a more equal society.

It is a fact that a law prohibiting the buying of sexual services is not a new phenomenon. Such laws already exist in other countries, such as Canada and the United States, as part of the legal regulation of immoral behaviour in public places. However, this is where the Swedish law differs from its predecessors: it is not about moral behaviour in public places but about gender relations. As it stands, the law is a part of a whole new package of legal measures combating men's violence against women. Undoubtedly, it is historically and globally unique, firmly located as it is within an explicit pro-feminist ideological framework, presupposing that a real change in gender relations calls for a radical reconsideration of men's responsibility in prostitution. The basis of such a reconsideration is that prostitution must be defined as a male issue; that prostitution is about men's sexuality, not women's.

This point was not arrived at overnight. The official Swedish position on prostitution is the result of a long and laborious process, lasting more than twenty-five years. On a general level, it is a result of Swedish society's drive towards equality between men and women. However, it has taken several national commissions on prostitution and sexual violence, and intensive public debate to reach the present position. Without doubt, an important feature of this process has been the marked and rather long-standing interest among Swedish (and other Scandinavian) social researchers with men's role as clients in prostitution. In many ways, this interest has meant a decisive shift in perspective on the issue. For whenever questions are posed about the men, earlier hidden aspects of the phenomenon become unveiled. Although the male client has occasionally been visible, it was only peripherally. Both in conceptualization and definition it was the female prostitute that was the subject of research; which often dealt with how and why women enter prostitution. To talk about how a demand can be met, however, does not shed light on the whole picture. One of the central questions for understanding prostitution must deal with *what* is purchased, that is to say, in the case of heterosexual prostitution, it must deal with men's motives and demand for prostitutes.

In this chapter, I intend to present and discuss some of the results of Swedish and other Scandinavian research about prostitutes' clients. However, whenever called for, I will compare these findings with the results from research in other countries. Clearly, the demand for prostitutes is a global issue, and drawing upon research only in a Swedish context has its limitations. Nevertheless, I do think that some of the observations made in Scandinavian research have some general implications for understanding men's role in prostitution. The three main questions asked are: (1) Who are the men seeking out prostitutes? (2) What are their motives? And (3) How can these motives be understood in the context of changing gender relations in society?

Who are the Men Seeking out Prostitutes?

We know that by no means all men buy sex. Some do, others don't. In his pioneering research on North American men's sexual behaviour in 1948, Alfred Kinsey stated that the majority (69 per cent) of all grown (white) men had had experiences of paid sexual encounters. This was probably an exaggeration.[2] Recent research in the United States and in Europe provides a somewhat different picture. Only 16 per cent of men in the United States have ever visited a prostitute according to a nationwide survey conducted in 1992 (Michael et al. 1994: 63). A similar study in Sweden in 1996 showed that about every eighth man over eighteen years of age (approximately 13 per cent) had at some time in their life paid for sex (Månsson 1998: 236). Even if the figures from Sweden and the

United States happen to be almost the same, there is evidence that men's disposition to pay for sex varies strongly from country to country, or rather from culture to culture. Table 9.1 is based on a review of studies of sexual habits in a number of West European countries carried out between 1989 and 1992 (Leridon et al. 1997).

TABLE 9.1 The proportion of men in various countries who have paid for sex at some time in their lives.[3]

Country	Per cent	Base rate (n)	Year
Finland	9.9	664	1992
Netherlands	14.3	392	1989
Norway	11.3	1,617	1992
Spain	38.6	409	1992
Switzerland	18.7	1,260	1992
UK	6.6	6,053	1991
Sweden	12.7	1,475	1996

The table shows that Spanish men top the 'sex-buying league'; almost four out of ten Spanish men have paid for sex at some time during their life. British men have least experience of paying for sex. A comparison of the results of studies carried out in Scandinavia shows that more men in Sweden than in Norway and Finland have paid for sex. The figure from the Dutch study is unexpectedly low taking into consideration the extensive sex trade that exists in this country, and the official liberal approach to it. One possible explanation of the low figure may be that the proportion of foreign visitors among purchasers of sex is very high, which is not reflected in the nationally-based statistics. It should be noted that the figures from the Netherlands and Spain (and to a certain extent Finland) are relatively uncertain due to low base rates.

Apart from statistical uncertainties there is, of course, every reason to question the reliability of this type of data. The actual act – paying for sex – is considered to be a clear violation of norms in many countries and something that people therefore wish to keep concealed from those around them. An interesting example of this can be seen in a study of 661 German-speaking men on vacation in Thailand, the Philippines, the Dominican Republic, Kenya and Brazil. All of them reported having had sex with one or more local women. Thus the researchers classified them as 'sex tourists'. However, as it appeared, this classification did not coincide with the men's self-definition. Probably well aware of the strong public condemnation of sex tourism, a vast majority of the men (almost 80 per cent) rejected the label (Günther 1998: 71). Furthermore, for some men, purchasing sex does not fit in with a strong, positive sexual self-identity. To admit, to oneself and others, that one is obliged to – 'needs to' – go to prostitutes can be felt to be the same as not being good enough on the 'normal' sex market. On the other hand, it is, of course, also quite conceivable that the opposite applies. Any shame involved in going to prostitutes is subordinated to another important norm in male society, namely having many different sexual experiences. Thus, for example, we can see a clear pattern in the 1996 Swedish study that the experience of paying for sex is greatest among men with a lot of sexual partners (Månsson 1998: 240). This is probably a fact that goes against the popular notion of the client as being 'lonely' and 'sexually needy'. In the North American study mentioned before, approximately three out of every hundred men who had at least three partners in the past year said that they had paid someone for sex. Essentially no one who had fewer than three partners in a year paid for sex (Michael et al. 1994: 196). Similarly, sociologist Martin A. Monto, who compared his sample of 700 clients to a national sample of North American men, found that clients were much more likely than men in general to report that they had more than one sexual partner over the past year, 56 per cent as compared to 19 per cent (Monto 2000: 72). Furthermore, in the Swedish study it was also noted that men with prostitution contacts seem to have greater problems than others in maintaining regular relationships with women. There were more divorces and broken-off cohabitation relationships among this group than among non-purchasers (Månsson 1998: 240).

In this context, it may be appropriate to underline that the expressions and forms of prostitution are moulded by the prevailing social conditions at different times in history. The activity changes continually and new forms for contacts between buyers and sellers arise, something which, of course, also affects the number of men who become involved in prostitution. Today, prostitution is part of a continually expanding sex industry with a global range. A marked component of this development is the extensive traffic over national borders for the purpose of prostitution. In the one direction, there is a more or less organized import of women from the 'third world' and the East European countries to the brothels of the rich countries in the western world. Estimates say that approximately 500,000 women were trafficked across borders into the countries of the European Union during a single year for the purposes of prostitution and sexual exploitation (EU Rapport 1996). In the other direction, there is a more or less organized transport of sex buyers from the rich to the poor part of the world. Important reasons for clients resorting to the foreign sex trade are the extensive supply, low prices, the good 'level of service', and the higher level of anonymity associated with purchase of sex abroad. When asked where the last sexual contact for payment took place, 69 per cent of the Swedish sex buyers said that it took place abroad, either on holiday or on a work or business trip (Månsson 1998: 241).

Another recent change in the structure of the global sex industry concerns the development of 'computer pornography' and the buying and selling of sexual services via the internet. There is no doubt that the introduction of this new technology has increased the availability of sex for money. In 1998, internet industry analysts estimated that 1 billion US dollars were spent online on 'adult content'; this comprised 69 per cent of the total internet sales (Hughes 2000: 4). So far, we have very little knowledge as to how exactly this has affected or maybe even changed the content and structure of demand. However, as sex industry analyst Donna Hughes argues: 'Men are usually secretive about their exploitation of women and children and one of the factors in the success of the online sex industry has been men's ability to download pornography or engage in online prostitution from the privacy of their homes and offices' (Hughes 2000: 10). Furthermore, tentative results from a Swedish case study which analysed the content of over one thousand emails from clients (given to the researchers by a woman who had decided to exit prostitution) suggest that the clients on the internet are much younger and have a better socio-economic situation than, for example, the clients of street prostitutes (Nordvinter and Ström 2000: 37).

Why Do Men Seek out Prostitutes?

In the following section, I shall discuss in a more in-depth manner what we know today about men's motives for buying sex. A central point in my reasoning is that the buying of sex is an action that carries meaning at many levels. It has both individual and social dimensions, and in order to understand it completely we must comprehend the complex interplay between these dimensions. On the psychological or social-psychological level, it seems to concern the satisfaction of different sexual demands and/or the solution of problems that men have in their relations with non-prostitute women. However, at the same time, it is a fact that most women in the same situation do not choose the same solution. Prostitution use is predominantly a male practice and in order to reach an understanding of what men seek in prostitutes, it is necessary to take into account men's sexuality and gender relations. At the same time, it is clear that both sexuality and gender are socially constructed, which makes it fair to argue that in many ways the buying of a prostitute has other implications today than it had a hundred years ago, both on a social and individual level. The act also carries different meanings in different cultural contexts, as indicated above.

Most of the Scandinavian studies conducted so far have been qualitative studies based on in-depth interviews with clients.[4] Analyses of motives based on these interviews show relatively unanimously that a rough division can be made into two major groups of men with regard to their motivation for paying for sex. These are:

1. Men who live in more or less regular relationships with women but are looking for something different – a typical saying would be: 'I buy what I want to have'.
2. Men who don't live in relationships with women and/or who consider they have big difficulties in making contact with women – a typical saying would be: 'There are no other women'.

The assertion 'there are no other women' does not necessarily mean that the men have no opportunities for making contact with women. The expression rather covers the man's own subjective view of what is available for him on the sex market. Underlying this may be shyness and fear, advanced age, physical or mental disabilities, etc. For men who live in more or less permanent relationships, purchase of a prostitute can be experienced as a rational and undemanding alternative in a situation where sex in the regular relationship is not working satisfyingly or has ceased. It also involves sexual wishes that the men say they do not dare or cannot express together with their steady partners (Borg et al. 1981; Månsson and Linders 1984; Sandell et al. 1996).

An interesting observation is that there are only a few men (approximately one in ten) who explicitly discuss sexual need as the reason why they visit prostitutes (Månsson and Linders 1984: 102). It seems possible that the emotional meanings and overtones involved in visiting a prostitute are much more salient for the man than a desire for a sexual experience. This means that sometimes the actual content of the visit to the prostitute is of less importance than the meaning that it has in the man's fantasy, for example as a symbolic representation or proof of masculinity. Notably, this is not the same as saying that it is usual for men to have no sexual needs or desires when they buy sex. It only means that they do not talk about this when they discuss why they visit prostitutes. They talk about other things, however, through which this demand expresses itself. For example, they frequently talk about things like 'curiosity' and 'excitement'.

Such statements seem to reflect a desire or a fantasy in the men of being able to have a certain type of sex which only in exceptional cases can be experienced in encounters with non-prostitute women. In their analysis of interviews with sixty-six Swedish sex buyers, Månsson and Linders (1984) demonstrate a whole complex of motives, which in different ways express a desire in the men to be able to experience a sexual encounter with a 'whore'. Partly these motives appear to have their origin in the extensive myth-building around prostitution and in the widespread conceptions about constantly accessible women who fulfil men's sexual 'needs' and fantasies. Also the prostitution milieu itself seems to evoke curiosity and excitement. In the red light districts or other places where sex trade occurs, the milieu itself functions as an 'invitation' to sex. This is underscored by the pornographic framework, for example the sex clubs and porn stores, that border 'the stroll' in the big cities, or the porn advertisements on the websites of the internet. In no other places are women found who so openly offer themselves for sale.

For some clients, the image of the 'whore' is sexually exciting. As an expression of the darker side of men's image of women, the 'whore' is connected with enticement, but also with contempt and disgust, and she is defined exclusively by her sexuality that can be purchased with money. Interestingly enough, around the man as a consumer there are no such emotionally charged images. He is anonymous or entirely invisible. *If* there is an image of the client, it mainly builds upon a very rigid and one-dimensional view of men's sexuality. It is a biologically deterministic view of men's sexual desires as being constantly high and never changing. Of course, this view disregards the fact that sexuality is socially and culturally constructed and should be understood in that perspective. As I have demonstrated, surveys on male sexual behaviour made in different countries show that the number of men who visit prostitutes ranges from a few per cent in one country to 40 per cent in another!

At the same time as men's fantasies around prostitution often involve encountering a sexually advanced and experienced woman, it is interesting to note that some men openly demand a different and more passive sexual role for themselves in their contacts with prostitutes, compared to how they behave in their ordinary relationships. In other words, the man buys himself the right to be passive and to be 'seduced' by the sexually aggressive 'whore'. In a study conducted by American sexologist Martha Stein (1974) on the clients of call-girls, it appeared that the act most requested was the woman performing oral sex on the man. Many clients expressed displeasure with their wives' unwillingness to perform this particular act. The second most requested act was the woman sitting on top of the man. According to Stein, about half of the men assumed a passive role and left it to the prostitute to lead the encounter and take all the initiatives. It therefore appears as though some men, when possible, prefer to abandon their socially constructed power position and take a role that allows them to release control and ignore all demands concerning the sexual performance.

In her book *Prostitution, Power and Freedom* (1998), British sociologist Julia O'Connell Davidson also discusses men's eroticizing of the prostitute as a sexually powerful woman. Her focus is a bit different from Stein's as it primarily deals with clients who pay prostitutes to be sexually dominated by them, to be hurt and humiliated, dressed as a woman or as a 'slave'. After having interviewed a number of such clients, she concludes that these men 'want to construct the prostitute as an immensely powerful, "phallic" woman, for it is her (illusory) power to debase them as masculine and sexual beings which they find erotic' (O'Connell Davidson 1998: 148). The author underlines the fact that these men are not interested in having sex with any one 'dirty whore'; and they don't like 'cheap' places but 'prefer to visit entrepreneurial prostitutes working from "classier" set-ups. They state most emphatically that they never use street prostitutes, and this is because they strongly associate street prostitution with powerlessness and vulnerability on the prostitute's part' (O'Connell Davidson 1998: 148).

The author's analysis displays a power game that is both complex and contradictory. Obviously, the man does not surrender to the woman in any real way. On the contrary, he uses his power to construct a situation where the traditional gender roles are reversed. However, the woman's power is only illusory and so is the man's willingness to release his control. In short, says O'Connell Davidson, the woman's value is attached to the fact that 'the prostitute *is* a prostitute'. She doesn't have any value as a full human subject. Instead, the client dehumanizes her and refuses to recognize her as anything more than her body and her sexual agency (O'Connell Davidson 1998: 150).

Contact Problems and Loneliness

The other major complex of motives that have appeared from interviews conducted by myself and other Scandinavian researchers can be brought together under the heading 'contact problems and loneliness'. Most of these motives have in common that they express a longing for *women*, not primarily prostitutes, but rather women in general. First of all we are talking about men who do not live in relationships with women or who consider themselves having great difficulties in making contact with women. These observations are substantiated by Martin A. Monto's North American study, where the data suggest that some men pay for sex because they have difficulties becoming involved in conventional relationships. 'Forty-two per cent [out of 700 interviewees] agreed that they were "shy and awkward" when trying to meet women, 23 per cent felt unattractive physically, and 23 per cent "had difficulty meeting women who were not nude dancers and prostitutes"' (Monto 2000: 80).

As mentioned earlier, an expression like 'there are no other women for me' does not necessarily mean that those who say it in reality have no opportunities for making contact with women. It rather refers to men's subjective view of what is available on the sex market. O'Connell Davidson criticizes what she calls the discourse about prostitution as a form of sexual therapy or healing; a discourse 'which some journalists and academics, even some prostitutes as well as clients, buy into' (O'Connell Davidson 1998: 152). She argues that presenting the prostitute as a kind-hearted 'comforter' permits the client to tell himself that it is not simply lust but rather his loneliness that makes him seek out prostitutes. 'But behind such narratives there are generally sexual scripts which have as much to do with vengeance and control as those enacted by any other client,' says O'Connell Davidson (1998: 152).

Losers and Cheats – or Buying Sex in a World of Changing Gender Relations

Generally speaking, there is a disagreement as to the way the gender system has changed during the past decades. On the one hand, there is no doubt that women have moved forward in the public arena. Women are now involved more in politics, education and gainful employment than earlier. On the other hand, many insist, and not least those in women's studies, that the equality women have received is an equality on men's terms. One side-effect of the so-called sexual revolution, it is argued, is that men have been strengthened in their feelings that they have a right to have unlimited access to sex. Men's sexual 'needs' seem to have become even more taken for granted than they already were, and as the general preoccupation with sexuality in society increases, the appeal of commercial sexuality to many men seems to increase along with it. This development, however, does not take place unchallenged. Alongside the increasing sex industry there is an ongoing public discourse about destructive male behaviour; a new phenomenon from a historical point of view.

Besides, it is a fact that many women nowadays will no longer accept male sexual dominance. Today's women expect to both give and receive sexual satisfaction. And both partners in a relationship have greater demands and expectations for sexuality than in the past. Taken together, these changes have great consequences for men. They drag behind in change, and are often very ambivalent about that which occurs.

Against this background, Norwegian sociologists Prieur and Taksdal (1993) see at least two sorts of sex-buyers today. The first is a group of, particularly, older men who will not or cannot accept the changes in the relations between men and women. The authors call these men traditionalists and *losers*. These are men who cling to the old notions of men's dominance over women, but, due to various personal or social reasons, lack the possibilities to enact this dominance in their real lives. The task of prostitution is to compensate for this deficiency; the only thing that is demanded is money. 'This view sees clients of prostitutes as traditional men who do not face the changes in gender relationships. In prostitution the ancient order is restored' (Prieur and Taksdal 1993: 111).

There is also another group, consisting primarily of younger men, whose views about gender and sexuality are shaped by modern society's mass-produced illusions about sexuality in pornography, advertisements and TV talk-shows. For these men all is understood as possible, not least in the area of sexuality. Such expectations also provide fertile soil for prostitution. Within prostitution the possibilities seem to be endless, as long as the customer is willing to pay. This points to a commodified perspective towards sexuality, in which sex can be compared to a consumer product rather than an aspect of intimate relationships. This kind of self-focused sexuality and the idea of shopping for a sex partner leads to what Blanchard calls *McSex*. According to one man he interviewed: 'It's like going to McDonald's; most people are looking for a good quick cheap meal. It's satisfying, it's greasy, and then you get the hell out of there' (Blanchard in Monto 2000: 80).[5] But this attitude does not only entail having as many sexual contacts as possible, it also means being able to transgress norms and borders, which is not allowed in other contexts and relations. Thus, the old gender order is maintained here also, though with new and different means of expression.

Prieur and Taksdal call this buyer of sex *the cheater*. Cheaters, they say, are 'the most modern players of the sexual game', men who avoid actual meetings with women out of fear of losing themselves in a relation with an equal partner – 'disenchanted, but safe'. Afraid of being seduced, the cheater/sex-buyer withdraws to a world he can control through the power of money. Women-abusers and rapists also belong in the category of cheaters, maintain Prieur and Taksdal, for they dare not expose themselves to others' desires and demands; they dare not meet challenges. Their means of power is violence, which is justified as a means to restore 'equal weight' in the relationship. Thus, the man hits and rapes in order to establish his position of power. At the same time, this demonstration of power is an illusion, for in the end he hits back at himself. Through reducing women to an object in his desire to control, he loses the possibility for love, her love. Another Norwegian researcher, Kristen Skjørten, has interviewed men who abuse women, and has found that in many of the men's stories paradoxical intentions come forward. The man wants both love and positive reinforcement from the woman, while at the same time demands power and control over her (Skjørten 1993: 112).

This ambivalence – simultaneous demands to maintain and give up power – can at least partly be attributed to the modern disruptions of male lives (as discussed in Susan Faludi's book *Stiffed* 1999). The studies by Prieur, Taksdal and Skjørten reveal that even if traditional male ideals have a firm grip on many men, there is a strong tension between these ideals and real life. Many cannot handle it, do not have the resources, do not want to follow these ideals. Men long for a new means of relating, but cannot express this. Many men complain that women have too high expectations of them, and are afraid they will not to be able to meet the demands of family, employers and society. They are tired of all the responsibility. In prostitution, on the other hand, no demands are made, and men are free to go their way after paying up, no fuss about feelings and no ties.

Everything is Possible?

The public revelations in books and media of men's sexual violations in the family, prostitution and in other arenas can be understood as a clear expression of these changes. It is a painful change for many men, but it is also one that carries unsuspected possibilities. We can, for instance, speculate about the consequences of the anonymity around prostitution being broken, with the client to a great extent being forced to confront the social and human implications of his actions, as is the case with the new law in Sweden prohibiting the buying of sexual services.

Even if, at present, there is not much to be said about the concrete effects of the law, it is clear from the public debate that it has stirred considerable feelings, particularly in the male community.[6] Shifting the focus from women to men and suggesting that prostitution is primarily about men's sexuality not women's in fact leads to a radical consideration of men's responsibilities in prostitution. And, no doubt, in the short run, this will give rise to frustration regarding questions of men's sexual comfort and privilege. In the long run, however, it may mean that the 'cheating' may end. Confrontations provoking men's consciousness about the implications of their purchase of prostitutes may, interestingly enough, mean freedom for the man to choose the challenges that lie in a relationship between socially equivalent partners.

We know, however, that many men defend themselves against such a development. There are strong regressive and anti-feminist elements in certain men's reactions and behaviour. These reactions express an obvious feeling of loss and a need to compensate for this through suppressing or misdirecting aggression towards women in various contexts. And many men's compulsive sexual odysseys into prostitution can probably be seen in light of this relative loss of gender power.

Discussion

An obvious question concerns how far this hypothesis about anti-feminist reactions as an expression of compensation for changes in gender relations can be taken. It is probably not unfair to interpret the rising demand for trafficked and imported women in this perspective. This demand and behaviour can be seen as a defence against anxieties around entering into close and dependent relationships with non-prostitute women (O'Connell Davidson 1998: 160). This becomes clear just by looking at the marketing of these women, in which sexual, racist and ethnic stereotypes play a big role; Asiatic women are portrayed as loving and submissive, African women as wild, and Latin American women as free and easy (Månsson 1995). It is not difficult to visualize how these stereotypes can give rise to men's fantasies about compensation for the reduction of masculine and sexual power in their own everyday lives.

However, the final answer to the question naturally depends upon, among other things, how strong a grip traditional ideals have on today's men. It is clear that there are men in modern society who experience strong inducements to develop new and more democratic strategies for male life, in relation to both women and children. At the same time, it is a fact that all men do not have the same goals. The older ideals for men still exist, in both open and hidden forms, because many, perhaps most, men benefit from the subordination of women. This means that even though the number of men who rigorously and openly practise the traditional patriarchal or male chauvinist patterns may be diminishing in some areas, it is a fact that the majority of men still take advantage and benefit from the overall subordination of women. This is true also for the Scandinavian countries, which are supposed to be the most advanced concerning 'equal opportunities' between men and women.

A more radical change of this situation presupposes a fundamentally different division of power between men and women. Until now it has been women who have played the leading role when it comes to working for such a change. A really revolutionary change, however, would presuppose men's participation. If so, the crucial question is: is there reason to believe that a substantial number of men are prepared to engage in counter-sexist politics that go against the interests they share, being men in a patriarchal society? New, exciting research on men's lives indicates that in quite a few cases – at least in Scandinavia and parts of Europe and North America – men are moving towards a greater involvement in their families and in their children's lives. Promoting such a development on a larger scale presupposes certain material conditions. From a Swedish point of view, it is clear that one of the main facilitators so far has been the very generous parental leave system that we have, guaranteeing men the right to long-term participation in their children's lives.[7]

What I am referring to here, though, are long-term changes, meaning that the effects of some men's greater involvement in their families and in their children's lives is, above all, an investment in the future. However, at this moment in history, we have to conclude that, globally speaking, the project of transforming masculinity carries almost no political weight or impact at all. Exceptions to the rule, such as the new Swedish law prohibiting the purchase of sexual services, are all too few. The truth of the matter is that men's interests in patriarchal power are consolidated and defended by most of the cultural machinery surrounding our everyday lives (Connell 1995: 241). This machinery is institutionalized in the state as well as in the market, not least within the framework of the global sex industry dealing in prostitution, trafficking in women and other forms of human and sexual exploitation. Challenging this industry is of major importance. And, no doubt, the public discourse on this issue is a process both painful and necessary for most men. However, as I stated earlier, the silence seems to be broken, and the way back to the old order is definitely a blind alley, for both men and women.

Acknowledgment

Thank you to Julia O'Connell Davidson, University of Leicester, for her valuable suggestions and thoughtful comments on this paper.

Notes

1. The Act Prohibiting the Purchase of Sexual Services entered into force on 1 January 1999 (Penal Act 1998: 408). It says that 'a person who obtains casual sexual relations in exchange for payment shall be sentenced – unless the act is punishable under the Swedish Penal Code – for *the purchase of sexual services* to a fine or imprisonment for at most six months. Attempt to purchase sexual services is punishable under Chapter 23 of the Swedish Penal Code.'

2. This is at least partly due to the fact that the research was based on a convenience sample rather than a probability sample, making it impossible to extend the findings to North American men in general (Monto 2000: 68).

3. The original presentation does not include data from Sweden, but for the sake of comparison, I have here added the figures from the 1996 nation-wide survey of sex life in Sweden (Månsson 1998: 236).

4. Borg et al. (1981); Persson (1981); Månsson and Linders (1984); Varsa (1986); Prieur and Taksdal (1989); Andersson-Collins (1990); Hydén (1990); Lantz (1994); Sandell et al. (1996); Månsson (1998).

5. This sexual lifestyle is also discussed in a Swedish study (Sandell et al. 1996). The men who display this pattern are called 'omni-consumers' by the authors and their

relation to women is described as 'sexualized'. They are big consumers of both pornography and prostitution and have a 'businesslike' attitude towards sex purchase.

6. Opinions differ whether it has been a success or a failure. Facts show that only twelve men were convicted for breaking the law during the first year. The low figure has mainly been attributed to juridical-technical factors concerning (1) the demarcation of the criminal offence and (2) problems of demonstration (BRÅ-rapport 2000: 4).

7. The benefit period for parental leave has been gradually extended and today it covers fifteen months which parents can, more or less, distribute between themselves as they prefer. In 1994, half of the Swedish fathers used parental leave with an average of forty-eight days. This corresponds to approximately 12 per cent of the days used in parental leave that year (in 1986 the corresponding figure was a little more than 6 per cent).

References

Andersson-Collins, G. (1990) *Solitärer: En Rapport Om Prostitutionskunder*, Report No. 124, Stockholm: FOU-byrån.

Borg, A. et al. (1981) *Prostitution: Beskrivning, Analys, Förslag Till Åtgärder*, Stockholm: Publica (Liber).

BRÅ-rapport (2000) *Förbud Mot Köp Av Sexuella Tjänster: Tillämpningen Av Lagen Under Första Aret*, Stockholm: BRÅ.

Connell, R. W. (1995) *Masculinities*, Cambridge: Polity Press.

EU Rapport (1996) *Angående Kvinnohandel Som Syfter Till Sexuellt Utnyttjande*, KOM (96) 567.

Faludi, S. (1999) *Stiffed: The Betrayal of the Modern Man*, London: Chatto and Windus.

Günther, A. (1998) 'Sex Tourism without Sex Tourists!', in Cognizant Communication Offices, *Sex Tourism and Prostitution: Aspects of Leisure, Recreation, and Work*, New York: Cognizant Communication Cooperation.

Hughes, D. M. (2000) 'The Internet and Sex Industries: Partners in Global Sexual Exploitation', *Technology and Society Magazine*, spring.

Hydén, L-C. (1990) *De Osynliga Männen. En Socialpsykologisk Studie Av Manliga Prostitutionskunder*, Report No. 122, Stockholm: FOU-byrån.

Lantz, I. (1994) *Torsken I Fittstimmet. Om Prostitutionskunder I Stockholm*, Stockholm: Citysektionen, Socialtjänsten.

Leridon, H., G. van Zessen and M. Hubert (1997) 'The Europeans and Their Sexual Partners', in M. Hubert et al. (eds), *Sexual Behaviour and HIV/AIDS in Europe: Comparisons of National Surveys*, London: Taylor and Francis.

Månsson, S.-A. (1994) 'Kuinnomisshandel: ur Mannens Perspektiv', *Nordiskt Socialt Arbete*, No. 1: 13–28.

— (1995) 'International Prostitution and Traffic in Persons from a Swedish Perspective', in M. Klap et al. (eds), *Combating Traffic in Persons*, Utrecht: SIM Special No. 17.

— (1998) 'Den köpta sexualiteten', in B. Lewin (ed.), *Sex i Sverige. Om Sexuallivet i Sverige 1996*, Stockholm: Folkhälsoinstitutet.

Månsson, S.-A. and A. Linders (1984) *Sexualitet Utan Ansikte. Könsköparna*, Stockholm: Carlssons; in English, S.-A. Månsson, *The Man in Sexual Commerce*, Lund: Lund University, School of Social Work, 1988; in French, 'L'homme dans le commerce du sexe', in P. Van der Vorst and P. May (eds), *La Prostitution – quarante ans après la convention de New York*, Bruxelles: Bruylant, 1992.

Michael, R. T., J. H. Gagnon, E. O. Laumann and G. Kolata (1994) *Sex in America: A Definitive Survey*, Boston: Little, Brown.

Monto, M. A. (2000) 'Why men seek out prostitutes', in R. Weitzer (ed.), *Sex for Sale. Prostitution, Pornography and the Sex Industry*, London: Routledge.

Nordvinter, I. and A. Ström (2000) *Torsk på natet: En studie av den manlige sexköparen på Internet*, Göteborg: Institutionen för socialt arbete, C-uppsats Vt00.

O'Connell Davidson, J. (1998) *Prostitution, Power and Freedom*, Cambridge: Polity Press.

Persson, L. G. W. (1981) *Horor, Hallickar och Torskar*, Stockholm: Norstedts.

Prieur, A. and A. Taksdal (1989) *Å Sette Pris på Kvinner: Menn Som Kjøper Sex*, Oslo: Pax.

— (1993) 'Clients of Prostitutes – Sick Deviants or Ordinary Men? A Discussion of the Male Role Concept and Cultural Changes in Masculinity', *NORA*, No. 2: 105–14.

Sandell, G. et al. (1996) *Könsköparna. Varför Går Män till Prostituerade?*, Stockholm: Natur och Kultur.

Skjørten, K. (1993) *Voldsbilder i Hverdagen. Om Menns Forståelser av Kvinnemisshandling*, PhD thesis, Institutt for kriminologi, Oslo.

Stein, M. L. (1974) *Lovers, Friends, Slaves ... The 9 Male Sexual Types. Their Psycho-Sexual Transactions with Call Girls*, New York: Berkeley Publishing Co. and Putnam.

Varsa, H. (1986) *Prostitutionens Osynliga Aktörer: Kunderna*, Helsingfors: Kvinnoforskningsstenciler, No. 5.

10

Towards the End of 'Black Macho' in the United States: Preface to a (Pro)Womanist Vision of Black Manhood

Gary L. Lemons

Out of his sense of urgency came a struggle called the Black Movement, which was nothing more nor less than the black man's struggle to attain his presumably lost 'manhood.' And so America had tightened the noose, although it did not know it yet; by controlling the black man's notion of what a black man was supposed to be, it would successfully control the very goals of his struggle for 'freedom.' (Wallace 1979: 32)

An Open Letter to Every Black Man in the United States: Dare I Speak These Words to You?

In my heart, I possess a deep love for you – my fathers, brothers, my allies in the struggle. As a black man in the United States, I am always aware of white supremacist patriarchal myths of our existence and the heavy weight of them tied to our black bodies. We carry their enormous load with us daily – to our jobs, our homes, our relationships, even to our graves. They have become our emotional, social, political, personal and physical weights. I am always aware of their heaviness in the ways we treat each other and the treatment we receive from others (who love, despise and/or simply do not care about us at all). I am tired of the weight of these myths, for they keep me from seeing you, from reaching out to you – to embrace you lovingly. I want to see you with eyes made new. I want to see you with eyes that revealingly penetrate your beauty, joy and pain, your deepest yearnings, your humanity.

In my visionary imaginings, I have seen you. I see us struggling side by side – together – against the myths of our manhood that never meant for us to survive the holocaust that was American slavery. I want to fight shoulder to shoulder with you against its legacy – as your ally – without fear in loving recognition of all the ways we are different yet the same. I want to see our spirits rising together in Holy Communion, unfettered by the chains of manhood ideas that brutalize and essentialize our masculinity. I refuse to see you as a myth. I stand with my arms stretched wide, waiting for you to see my heart. The mere thought of our embrace even now makes me weep for joy.

In the United States today, where notions of manhood remain bound up by the power of patriarchal relations under white (male) supremacy, it should come as no surprise to anyone studying 1960s Black Power movement gender politics that Nation of Islam leader, Louis Farrakhan, would promote the Million Man March as a show of black (male) power demonstrated as 'patriarchal atonement'. Invoking black nationalist, male-centred rhetoric from the 1960s, Farrakhan's masculinist pronouncements politically linked patriarchal ideas of black manhood with the struggle. In fact and fiction, the 1960s became the reigning signifier of black machismo.

As Michele Wallace boldly proclaimed in *Black Macho and the Myth of the Superwoman*, 'black macho' is a sexist dogma – working in allegiance with white supremacy – to attain patriarchal control over the bodies of black women. I agree with Wallace. Black men face an ongoing struggle against images of us that perpetuate a history of sexualized racism that many of us play out in the practice of sexism in our daily lives. For example, when Supreme Court Judge Clarence Thomas conveniently referred to his (televised) US Senate Confirmation Hearings in 1991 as a 'high-tech lynching' (conducted by a panel of all white men), under the charge of sexual harassment by black woman law professor Anita Hill, he ignored the fact that, at the same time, she was experiencing the enormous power of white male supremacy bent on discrediting her testimony.

Since the 1960s movement for Black Power and as recently as the Million Man March more than thirty years later, ideas of black manhood and masculinity rooted in sexist and misogynist dogma continue to under-mine gender solidarity in our communities. In *Black Macho and the Myth of the Superwoman*, Michele Wallace boldly proclaims: '[W]hat most people see when they look at the black man is the myth ... [I]t has also been used by the contemporary black man to justify his oppression of the black woman' (Wallace 1979: 18). Against the myth of black manhood, I argue that the liberation struggle of African Americans is doomed to fail as long as it remains bound to masculinist dictates and sexist pronouncements of manhood. I claim that the most emancipatory ideas of black manhood have emerged not from a masculinist discourse of loss, but from a vision of liberatory gender power grounded in *womanist* thought. When Alice Walker brought into being the revolutionary term in *In Search of Our Mothers' Gardens* (1983), she named the project of black feminism in gender-inclusive terms – stating that a womanist is 'committed to the survival and wholeness of entire peoples, male and female' (Walker 1983: xii). In doing so, Walker – as I have asserted in a chapter entitled 'To be Black, Male, and *Feminist*: Making *Womanist* Space for Black Men on the

Eve of the New Millennium' (1998b) – conceived a place in feminism where black men could work as allies with (black) women struggling most directly against the interrelated oppressions of racism, classism, homophobia and *sexism*.

My aim in this chapter is to pose a direct challenge to an ideology of black manhood rooted in sexism. Moreover, I contest a rhetoric of manhood that seeks to patriarchalize black men as its goal. Against sexist practice(s) in black communities, I am (pro)womanist – supporting black men who believe in the necessity of education within an *anti*-sexist consciousness. I want to affirm black men who are actively working to unlearn sexism. Calling black men into a (*pro*)womanist alliance with black women to end sexism, I advance a feminist vision of manhood that rejects a discourse of liberation that denies the existence of sexism in our communities. Progressive black men advocating womanist feminism believe that sexism is as injurious to the survival of black people as white supremacy. We know that black women are not our enemies. As bell hooks strategically argues, 'white supremacist capitalist patriarchy' is the enemy of all men (hooks: 1992). (Pro)womanist black men working to end female oppression affirm a vision of a liberatory manhood struggle for the liberation of black women, actively opposing the ways they are multiply oppressed.

I situate my argument for the political viability of (pro)womanist manhood in an analysis of two critically important documents on the relationship between black manhood and the African American struggle for self-determination. One of the documents is the little-known 'feminist/womanist' manifesto of an even more obscure organization called Black Men for the Eradication of Sexism (first organized in the mid-1990s at Morehouse College in Atlanta, Georgia). The other is widely known as the 'Mission Statement' of the Million Man March. Vastly differing on the subject of black manhood, both espouse the equality of women. However, their views on black women's involvement in the political struggle of black people in the USA add to the long history of and considerable debate around feminism in black communities. Before turning to a critical examination of the two texts, I continue a discussion of Michele Wallace's critique of black manhood from the 1960s, relating it to her commentary on the politics of the Million Man March to advance a (pro)womanist vision of black manhood.

Black Macho and the Myth of the Superwoman: More than Two Decades Later

At the end of the 1970s, Michele Wallace, in a highly contested slender volume of feminist critique, took on the subject of gender/sexual politics in the Black Power movement. Controversial and irreverent, *Black Macho and the Myth of the Supermoman* (1979) initiated a turbulent debate about black men's relation to sexism: 'The black man ... since the black Movement, has been in the position to define the black woman. He is the one who tells her whether or not she is a woman and what it is to be a woman. And, therefore, whether he wishes to or not, he determines her destiny as well as his own' (Wallace 1979: 12–13).

More than twenty years later, Wallace's words sound prophetic. Since the 1970s, the gender politics of black women and men have been infused by an intense debate on the pervasiveness of black sexism. The 'Black Sexism Debate' was spawned by a rather scathing critique written by black sociologist Robert Staples of Wallace and Ntozake Shangé's representation of black men in their work. From the feminist writings of Wallace and Shangé to the woman-identified work of Alice Walker and Toni Morrison in the 1980s, to the female-centred novels of Terry McMillan in the 1990s, among others, black women writers have been accused of nothing short of a discursive castration of black men (Lemons 1998a).

Two decades after *Black Macho*, Wallace continues to speak (with a cadre of other black feminist voices) in resistance to patriarchy and sexist practice in our communities. Nevertheless, according to Wallace, the battle against black sexism in the political arena appears to be moving without much realized effect. Reflecting on her participation at a teach-in staged in response to the March (sponsored by a group of black progressives known as African American Agenda 2000), Wallace lamented their failure to produce a nuanced critique of the gender/familial politics of the Million Man March:

> First: What about the men at the march? Weren't they our brothers, our fathers, our kin? Where were the statistics on them? Second: How and when are we ever going to acknowledge the fear and desperation of the marchers? Last: Did the people ... at the teach-in really need empirical support for a progressive agenda? Shouldn't we have been focusing on what to do now? No one 'teaching' the teach-in was prepared to say. (Wallace 1995)

Here Wallace speaks to the fundamental ways that black women and men are tied together through familial bonds and historical struggle. Like Wallace, I could not divorce myself from those men who marched on Washington, nor could I deny my own yearning for the feeling of brotherly kinship that had compelled them to make the journey. But what I have long realized is that black men can no longer determine black women's service to any movement for the liberation of black people.

Black feminism offers a critical analysis of systemic domination that exposes the mechanics of white supremacy as integrally linked to sexism.

Of black feminists calling out the gender politics of black liberation struggle in the 1960s, Paula Giddings painstakingly documents this period as 'The Masculine Decade'. In her chronicle of the rise and the decline of the movement for black power in *When and Where We Enter: The Impact of Black Women on Race and Sex in America* (1984), she shows with one striking example after another how black women's active participation in black anti-racist organizations represented a threat to their male leaders. From sexism confronting them in the Southern Christian Leadership Council and the Student Non-Violent Coordinating Committee (SNCC) to sexist practice experienced in the Black Panther Party, black women not only had to combat racism, they had to defy gender oppression exercised by the same men with whom they struggled. Of those women, Angela Davis and Kathleen Cleaver would become the most widely known. Looking back, Davis reflects upon her experience in SNCC (the Los Angeles branch):

> Some of the brothers came around only for staff meetings (sometimes), and whenever we women were involved in something important, they began to talk about 'women taking over the organization' – calling it a matriarchal coup d'etat. All the myths about Black women surfaced. (We) were too domineering; we were trying to control everything, including the men – which meant by extension that we wanted to rob them of their manhood. By playing such a leading role in the organization, some of them insisted, we were aiding and abetting the enemy, who wanted to see Black men weak and unable to hold their own. (Davis quoted in Giddings 1984: 316–17)

She further observes that this was 'a period in which one of the unfortunate hallmarks of some nationalist groups was their determination to push women into the background. The brothers opposing us leaned heavily on the male supremacist trends which were winding their way through the movement' (quoted in Giddings 1984: 316–17). Giddings herself concludes, 'Ironically, the most "nationalist" groups were also the most sexist, often to the point of downright absurdity' (Giddings 1984: 317).

We Can't Go Back: Patriarchal Atonement Just Won't Do

In 1995, the same year black men across the nation marched in the nation's capital, heeding the patriarchal call of black nationalist leader Louis Farrakhan in a demonstration of self-empowerment, a group of young black men at Morehouse College organized a counter-revolutionary group called Black Men for the Eradication of Sexism (BMES). The next year, it staged with meagre funding the historic anti-sexist conference 'To be Black, Male, and Feminist/Womanist'. BMES proclaimed: 'We believe that although we are oppressed because of our color, we are privileged because of our sex and must therefore take responsibility for ending that privilege.' The small group of (pro)womanist men asserted that the time had come for black men to protest sexual oppression, articulating a radical transformation of gender relations in black communities. They called for a 'revolutionary change' that would mean an end to the concept and practice of male supremacy. Refusing to gloss over the evils of sexism and homophobia in anti-racist rhetoric, BMES further declared: 'Sexism is a radical problem that requires a radical solution. It will not be solved by simple reform. We support feminism/womanism and all efforts to eradicate sexist oppression. We ultimately demand a complete and fundamental revolutionary change that eradicates oppression based on sex, race, class, and sexual orientation, both within and without' (BMES, 31 July 1996: internet). The revolutionary position BMES proclaims marks a critical departure from black nationalist, male propaganda claiming that racial justice will be served when 'the Black man' receives his rightful share of patriarchal power.

In contrast to the 'feminist/womanist' stance of BMES, one of the most vocal proponents of a neo-nationalist, patriarchalized version of black manhood today is Louis Farrakhan, credited with the idea of the Million Man March. Counter to the sexist rhetoric for which Farrakhan has become notoriously known, the organizing committee responsible for publishing the March's 'Mission Statement' advances the idea of a black male identity connected to the need for 'transformative and progressive leadership' that pointedly addresses the existence of black male sexism. In a section titled 'Atonement', it states that black men must atone 'for not resisting as much as we can sexist ideas and practices in society and in our own relations and failing to uphold the principle of equal rights, partnership and responsibility of men and women in life, love and struggle' (1995: 7). Fundamentally, however, on the subject of women's rights, the 'Mission Statement' is framed in duality. It never mentions feminism or womanism nor overtly aligns itself with any movement for women's rights. On the one hand, it promotes an anti-sexist model of struggle. On the other, it conceptualizes and advocates a double standard of political labour in which women are assigned the perennial role of domestic worker.

The Million Man March fuelled intense discussions about the existence of sexism in black political movements. The decision that black men should march (without black women) ignited heated debate on the presence (or in this case the absence) of black women in the national struggle for African American self-determination and triggered an outpouring of female con-testation. In light of the stand taken against sexism in the Million Man

March's 'Mission Statement', it remains surprising that so little attention was given to its pro-active content – obscured by the rhetoric of patriarchal atonement on the day of the event. Ironically, both MMM and BMES condemn the practice of sexism, challenging black men to accept the equality of women:

> [We] self-consciously emphasize the *priority need* of Black men to stand up and assume this new and expanded responsibility without denying or minimizing the equal rights, role and responsibility of black women in the life and struggle of our people ... [T]he quality of male/female relations, and the family's capacity to avoid poverty and push the lives of its members forward all depend on Black men's standing up. (1995: 2–3)

Like BMES, the organizing committee holds that it will be essential for black men and women to unite in the struggle for black empowerment and social justice. BMES asserts, 'As we fight alongside our sisters we struggle to become whole; to deprogram ourselves. We have organized into one body because we know in our hearts and minds that as we hold our sisters back so will we hold ourselves back.' The organizing committee of the March declares, 'those of us [black men] who have stood up, must challenge others to stand also; and that unless and until Black men *stand up*, Black men and women cannot *stand together* and accomplish the awesome tasks before us'. The March's statement denounces sexism and gender oppression. It strongly urges the government 'to increase and expand [its] efforts to eliminate race, class and gender discrimination' (1995: 12).

Yet by requesting that women should stay home on the day of the march, the organizing committee (which included women) not only attempted to (re)domesticate black women, but its male-centred rhetoric conjured up sexist imagery from the Black Power movement of the 1960s. It advocated a patriarchal model for the black liberation struggle that supports female subordination. The following quote is a striking illustration of the point: 'We call on those who do not come to Washington, *especially, Black women* [emphasis added], to mobilize and organize the community in support of the Million Man March and its goals' (Million Man March 1995). Many black women (and men) wholeheartedly rejected the image of black men marching at the front line, while black women served the domestic needs of the struggle on the home front. Surely the organizers of the March and writers of the 'Mission Statement' realized the implications of this call, though they attempted to smooth over the glaringly obvious with the rhetoric of joint participation (points 31 and 32 of section VI):

> The Day of Absence [irony abounds here] is a parallel activity to the Million Man March and a component part of one joint and cooperative project: *the*

standing up and assumption of a new and expanded responsibility by the Black man in particular and the Black community in general [emphasis added].

Women are in the leadership of the Day of Absence without exclusion of men as men are in the leadership of the Million Man March without exclusion of women. *And both activities are equally essential* [emphasis added]. (1995: 15)

Even if the language in the equation of equality stated above includes such phrases as 'component part of one joint and cooperative project' and 'both activities are equally essential', certain questions remain: Why the exclusion of females in the actual March? If the sexes worked together at the organizational level of the march, and co-wrote its 'Mission Statement', and women worked 'without exclusion' in a leadership capacity in the March, would not a visible, united coalition of men *and women* marching together have been a more powerful show of black solidarity? Thus, the premise that 'unless and until Black men *stand up*, Black men and women cannot *stand together* and accomplish the awesome tasks before us' functions as an empty rhetorical gesture, little more than a veiled attempt to convince black women that they share power. The truth is that the MMM reinforced the myth that black liberation remains the pre-eminent domain of black men.

Black women's critique of patriarchy and sexism in the black liberation struggle has long shown that a division of political labour that privileges male status over that of the female is not only counter-productive but strategically wrong-headed and politically divisive. In spite of the progressive rhetoric of the MMM 'Mission Statement', it consciously works against itself – progressive on the one hand, while reinforcing male domination on the other. In the end, its vision of the 'stand' black men took on the 'Day of Atonement, Reconciliation and Responsibility' remained tied to a patriarchal imperative to consolidate black male power.

Anchored in a discourse of black male empowerment as the key element to gender unification in black communities, the MMM statement's *stand up* manhood rhetoric more often than not places black woman in the position of domestic workers behind the scene of battle. How could progressive-minded black women take seriously a call to co-operative political work that did not genuinely contest patriarchal edicts and sexist dogma?

It is a mistaken notion that the struggle for black self determination will happen in the USA when black men have gotten themselves together. A struggle whose mission is liberatory for both sexes is one whose aims resist the trappings of patriarchy, where male prerogative operates as the chief determinant of female value. Until black men begin to call out sexism in black communities, its practice will continue to undermine even the most progressive black male calls for gender solidarity.

Not only that, any document seriously proposing strategies for black male empowerment must oppose male supremacy while vigorously denouncing homophobia. Nowhere in the Million Man March 'Mission Statement' is there any inclusive mention of gay and lesbian black folk. The heterosexist representation of the March would have us believe that all men who participated were heterosexual. Such was clearly not the case. James Hannaham (a member of Black Gay and Lesbian Leadership Forum) writing in the *Village Voice* (25 October 1995) about his and other black gay men's experience at the March noted: 'Though Maya (Angelou) clapped, Jesse (Jackson) failed to enunciate, and Stevie (Wonder) plugged his album, none of them came close to even uttering the word "homophobia", as we'd hoped.' With all the 'Mission Statement's insistence upon black men 'standing up' and being responsible, the question remains – to whom are we to be responsible? Only those in our communities we choose to recognize?

Furthermore, the conspicuous silence on AIDS and its impact on African Americans flies in the face of the alarming statistics on HIV and black females. Can we be so naïve as to believe that simply by not speaking about certain issues they will go away? Can we ignore the reality of the sexual oppression of gays and lesbians in our communities, just as we continue to deny the existence of black sexism? AIDS has emerged as one of the fastest-growing killers of blacks in the USA. Is saving our manhood worth risking the survival of an entire people? For all its good intention, these are questions the 'Mission Statement' failed to ask. Black men marching together in the nation's capital was a powerful and historic sign of gender solidarity, on a scale we had never before witnessed. Even as I personally supported a number of men from my community who participated in the March and was awed by the sight of thousand upon thousand of black men standing together in solidarity, I could not support its separatist politics. Having been a committed advocate of women's rights ten years before the Million Man March, I was not swayed by a call – no matter how heartfelt – for black male comradeship predicated upon the exclusion of black women.

Black Women are not Our Enemies: Womanist Facts and Masculinist Fictions

Collectively we can break the life-threatening choke-hold patriarchal masculinity imposes on black men and create life-sustaining visions of a reconstructed black masculinity that can provide black men ways to save their lives and the lives of their brothers and sisters in struggle (hooks 1992: 113).

Radical black film-maker Marlon Riggs in *Black is, Black ain't* (posthumously released in 1995) speaks passionately about the necessity for black people to engage the subject of sexism and misogyny In the film, Riggs includes a telling clip of Mike Tyson (as a pageant judge) observing a black beauty contestant rehearsal. Tyson looks on with adulation as the women perform a dance routine. Informed viewers watching this clip know that Tyson ultimately would be charged and found guilty of raping one of the contestants shown. Through strategic editing, Riggs enables us to make a critical connection between what we witness in this scene and the clip he splices into it. Provocatively, the film-maker juxtaposes the scene of Tyson and the beauty contestants with footage showing Louis Farrakhan before an audience contesting Tyson's conviction.

In defence of Tyson, Farrakhan argues that the fighter is the victim, the unsuspecting prey of a more than willing 'sista'. In this misogynist scenario, a female vulture entraps Mike Tyson. Farrakhan insists that Tyson should not be blamed for his actions (regardless of intent?) but rather the woman who charged him. In mocking and sarcastic tones, the Nation of Islam leader calls all black women liars. Not only that, he says they need 'to come clean' (and stop falsely charging black men with sexual aggression) and admit that when they are saying 'no' (even to male sexual violation?), they actually mean 'yes'. Farrakhan's anti-black woman position stated here is no different from that voiced by many of the black men (and women) who supported Mike Tyson. In fact, many pro-Tyson voices came from the pulpit of black churches across the country.

When I was a graduate student, I read bell hooks's *Feminist Theory: From Margin to Center* (hooks 1984) for the first time. Its insistence that men must join the struggle to end sexism convinced me that black men's commitment to feminism is a revolutionary act of gender solidarity necessary for the liberation of black people. Holding men accountable for perpetuating sexism, bell hooks says:

> In particular, men have a tremendous contribution to make to feminist struggle in the area of exposing, confronting, opposing, and transforming the sexism of their male peers. When men show a willingness to assume equal responsibility in feminist struggle, performing whatever tasks are necessary, women should affirm their revolutionary work by acknowledging them as comrades in struggle (hooks 1984: 81)

hooks's belief that men must work in feminist alliance against sexism represents a radical gesture of political partnership between black men and women: 'Men who actively struggle against sexism have a place in the feminist movement. They are our comrades.' hooks calls for pro-feminist men to declare their anti-sexist beliefs publicly. She states that '[m]en who advocate feminism as a movement to end sexist oppression must become more vocal and public in their opposition to sexism and sexist oppression' (hooks 1984: 80).

Even while she challenges men who advocate feminism to go public, hooks (1984: 73) argues that all men do not equally share in male privilege because of class difference. According to her, sexism is particularly de-humanizing for men without class and race privilege. It leads us to believe that we are exercising genuine male power when, in reality, we remain powerless. hooks (1984: 73-4) maintains that sexist behaviour for the man without race and class privilege is ultimately devoid of self-gratification, an empty gesture of power. Moreover, she dismantles the myth that feminism is a middle class, 'woman-only' ideology. Simultaneously, she asserts that class oppression was the chief reason why poor, working-class white women, and black women from all classes did not join the women's liberation movement in the 1960s and why many working-class and poor women (from all race and ethnic backgrounds) still have not claimed feminism as a viable location for struggle.

As a major proponent of male involvement in the feminist movement, hooks (1984: 77) argues that men are not enemies of women. While men are the perpetrators of sexism, she believes that ending sexist practice is about shared responsibility. Men *and women* must work together to unlearn sexism. hooks promotes alliance-building between the sexes that enables men to understand that male supremacy is not an attribute or an inherent biological characteristic of manhood.

Of radical feminists today in the USA, more than any other, hooks has written specifically on the necessity of black male participation in the feminist struggle to end sexism. From the political, social, personal and economic relationship of black men to feminism to its impact upon us historically, she has been relentless in her critique of the effects of sexism in the daily lives of black men. Refusing to excuse sexism perpetrated by black males, hooks clearly will not abandon them: 'It is useful to think of misogyny as a field that must be labored in and maintained both to sustain patriarchy but also to nourish an anti-feminist backlash. And what better group to labor on this "plantation" than young black men' (hooks 1995: 116).

Why young black males? Evoking imagery from slavery to illustrate the exploitative nature of black male rappers, she compares it to a slave/master arrangement – only in this scenario the master comes bearing lucrative gifts:

When young black males labor in the plantations of misogyny and sexism to produce gangsta rap, white supremacist capitalist patriarchy approves the violence and materially rewards them. Far from being an expression of their 'manhood,' it is an expression of their own subjugation and humiliation by more powerful, less visible forces of patriarchal gangsterism … The tragedy for young black males is that they are so easily duped by a vision of manhood that can only lead to their destruction. (hooks 1995: 122–3)

hooks insists upon social accountability, adamantly defending black female resistance to it, while contesting accusations of racial betrayal when black women challenge black male sexism. It cannot simply be reduced to male-bashing. Black women have no other choice but to defend themselves, hooks contends. By doing so, she asserts, they save themselves. Never allowing us to forget our own power as men to perpetuate sexual domination, she opposes critiques of sexism that vilify black men (hooks 1995: 123). Even in white supremacist culture, where the humanity of black people remains under constant threat and assault, liberation struggles modelled on a vision of beneficent, hetero(sexist) patriarchy just won't do. When the power of male supremacy denies the power of women to be self-determining, none of us is free. The passionate manifesto of Black Men for the Eradication of Sexism illuminates a visionary path of liberated manhood away from the dictates of patriarchal atonement. In womanist ideas of political struggle against domination, confronting white supremacy necessarily means fighting against sexism (in and outside black communities). A progressive agenda for black liberation will necessitate (1) a critique of patriarchy that calls out its relationship sexism; (2) the eradication of masculinist notions of black liberation; and (3) the transformation of black manhood linked to emancipatory ideas of masculinity.

Womanist-identified black men committed to progressive ideas of black manhood and masculinity challenge the notion that feminism has no place in the lives of black males; we reject the myth of black macho. Embracing womanism as a strategic location to contest (hetero)sexism and white supremacy, I practise a manhood politics lived in patriarchal defiance as a matter of personal, emotional and spiritual health. I contend that black men who long for racial justice must be the same men who denounce sexism – even as we oppose homophobia in our communities. Until we acknowledge, on a national level, that sexism poses a major threat to our political, social and intimate relationships with black women, there exists little hope for a progressive vision of shared struggle between us.

In a climate of neo-black nationalism grounded in (hetero)sexist and homophobic notions of black manhood, (pro)womanist black men must begin organizing to launch a counter, *anti*-sexist movement that publicly protests the overt erasure of black feminist women's critical presence in the struggle for black self-determination in the USA. Black men opposing sexism resist the rhetoric of 'patriarchal atonement' that presents our manhood (is defined?) solely in opposition to the ideology of ruling-class, white supremacist patriarchy. In a womanist vision of black manhood, we work as allies of black women to end sexism. Our survival as men depends upon this. Together, we bear the burden of a history mired in racist mythology. As a critical piece in the radical work of feminist/womanist black women has been to undo 'the myth of the (black) superwoman', so the manifesto of Black Men for the Eradication of Sexism critically works as a revolutionary (pro)feminist/womanist declaration to begin dismantling the myth of 'black macho'. This work must continue.

References

Giddings, P. (1984) *When and Where We Enter: The Impact of Black Women on Race and Sex in America*, New York: Bantam Books.

Hernton, C. (1995) 'The Sexual Mountain and Black Women Writers', *Black Scholar*, Vol. 16, No. 4: 2–11.

—— (1987) *The Sexual Mountain and Black Women Writers*, New York: Anchor Press.

hooks, b. (1984) *Feminist Theory: From Margin to Center*, Boston: South End Press.

—— (1992) *Black Looks*, Boston: South End Press.

—— (1995) *Outlaw Culture*, New York: Routledge.

hooks, b. and C. West (1991) *Breaking Bread: Insurgent Black Intellectual Life*, Boston: South End Press.

Lemons, G. (1998a) 'A New Response to Angry Black (Male Anti) Feminists: Reclaiming Feminist Forefathers, Becoming Womanist Sons', in T. Digby (ed.), *Men Doing Feminism*, New York: Routledge.

—— (1998b) To be Black, Male, and Feminist: Making Womanist Space for Black Men on the Eve of the New Millennium', in S. Schacht and D. Ewing (eds), *Men in Feminism*, New York: New York University Press.

The Million Man March/Day of Absence Mission Statement (1995), Los Angeles: University of Sankore Press.

Walker, Alice (1983) *In Search of Our Mothers' Gardens: Womanist Prose*, New York: Harcourt Brace Jovanovich.

Wallace, M. (1979) *Black Macho and the Myth of Superwoman*, New York: Dial Press.

—— (1995) 'Let's Get Serious', *Village Voice*, 25 October.

11

Masculinities in Brazil: The Case of Brazilian Television Advertisements

Benedito Medrado, Jorge Lyra and Marko Monteiro

In Brazil, unlike in other countries (especially Canada, the United States and Australia), the debate on men and masculinities did not come about as a result of pressures arising out of men's movements, be they pro-feminist or masculinist; on the political level, discussions concerning male participation in health and reproductive rights issues came about as a result of feminist activism, especially after the Fourth International Conference on Population and Development (Cairo 1994) and the Fourth World Conference on Women (Beijing 1995).

Leading activists of the Brazilian feminist movement were present at both conferences. One of the main questions raised as the result of those debates was the necessity of greater male participation in the promotion of sexual and reproductive rights. On the academic level, such discussions have been conducted under the rubric of gender as an analytical category, from the point of view of different disciplines, such as anthropology, psychology, social psychology and demography among others.

Men, Feminism, Gender Politics and Theory

In general terms, the current interest in masculinity as an object of study began in the 1960s. This was due, on one hand, to the influence of the feminist movement and the search for a critical examination of the social asymmetries based on sexual differentiation. On the other hand, it was also the result of the gay movement that, while struggling for gay rights, demanded a new consideration of sexual identities based on a historical reading of the social construction of sexualities (Kimmel 1992a; Morgan 1992; Almeida 1995; Connell 1995; Lyra 1997; Medrado 1997; Arilha et al. 1998; Monteiro 2000, among others).

While seeking to define, in a broad manner, their space in politics, in the economy, in sexuality-related issues, at both the public and private level, feminists and gays struggled against oppression and proposed new thought patterns, new behaviour and new perspectives for the relations between the genders, by directly questioning the so-called hegemonic masculinity: white, heterosexual and dominant.

In Brazil, although later than in Europe and the United States, theoretical and political discussion has followed the feminist debates. Traditionally, the starting point of the contemporary Brazilian feminist movement is located in the second half of the 1970s, particularly in 1975, the United Nations' International Year of Women (Goldberg 1989; Rosemberg 1993; Sarti 1988; Lyra 1997).

A remarkable trend in the academic and political output of Brazilian feminism at that time was to approach or to attempt a dialogue with Marxism, highlighting the working woman as a theme (Sarti 1985). Women's conditions were described, discussed, denounced and alternatives were proposed, in various areas of women's lives. From that discussion, men, or masculinities, were excluded – and excluded themselves – or they served only as a counterpoint for the studies on women. Men have always been present, directly or indirectly, but the focus on masculinity as such was very restricted.

Groups of women activists formed, either independently or associated with broader institutional spaces. Women's consciousness-raising groups (Costa 1988) and women's organizations were created within the political parties, in trade unions (Moraes 1985) and in post-graduate associations (Costa et al. 1985). At this time 'compulsory' motherhood became an issue in the fields of health (Barroso 1987) and social and psychological life (Moraes 1985). Binding the sexual, emotional and creative destiny of women to maternity was questioned intensely with slogans such as: the right to one's own body, the right to work outside the home, the right to social facilities to collectivize domestic activities and child raising (Moraes 1985), and especially the right to child-care centres (Rosemberg 1987).

In the context of the theoretical and political dialogue with Marxism, or with the Brazilian political left, the claims and the proposals of Brazilian feminism were aimed more at government policies. For example, the feminist press in the 1980s postulated as an alternative to compulsory maternal child-raising, the right to day-care centres; much less strongly, they demanded that fathers should share in the care and education of their children (Campos et al. 1988). At that time, paternity was not an issue raised by feminists, and Brazil had no movement for the organization of men, either heterosexual or gay.

Both in northern and southern hemisphere countries, including Brazil, the theoretical and political output of feminism has been varied, embracing different tendencies (Goldberg 1989; Barbieri 1991; Izquierdo 1994; Scott 1988). Because feminism brought the 'woman issue' to the centre of academic discussions, it also revealed the hidden assumptions on which social investigations are based. That is, one talked (and still talks) supposedly of 'mankind'; thus women as an oppressed category are made invisible. At the same time, the change of emphasis in feminist theory towards gender in the 1980s revealed the need to denaturalize the categories of 'man' and 'woman' by seeking to separate the biological body from the social categories which give it meaning, understanding how bodies are *socially* perceived as 'biological' (Butler 1990; Lauretis 1990).

Also, in Brazil, an international perspective – apparently hegemonic nowadays – was assumed. Feminist studies apparently would no longer raise the issue of woman by herself; we would have to talk about gender relations instead. A complex perspective was then opened: that of conceptualizing gender as a relational category that would allow an understanding or an interpretation of the social dynamics that make hierarchical the relations between masculine and feminine. The category 'gender' revealed the importance of not limiting research to women, but to include in investigations traditionally aimed at women, particularly in the context of health and sexual and reproductive rights, the topic of men from a critical viewpoint. That is, to investigate the social construction of masculinities, in order to denaturalize the 'masculine condition', showing how genders are conformed in a complex and relational manner, where the social hierarchies separate not only men from women but separate men from each other in asymmetric relations of power (Almeida 1995).

According to the *Epidemiological Profile of Masculine Health in the Americas* (*Perfil epidemiológico da saúde masculina na região das Américas*), developed by Rui Laurenti and others in 1998, ever since countries began systematically to calculate the average age of their populations, it has been clear that men always have a shorter life expectancy than women. In Brazil, for example, in the first half of the 1950s, life expectancy was 52.8 years for women and 49.3 years for men. In the second half of the 1980s, these figures were, respectively, 67.6 and 62.3. Similarly, in analysing mortality rates according to sex and age, men have a higher rate in all age groups, especially in the younger.

Social and demographical data also suggest that, even if a feminization of the AIDS epidemic occurs in Brazil, there is a prevalence of male victims in various social-demographic sectors, such as by age group and household, and in most categories of virus transmission, especially through sexual contact and blood. Data from the Brazilian Health Ministry for 1998–99 show that, in Brazil, 67.5 per cent of the population infected with HIV is male. With the exception of babies infected at birth, since 1980 men show consistently higher rates of infection than women (source: *Boletim Epidemiológico*, CN-DST/Aids).

In general terms, such statistical data can be interpreted as indicators of violence or abuse of power, be it against women, children, property or the self. However, the association of masculinity with power and violence is not exclusively due to (nor is it reducible to) biological or genetic factors. This association is constructed and reproduces itself in social relations, historically and culturally; it is also reinforced in the social division of labour, in socialization processes within the family, schools, and other more or less ritualized forms of social interaction. As it is a cultural construction, this association can be reconstructed.

In Brazil, these reflections have constituted the central axis of political action and academic thought on this matter. Thus, reviewing political action and intervention initiatives in order to include a greater focus on masculinities, encouraging men to reflect upon their own sexual behaviours and practices, and paying attention to issues such as violence and reproductive rights are fairly recent developments in Brazil. With the support of financial institutions and the co-operation of international agencies, Brazilian institutions involved in public policy towards reproductive and sexual issues are ever more aware of the importance of taking masculinity into account, something that was not seen as helpful in the discussion of greater gender equity.

In 1995, the non-governmental agency ECOS (Studies of Communication in Sexuality and Human Reproduction), based in São Paulo, founded the GESMAP (Group for the Study of Male Sexuality and Paternity). This initiative, the first of its kind in the country, has become a focus for various interested professionals and institutions. GESMAP brought together professionals from a variety of fields who organize events and published a book and several pamphlets, among other initiatives, in order to broaden the debate on masculinity.

In 1997, the PAPAI initiative was founded in Recife (state of Pernambuco). Based at the Federal University of Pernambuco, and funded by the MacArthur Foundation, PAPAI (Dad, in Portuguese) is a programme that involves research activities on gender and masculinities, on a national and international level, through partnerships. The group is also involved in social intervention at a local level, working with young male populations in the city of Recife. The group brings together researchers with an academic background and a body of assistants, generally undergraduate social sciences students, besides numerous direct and indirect collaborators, in order to develop the research and activities.

The main themes addressed by the group are: (1) health and reproductive rights; (2) sexuality and AIDS prevention; (3) violence; and

(4) communication in health-related issues. In 1998, the PAPAI group founded the Work Group in Gender and Masculinities (Gema), after the successful GESMAP model.

In research and policies focused on the question of masculinity, media productions have a prominent role, since the media introduced substantial changes in everyday discursive practices, that is, in the ways people produce meaning about social phenomena and stand before it. In general terms, the media are not only powerful means of creating and circulating repertoires, but they have a changing power that restructures the interaction spaces, allowing for new configurations in the new efforts of meaning production. The fluid space, without spatial and time borders, generated by the media leads, inevitably, to re-conceptualizations of the division established in classical modernity between the private and the public spheres (Giddens 1977; Thompson 1995; Spink 1997; Medrado 1999).

Media as a Discursive Practice

The visibility of social phenomena generated by the interaction mediated by technical devices or via mass communication thus takes an important place in contemporary discussions. It becomes increasingly necessary to manage contents. Similarly, it is necessary to construct a methodological approach to analyse media processes and products, de-familiarizing concepts still tied to the type of face-to-face interaction and understanding the complex dynamics that is set in *mediated* and *quasi-mediated* interactions (Thompson 1995).

We may define *discursive practices* as language in action, that is, the ways in which people produce meanings and take a stand in everyday social relations. That is, it is necessary to understand that language is action and produces consequences.[1] Our work as social scientists who analyse discursive practices is to study the construction of linguistic repertoires, focusing on the performing dimension of the use of language, working with broad but not always intentional consequences. In the processes involved in arguing, in rhetorical exercise (Billig 1991), and when we talk, write or produce media, we are invariably performing an action – accusing, asking, justifying and so on – producing a game of positions towards our interlocutors (direct or indirect, specific or generic), no matter if we intend to do it or not.

Of course, this process is not restricted to oral productions. A written text, a painting or a commercial, for example, constitute printed (or virtual) acts of speech, elements of oral communication which provoke active discussions; they may be complimented, commented on, criticized, they may guide further actions. Thus, nowadays, the radio, television, websites and so on may also be considered *acts of speech*.

In everyday life, meaning arises from the use we make of the interpretative repertoires we possess. *Interpretative repertoires* are, in general terms, the construction units for the discursive practices – the collection of terms, descriptions, common places and figures of speech – that delimit the list of possibilities of discursive constructions, whose parameters are the context in which these practices are produced and the specific grammatical styles or speech genres.

Potter and Wetherell (1987), based on the works of Gilbert and Mulkay (1984), define the interpretative repertoires as linguistic devices that we use to construct versions of the actions, events and other phenomena around us. They are present in a variety of linguistic productions and serve as substratum for an argument.

Interpretative repertoires are essential components for the study of discursive practices, particularly in the media context, as it is through them that we can understand the stability, the dynamics and the variability of human linguistic productions. In other words, this concept is particularly useful for understanding the variability usually found in everyday communication, when repertoires inherent to various discourses are combined in less usual ways, complying with a line of argument, but often giving rise to contradictions.

The focus of the studies that adopt this concept is, then, no longer only regularity, the invariable, the consensus, but will also include the very variability and polysemy which characterize the discourses. Polysemy is here understood not as a 'semantic phenomenon in which a word extends from a primitive meaning to several other meanings', but as 'the property that a word has (in a given time) to represent several different ideas' (Lalande 1996).[2]

Admitting that the discursive practices are polysemic does not mean to say, however, that there is no tendency towards hegemony or that the meanings produced have the same power to cause changes. On the other hand, the polysemic nature of language allows people to transit among a number of contexts and experience varied situations.

Grasping repertoires on masculinity in television commercials allows us to identify those meanings (consensual and contradictory) that circulate in people's everyday lives, and that serve as a substratum for their discursive practices. The purpose of this chapter is to present some analyses from data collected for Medrado's (1997) Master's dissertation in social psychology under the title *O masculino na mídia* (The Masculine in the Media). This research was conducted between 1995 and 1997 and its general goal was to identify repertories on masculinity disseminated by Brazilian TV advertisements. Semi-structured interviews were conducted with professionals who work directly in the production, dissemination and regulation of advertising campaigns. In addition, programmes were taped throughout 1996, one day in each month, during prime-time (from 8 to 11 p.m.) from Rede Globo. According to the Brazilian Institute of Public Opinion and Statistics (IBOPE), Brazil's largest institute for viewer audience assessment, Globo's prime-time has the largest audience in Brazilian television. Thirty-six hours of programming were taped, which meant a total of 1,072 adverts, an average of 90 per day. For this article we focused the discussion on adverts that were seen nationally, which meant 793 or 74 per cent of the total sample collected.

Men in Brazilian Media

Some authors (Nolasco 1993; 1995; Jablonski 1995; Pereira 1995; Monteiro 2000, among others) have produced interesting speculations about masculinity in the Brazilian media. Bernardo Jablonski (1995), for example, suggests that Brazilian television advertising tends to maintain the traditional stereotypes:

> in most commercials, women feature as objects of desire and consumption, as dependent, anxious for support and protection, within the home, and happy only as a 'good mother and wife'. Still according to the classic definition by Parsons, men are instrumental and women are expressive. Instrumentality is meant to be the economic and political responsibility of society. Expressiveness would be, in turn, essentially connected with the care of the home and assistance to the offspring. (Jablonski 1995: 159)

However, according to Sócrates Nolasco (1993), from the late 1980s on, Brazilian media have shown structural changes in the dissemination of male images, generating some 'social permission' for men to take part in activities previously considered as feminine. This phenomenon is similar to what is happening in countries such as the USA and the UK, as we saw above. In his opinion: 'in Brazil, in the last five years, the media have been responsible for raising issues about men's behaviour, disseminating therapeutic works, workshops, seminars and even news stories where men are shown changing diapers, taking children to school and going to beauty parlours to take care of their skin and hair' (Nolasco 1993: 17). These changes, however, as pointed out by the author himself, refer to the printed media, mainly women's magazine. Such ideas do not appear in similar vehicles aimed at men.

Although still superficial and in need of empirical studies, these speculations emphasize the importance of and the need to produce knowledge about the ways masculinity has been represented by national television advertising, by supplying background information for discussions in the arena of gender relations, taking into account that commercials are a very condensed form of information and tend to express selectively the social contexts from which and towards which they are projected.

In our own research, the images and the texts that compose the scenes and messages conveyed by the commercials analysed seem to be still rooted in the most traditional models of social relations against which both the organized women's movement and the homosexual rights movement position themselves, namely, the struggle against the crystallization of behaviour models which impose value on to individual freedom.

Concerning voice-over narration in the advertisements, for example, we found that out of 793 ads aired nationally in 1996, 86 per cent had male narrators, 2.5 per cent female and 11.5 per cent had no narration. This is particularly interesting when we realize that a male voice is considered to lend credibility to the product and to the message conveyed. There seems to be a consensus that male speech, in the media, guarantees reliability. Thus, male narration is a major element in television advertising production, as well as the empiricist repertoire in the formal scientific production (Potter and Wetherell 1987).

Regarding the type of product and the settings in which male characters are featured, we notice a dominance of men in commercials for more expensive products (priced higher than US$ 100) and those associated with non-domestic contexts, such as driving a car, relaxing on the beach, taking part in rodeos, horse-riding and so on.

This is worth highlighting because in everyday discursive practices men still represent the family's main financial provider (even if not the sole provider). For this characterization, scenarios are used that feature men being courageous, adventurous, competitive, and so on.

Both men and women portrayed in the sample analysed are, mostly, white and young or adult[3] and represent an exclusively hetero-erotic standard for relationships, producing a typically traditional scenario: men as workers or financial providers for the family and women as housewives, frivolous and submissive.

However, in contrast to this traditional view, a reference to male homosexuality is made in an advertisement in which the product (Salsaretti tomato sauce), the message and the setting (a kitchen) are aimed at a female target audience. This ad features well-known actors, who have a clear macho image in public, acting effeminately while talking about the sauce and how they use it in their recipes. In addition, the relationship between the actors and the virtual female viewers involves a certain competitiveness, made explicit in the product's slogan, 'A good secret, no woman tells it to another', promoting the idea that in order to compete with the enemy (women) in their own field, it is necessary to assimilate

their weapons. More than a reference to homosexuality, this is a feminization (in the cultural sense) of men.

The series of commercials aired by Bombril (a soft steel-thread mesh
used for cleaning), whose products are also targeted at women, is exemplary,
as it makes use of a clear strategy to disguise the male character by means
of both extreme infantilization and, in a certain way, exaggerated sensitiza-
tion/feminization.

The scenes where men and women interact are in general full of
sensuality and the male characters behave in a virile and active manner. This
characterization is not restricted to the adult world. In a chocolate commercial (Chocodisco Astro), for example, a boy of approximately thirteen
years old talks about the product while there are close-ups of female
characters (a young woman and a little girl) wearing short clothes and with
sensual expressions associated with 'beauty' and the 'care of the body',
whereas the product consumed by the boy is so described: 'Chocodisco
Astro is delicious and gives me a lot of energy!' His facial expression reflects
some sensuality. Likewise, but in a more explicit way, in another chocolate
commercial (Garoto) there are typical scenes of the 'awakening to sexuality'
in which kids observe, admire and flirt with extremely sensual women. The
musical background, the facial expression of the boys, the slow movements
and the swing of the women's hair help to compose the scene.

In commercials where only male characters interact, the plots tend to
emphasize a certain tone of male solidarity (e.g. beer commercials from
Kaiser showing a series of situations in which the character calls his wife
from a bar saying he's still at work, supported by his buddies) or, on the
contrary, a certain competitiveness. For example, in a CCE commercial two
friends talk about the products they have bought, and the success of one
is opposed to the failure of the other. Likewise, in a Mitsubishi commercial,
Zagalo (the Brazilian national soccer team ex-coach) tells Telê Santana
(another famous national soccer team ex-coach) that he's guaranteed until
the 2002 World Soccer Cup (referring to the TV set's warranty time limit).

We notice that, in general, the results obtained corroborate researches
conducted in other countries. On the other hand, as Potter and Wetherell
(1987) tell us, consensus is only one side of the discourse. We realize that
within consensual repertoires, we find space for other/new ways of con-
ceiving masculinities and femininities, further expanding the range of
repertoires available and allowing for changes in the field of gender and
sexuality.

In the context of seduction, discursive productions, especially in the
advertising context, also seem to have undergone some gradual changes.
Research developed by the international advertising network BBDO World-
wide between 1990 and 1991 highlights that this change of repertoires in

advertising is proceeding at a slow pace, and does not yet follow a change of values in society. That research, published by the magazine *Mercado Global* (Global Market) in the first quarter of 1992, was conducted in ten countries (France, Germany, Spain, Italy, UK, USA, Brazil, Colombia, Japan and Australia) and drew on three major sources: focus groups and in-depth interviews with 300 men and 100 women aged twenty to thirty-five from classes A and B; a survey of articles published in these countries about men and masculinities; and 100 commercials produced in the different countries. Each country selected those commercials that best represented different aspects of men.

The results provided evidence that, in advertising, from that point in time, a radical change was urgently needed in order to reach a new kind of consumer coming into the market and who therefore became an important target: 'the man who goes to the supermarket to shop for groceries, likes convenience stores, brands with a well-established image, is more sensitive and has a better humour' (Oliveira 1992).

In the seduction game, according to that research, men would no longer be seen as the 'strong gender', as pillars of protection and security; there was a tendency to highlight other attractive points such as insecurity and vulnerability. Thus, in recent years, the market has constructed new models of the seducing man. The repertoires identified in the construction of the *seducing men* would eschew muscles in favour of sensitiveness.

It is worth noting, however, that, in general, behaviour changes appear in the media in the form of humour, a basic strategy in the discursive production which introduces a breakdown in the linearity of the message at the end of the story, leading to the conclusion that there is a strong seduction power in the 'sensitive man'. What seduces, eventually, is not the whitish, skinny, tender, 'sensitive' boy but the product.

However, the Brazilian printed media, especially mass circulation magazines, seem more susceptible to social changes and include fewer consensual repertoires in their advertising messages. An example would be the controversial campaign from Duloren (a brassière maker) throughout 1996. For example, in celebrating the month of brides (traditionally May in Brazil), a two-page ad in *Folha Magazine* (a special Sunday insert in Brazil's largest nation-wide newspaper) presents on the right-hand·side two women embracing, eyeing one another, dressed only in underwear, one of them with bridal ornaments (veil, white gloves and a bouquet). On the left side, highlighted, is a marriage licence for Renata Pacheco Jordão and Maria de Fátima Vaz Rodrigues, supposedly the names of the two women on the right. The slogan says: 'You cannot imagine what a Duloren can do.'

In another ad, the composition is similar: to celebrate Valentine's Day, two men kiss each other dressed in suits and ties. The slogan contains a small but substantial change: 'You cannot imagine what the lack of a Duloren can do.'

We realize that the composition of new repertoires still oscillates between the traditional and the new. However, it is worth highlighting the importance of, and the need for gradually introducing other/new repertoires on the level of gender and sexual relations in order to make it possible to produce other/new meanings, other/new versions of the phenomena around us.

In terms of social intervention, for example through the Health and Media Work Group, Programme PAPAI[4] has sought to promote other/ new male images associated with contexts culturally identified as feminine, such as aesthetics, health in general, self-care and child-care. Significant among these strategies is the PAPAI mascot, a male doll 3.5 metres tall, displayed at public events, especially during Carnival. It is a young man carrying his son in a *baby-bag*; in general terms, it functions as a symbolic device that associates the male image with child-care, an arena culturally defined as belonging to the female gender.

It is worth noting that strategies such as the one described above cannot be used to find a common basis for masculinity and femininity, assuming mistakenly that it is possible to construct another *hegemonic masculinity*. By means of our reflections, we attempt above all to stress both the rupture and the permanence of repertoires, in an effort to present the co-existence of multiple meanings that the hegemony seeks to obscure and which may provide material for the construction of new meanings.

Notes

1. Discursive practices, in their performing character, constitute *speech acts*, an expression coined by ethnomethodology to refer to the orientation of the use of language for action.

2. The concept of polysemy is opposed to polylexia, used by contemporary linguists to designate the existence of various synonyms for the same idea (Lalande 1996).

3. White characters constitute 87.4 per cent of people shown in commercials. Out of a total of 199 commercials with human characters, aired nation-wide, 44.7 per cent have adult characters; 29.6 per cent young people, 18.1 per cent are mixed; and 7.5 per cent feature children and old people.

4. Formed in 1997, Programa PAPAI is dedicated to research, teaching and social intervention. It is located in the Federal University of Pernambuco (UFPE), and operates in the field of health studies and actions and gender relations, discussing and promoting the involvement of young people and men in the field of sexuality and reproduction. Medrado and Lyra founded this programme and are currently its co-ordinators.

References

Almeida, M. V. de (1995) *Senhores de si. Uma Interpretação Antropológica da Masculinidade*, Lisbon: Fim de Século.

Arilha, M., S. Ridenti and B. Medrado (eds) (1998) *Homens e Masculinidades: Outras Palavras*, São Paulo: ECOS/Editora 34.

Barbieri, T. de (1991) 'Sobre la categoría género. Una introduccíon teórico-metodológica', in S. Azeredo and V. Stolcke (eds), *Direitos reprodutivos*, São Paulo: FCC/DPE.

Barroso, C. (1987) 'Estudos sobre mulher: o descompasso na expansão do ensino e da pesquisa', in E. Oliveira (ed.), *Mulheres: da Domesticidade à Cidadania; Estudos Sobre Movimentos Sociais e Democratizaçã*, São Paulo, CNDM.

Billig, M. (1991) 'Thinking as Arguing', in *Ideology and Opinions: Studies in Rhetorical Psychology*, London: Sage.

Boletim Epidemiologico Brasilia: Coorenacao Nacional de DST/Aids (1998/99), Brasil: Ministerio da Asude (websites: http://www.aids.gov.br).

Bourdieu, P. (1998) *La Domination Masculin*, Paris: Seuil.

Butler, J. (1990) *Gender Trouble: Feminism and the Subversion of Identity*, New York: Routledge.

Caldas, D. (1997) *Homens: Comportamento, Sexualidade, Mudança*, São Paulo: SENAC.

Campos, M. M. M., F. Rosemberg and S. Cavasin (1988) 'A expansão da rede de creches no município de São Paulo durante a década de 70: a participação do grupo *Nós Mulheres*', Trabalho apresentado no XII Encontro Anual da ANPOCS. Águas de São Pedro/SP – GT. Mulher e Política.

CCSP (Clube De Criacao De Sao Paulo) (1996) *21º Anuário de Criação*, São Paulo.

Connell, R. W. (1995) 'Políticas da masculinidade', *Educação e Realidade*, Vol. 20, No. 2: 185–206.

Cornwall, A. and N. Lindisfarne (eds) (1994) *Dislocating Masculinity: Comparative Ethnographies*, London: Routledge.

Costa, A. (1988) 'É viável o feminismo nos trópicos? Resíduos de insatisfação. São Paulo, 1970', São Paulo, *Cadernos de Pesquisa*, No. 66: 63–4.

Costa, A. O., C. Barroso and C. Sarti (1985) 'Pesquisa sobre mulher no Brasil – Do limbo ao gueto?' São Paulo, *Cadernos de Pesquisa*, No. 54: 5–15.

Courtney, A. E. and T. W. Whipple (1974) 'Women in TV Commercials', *Journal of Comunications*, Vol. 24, No. 2: 110–18.

Craig, S. (ed.) (1992) *Men, Masculinity and the Media*, Newbury Park: Sage.

Dominick, J. R. and G. E. Rauch (1972) 'The Image of Women in Network TV Commercials', *Journal of Broadcasting*, No. 16: 259–65.

Doty, W. G. (1993) 'Baring the Flesh: Aspects of Contemporary Male Iconography', in B. Krondorfer (ed.), *Men's Bodies, Men's Gods: Male Identities in a (Post-) Christian Culture*, New York: New York University Press.

Fejes, F. (1992) 'Masculinity as Fact: A Review of Empirical Mass Commumication Research on Masculinity', in Craig (ed.), *Men, Masculinity and the Media*.

Giddens, A. (1977) *Intimacy: Sexuality, Love and Eroticism in Modern Societies*, Cambridge: Polity Press.

Gilbert, N. and M. Mulkay (1984) *Opening Pandora's Box: A Sociological Analysis of Scientists' Discourse*, Cambridge: Cambridge University Press.

Gilly, M. C. (1988) 'Sex Roles in Advertising: A Comparison of Television Advertisements in Australia, Mexico, and the United States', *Journal of Marketing*, Vol. 52, No. 2: 75–85.

Goldberg, A. (1989) 'Feminismo no Brasil contemporâneo: O percurso intelectual de um ideário político', Rio de Janeiro, *Revista BIB*, No. 28: 42–70.

Izquierdo, M. J. (1994) 'Uso y abuso del concepto de género', in M. Vilvanova (ed.), *Pensar Las Diferencias*, Barcelona: Universitat de Barcelona, ICD.

Jablonski, B. (1995) 'A difícil extinção do boçalossauro', in Nolasco, *A Desconstrução do Masculino*.

Kimmel, M. (1992a) 'La producción teórica sobre la masculinidad: nuevos aportes', in Rodrigues (ed.), *Fin de Siglo. Genero y Cambio Civilizatori*, Santiago: Isis International, Ediciones de las mujeres, No. 17: 129–38.

— (1992b) 'Foreword', in Craig (ed.), *Men, Masculinity and the Media*.

Lalande, A. (1996) *Vocabulário Técnico e Crítico da Filosofia*, 2nd edn, São Paulo: Martins Fontes.

Lauretis, T. de (1990) 'Eccentric Subjects: Feminist Theory and Historical Consciousness', *Feminist Studies*, Vol. 16, No. 1: 115–51.

Lovdal, L. T. (1989) 'Sex Role Messages in Television Commercials: An Update', *Sex Roles*, Vol. 21, No. 11/12: 715–24.

Lyra, J. (1997) *Paternidade adolescente: uma proposta de intervenção*, thesis (Mestrado em Psicologia Social), São Paulo: PUC/SP.

McArthur, L. and B. Resko (1975) 'The Portrayal of Men and Women in American Television Commercials', *Journal of Social Psychology*, Vol. 6, No. 4: 209–20.

Mazzella, C., K. Durkin, E. Cerini and P. Burall (1992) 'Sex Role Stereotyping in Australian Television Advertisements', *Sex Roles*, Vol. 26, No. 7/8: 243–59.

Medrado, B. (1997) *O masculino na mídia*, thesis (Mestrado em Psicologia Social), São Paulo: PUC/SP.

— (1999) 'Textos em cena: a mídia como prática discursiva', in M. J. P. Spink (ed.), *Práticas Discursivas e Produção de Sentidos No Cotidiano*, São Paulo: Cortez.

Monteiro, M. (2000) *Tenham Piedade dos Homens!: Masculinidades em Mudança*, Juiz de Fora: FEME.

Moraes, M. L. Q. (1985) *Mulheres Em Movimento: O Balanço da Década da Mulher do Ponto de Vista do Feminismo, das Religiões e da Política*, São Paulo: Nobel.

Morgan, D. (1992) *Discovering Men*, New York: Routledge.

Nixon, S. (1996) *Hard Looks: Masculinities, Spectatorship and Contemporary Consumption*, New York: St Martin's Press.

Nolasco, S. (1993) *O Mito da Masculinidade*, Rio de Janeiro: Rocco.

— (1995) *A Desconstrução do Masculino*, Rio de Janeiro: Rocco.

Oliveira, M. (1992) 'Um novo homem para a nova mulher', *Revista Mercado Global*, No. 87, August.

Pereira, C. A. M. (1995) 'Que homem é esse? O masculino em questão', in Nolasco, *A Desconstrução do Masculino*.

Postman, N., C. Nystrom, L. Strate and C. Weingartner (1987) *Myths, Men and Beer: An Analysis of Beer Commercials on Broadcast Television*, New York: AAA Foundation for Traffic Safety.

Potter, J. and M. Wetherell (1987) *Discourse and Social Psychology: Beyond Attitudes and Behaviour*, London: Sage.

Pyke, S. W. and J. C. Stewart (1974) 'This Column is about Women: Women and Television', *Ontario Psychologist*, Vol. 6, No. 5: 66.

Rosemberg, F. (1987) *As Feministas e a Luta Por Creche*, São Paulo: Fundação Carlos Chagas.

— (1993) 'Estudos sobre mulher e relações de gênero', in *A Fundação Ford no Brasil*, São Paulo: FAPESP/ Sumaré.

Sarti, C. (1985) '"É sina que a gente traz": ser mulher na pariferia urbana', thesis (Mestrado em Sociologia), São Paulo: USP.

— (1988) 'Feminismo no Brasil: uma trajetória particular', São Paulo, *Cadernos de Pesquisa*, No. 64: 38–47.

Scheibe, C. (1979) 'Sex Roles in TV Commercials', *Journal of Advertising Research*, Vol. 19, No. 1: 23–7.

Scott, J. (1988) *Gender and the Politics of History*, New York: Columbia University Press.

Spink, M. J. P. (1997), *A construção social do risco no cenário da AIDS*, Projeto de pesquisa apresentado ao Conselho Nacional de Desenvolvimento Cietífico e Tecnológio – CNPq, mimeo.

Strate, L. (1992) 'Beer Commercials: A Manual on Masculinity', in Craig (ed.), *Men, Masculinity and the Media*.

Thompson, J. (1995) *The Media and Modernity: A Social Theory of the Media*, Cambridge: Polity Press.

12

Unlearning Machismo: Men Changing Men in Post-revolutionary Nicaragua

Patrick Welsh

Introduction: 'Violence Against Women: A Disaster that Men *Can* Avoid'

'Violence against women: a disaster that men *can* avoid' is the catchy slogan of a multimedia campaign promoted in Nicaragua at the end of 1999. Organized by the feminist NGO Puntos de Encuentro and developed on the basis of previous research on masculinity and violence carried out in Nicaragua (Montoya Tellería 1998), it was implemented in co-operation with the Managua-based Group of Men Against Violence (GMAV). The campaign was aimed specifically at Nicaraguan men living in those areas of the country that had been most severely affected by a natural catastrophe almost a year previously: Hurricane Mitch. For a period of three to four months, the most popular prime-time soap operas were interspersed with professionally-produced TV spots inviting men to reflect upon their 'machismo' and violence, and encouraging them to change. The catchphrase of the campaign glared down from massive billboards on the country's major highways, its jingle was played on national and local radio stations, and glossy posters, calendars and car-stickers were posted in private and public places all over Nicaragua. Dozens of workshops on masculinity and violence were also organized by men for men, some in the most remote villages. Men were sat down together to talk about male gender identity, power and violence and to make concrete proposals for changing their own perceptions, conceptions and behaviour. The unlearning of machismo was in progress.

'Machismo'

To understand why and how men are changing men in post-revolutionary Nicaragua it is important to define what 'machismo' is and to examine the processes of 'unlearning machismo' within the context of contemporary Nicaraguan history. 'Machismo', in Nicaragua, constitutes a socio-cultural model of masculinity that, passed on from generation to generation, dictates the attitudes, values and behaviour that men should adopt in order to be considered men and to feel within themselves that they are men. It encompasses not only the way that men relate to women but also to other men and to children in both the domestic and public spheres of life. It is, in effect, an ideology built upon the erroneous supposition that men are naturally physically and intellectually superior to women, a concept that is instilled into both women and men from an early age. Consequently, men enjoy rights and privileges and have access to opportunities in society that are denied to women and a system of gender inequity is promoted and perpetuated.

While machismo is commonly associated with stereotypical images of gun-slinging, heavy-drinking cowboys, its manifestation in modern-day Nicaragua entails the quest by men to attain power (an important source of sense of identity, status and wealth) at all levels in society. As in many societies, power is conceived of as a means to ensure dominion and control over others, especially women, and gender-based violence in all its manifestations is an important mechanism to ensure the consolidation of personal and collective male power and to guarantee the perpetuation of rights and privileges.

Machismo, then, should not be considered as a phenomenon restricted to Latin American men, but rather as a universal system of male values, attitudes and behaviour whose development in a country like Nicaragua is intimately related to its specific cultural reality and social history. Indeed, the existence of machismo, understood as a paradigm of masculinity to which all men must aspire, inevitably leads to an array of different possible manifestations of masculinity, as individuals and different groups of men develop their own sense of identity. However, while a diversity of male identities or masculinities may exist, machismo is the framework within which men in Nicaragua internalize their sense of maleness and learn to be men, and social pressure inhibits all but a few men from developing significantly divergent alternatives.

Nicaragua: A 'Before and After' Land

Nicaragua is a country in which time and human experience are measured in relation to natural and historical phenomena. Phrases such as 'before/after the earthquake' (1972), 'before/after the triumph of the Revolution' (1979), or 'before/after Hurricane Mitch' (1998) are frequently used by people in reference to the tumultuous and dramatic events that have shaped their lives. Since the major earthquake that flattened Managua in 1972, Nicaraguans have suffered a series of hurricanes, tsunamis and volcanic eruptions that have left thousands of people dead and have had devastating psychological and economic effects upon the lives of the survivors. Add to these natural disasters a series of tragic and calamitous socio-political upheavals (war, dictatorship, revolution and counter-revolution, economic embargo) and you end up with a hefty batch of before-and-after situations with which to measure life, and death.

A significant before-and-after event in contemporary Nicaraguan history was the general election held in 1990 which the Sandinistas surprisingly lost. This marked the beginning of the post-revolutionary era in Nicaragua. Everything that took place 'before the elections' (free and improved education and health-care, increased literacy, land reform, etc.) began to be systematically dismantled 'after the elections'. The newly elected centre-right government, with the support of the IMF and World Bank, quickly began to pursue social and economic reforms that entailed the implementation of some of the harshest Structural Adjustment Programmes ever conceived. While the war was over, in military terms at least, electoral promises of peace, prosperity and reconstruction failed to materialize and as levels of misery began to soar, so too did levels of violence between men and women and between men.

Women and the Sandinista Revolution

During the revolution, however, people's political awareness and capacity for critical analysis blossomed. They became 'empowered'. Despite the anguish and hardship caused by the war and economic impoverishment, thousands of Nicaraguans discovered a new sense of inner strength as they struggled against the odds to defend their dignity and right to life and to determine their own human development. Many of these, of course, were women and perhaps one of the most important legacies of the revolution is the autonomous women's movement in all its rich diversity. Since the early days of the armed insurrection in the 1970s, and throughout the years of the revolution, women took on new roles and responsibilities at all levels in society and their vision of themselves, of their own potential and human capacities, was radically and irreversibly altered.

These advances, however, were invariably perceived by the predominantly male leadership of the revolution as a threat, and demands by women that their own agenda be incorporated into the revolution were, by and large, ignored. Margaret Randall in *Sandino's Daughters Revisited: Feminism in Nicaragua* says: 'Women's issues and the needs of the Revolution were too often placed in opposition to each other' (Randall 1994: 28). It was argued that once the war was over there would be time for women's rights but until that time everyone had to pull together to defend the revolution against the military, economic and political onslaught of the US government, the Contra revolution and the CIA.

By the late 1980s, however, a number of women's groups and collectives, while still militantly Sandinista, began to develop programmes and projects that went beyond the vision of AMNLAE, the official Sandinista women's organization. Demanding greater autonomy and respect for their own political agenda, they were greatly influenced by feminist theory and practice that incorporated a gender perspective and analysis. Initially, of course, the emphasis was a Women in Development (WID) one and focused mainly on the economic development and technical and organizational capacity-building of women's groups, an issue of vital importance to the revolution given the huge number of men in active military service. By the end of the 1980s, however, some women in Nicaragua were seriously questioning the validity of WID as a strategy for liberation and its appropriateness for their integral human development. More often than not, the introduction of projects designed to improve women's economic situation invariably increased their already high workload and failed to challenge culturally engrained gender stereotypes and relations. It had become clear that women's strategic needs, in general, were not being sufficiently addressed.

Without abandoning the need to attend to women's practical gender needs, the gradual shift by many groups and collectives to a Gender and Development (GAD) focus led to them beginning to take on important issues of gender identity, gender-based violence, sexuality and sexual and reproductive health. Women began to work on issues of power, self-esteem, conscientization and empowerment. The revolution supplied a class analysis that challenged discriminatory conceptions and practices imposed upon Nicaragua from the outside (and to a certain degree internally) that women could identify with and participate in. The emergence of an autonomous women's movement, feminism and gender theory provided the framework for the identification and challenging of machismo within the revolution and its particular effects upon women's development within a socialist revolutionary context.

Throughout the 1980s, therefore, a truly feminist agenda 'played second fiddle' to the strategic needs of the Sandinista Party and revolution and was consistently undermined by the macho values and attitudes that continued to permeate Nicaraguan culture and which inevitably had become enshrined in Sandinista institutions. After the elections of 1990, however, the critical women's collectives and groups that had been formed towards the end of the 1980s (and dozens of new ones that quickly sprang up in all parts of Nicaragua) began to gather momentum, mainly due to the fact that they no longer had to play a subservient role in society. Rooted in Sandinismo and building upon the advances women had achieved in the 1980s (basic freedoms, access to health, education, work, political awareness and participation), the early 1990s saw the emergence of an autonomous women's movement that today constitutes the most active, dynamic and wide-reaching social movement in Nicaragua. Indeed, according to Nicaraguan feminist Sofía Montenegro, 'the women's movement, after the FSLN electoral defeat, was one of the first to acquire autonomy and (since then) has been setting itself up as an emergent political force' (La Corriente 1997: 36).

In 1993 the National Network of Women Against Violence (NNWAV) was set up and currently brings together more than 320 women's groups, collectives, NGOs and so on, from all over Nicaragua, that at a local level offer support for women and families subjected to violence by men. On a political level the NNWAV has had major success in passing important legislation (Law 230, passed in 1996) to prevent and eliminate family violence. Indeed, one of the most impressive achievements of this legislation is the recognition of psychological lesions to women by their partners as criminal acts.

The Emergence of the Group of Men Against Violence (GMAV)

The appearance of the NNWAV in 1993 and increased public awareness as regards the extent and severity of gender-based violence in Nicaragua led in June of the same year to the setting up of the Managua-based Group of Men Against Violence (GMAV). Linked to the feminist NGO Puntos de Encuentro, the GMAV's major concern, initially, was how to contribute to the reduction and elimination of male violence against women. It quickly became apparent, however, that the focus of attention could not solely be on 'other men' perceived of as violent and in need of help to relinquish their violent behaviour. This was certainly a need, but the GMAV also became a focus for men willing to enter into processes of critical self-reflection and analysis, each member responsible for unravelling the violence in his own life in all its dimensions and manifestations and 'discover' its relation to the social construction of masculinity. To this day both foci remain relevant and the GMAV continues to provide spaces for men to reflect upon issues of violence and masculinity as well as to organize and participate in activities (workshops, campaigns) aimed at raising awareness and changing men's behaviour.

One of the most important activities that the GMAV has taken part in over the years has been the systematic support and accompaniment of the political initiatives of the NNWAV. In 1996, shortly after the Ministry of

Health's recognition of family violence as a public health issue/problem, the NNWAV instigated a campaign to introduce and pass legislation to prevent and eliminate family violence. Men from the GMAV helped to fill petitions and lobbied male representatives of the National Assembly to ensure their support for the bill. In 1998, the GMAV took a public stance in support of Zoilamérica Narváez when she accused her stepfather, Daniel Ortega (ex-president of Nicaragua and general secretary of the Sandinista Front for National Liberation), of having sexually abused her as a child and young woman. The NNWAV set up a commission to support Zoilamérica in her efforts to bring Daniel Ortega to justice and for the first time men from the GMAV were officially invited to participate.

In late 1999, a documentary, *Macho*, was made about the GMAV, commissioned by BBC television and written and directed by Lucinda Broadbent, an independent Scottish film-maker.

The membership of the GMAV has also been an important source of 'manpower' for other national and international NGOs working on issues of masculinity, gender and violence in Nicaragua and other parts of Central America.

Inspired by the experience of the GMAV in Managua and by work on masculinity and violence promoted by Nicaraguan NGOs such as Puntos de Encuentro and CANTERA (the Centre for Popular Education and Communications), men in other parts of Nicaragua began to set up groups. In August 1995 the GMAV organized and hosted the first National Encounter of Men Against Violence, bringing together a diverse group of 100 men from all areas of Nicaragua. In March 1999, the second National Encounter was held but participation had to be limited to representatives of the different regions in Nicaragua.

Masculinities and Popular Education: The Search for Appropriate Methodologies for Unlearning Machismo

An important resource for the membership of the GMAV and other men interested in unlearning machismo have been the courses on Masculinity and Popular Education developed and run in Nicaragua every year since 1994 by CANTERA, a Nicaraguan NGO specializing in the methodology of popular education. Since its foundation in the mid-1980s, one of its areas of specialization has been the development of participatory training methodologies for the conscientization and empowerment of women. Up until that time, in Central America, popular education had been associated with a predominantly Marxist analysis of society and its proposals centred on the need for objective changes in oppressive structures, at different levels, in order to achieve social justice. The fusion of popular education and gender analysis with women, in a sense, complemented processes of critical analysis of objective reality with one of subjective reality at a time when the personal dimensions of everyday life were being reinterpreted as political. As well as focusing reflection on external reality, forces and structures, women began to focus upon the analysis of themselves, using a popular education methodology. Their own complex and subjective reality became the centre of their reflections and analysis. The result of these processes led to the articulation of concrete proposals to improve their own lives through changes to attitudes, values, roles, responsibilities, opportunities, rights and duties, public and political participation. In essence, women were stripping down the social construction of their gender identities and discovering ways to work towards the realization of their practical and strategic gender needs.

By 1993, hundreds of women had benefited from participation in the courses, seminars and workshops offered by CANTERA and other Nicaraguan organizations, but they were also facing many obstacles in the implementation of concrete changes. In the majority of cases, one of the major obstacles identified was the intransigence of men's patriarchal attitudes, values and behaviour. Indeed, in some cases, these had become even more deeply entrenched in men as they counter-reacted to women's processes of conscientization and empowerment. It was becoming increasingly obvious to many women that if these processes were to be strengthened and consolidated 'something would have to be done with the men' in their families, workplaces and communities.

Simultaneously, discussions within CANTERA as regards the meaning of gender and its relation to popular education opened up debate on masculinity for the first time. The fusion of CANTERA's own popular education practice with women and theoretical advances in gender theory made it clear that the improvement in women's quality of life depended not only upon changes in women's perceptions, conceptions, values and actual behaviour but also upon similar processes in men. How would it be possible to modify gender power relations if half of the population was not even willing to enter into the gender debate?

For women within CANTERA working on issues of popular education and gender, it had become glaringly obvious that social justice, the ultimate goal of popular education, is unachievable if gender justice does not exist. Indeed, popular education itself falls short if it focuses only on objective reality and social and political structures. And men committed to and working in popular education fall short if they are not equally committed to gender justice. Gender justice, then, is obtainable only if both men and women work towards it, changing their ways of thinking, being and relating. For both, this entails processes of conscientization which for women mean empowerment, and for men the unlearning of machismo.

Recognizing Resistance, Fears and Contradictions

For many men, however, words like 'gender' and 'feminism' are like a 'red rag to a bull' and the men working in CANTERA at this time were no exception. Before they could take on board the intellectual arguments presented to them by women, they first had to come to terms with their own misconceptions, prejudices and fears as regards gender and feminism. Furthermore, they also had to begin to reflect upon the possible benefits that they themselves would reap if they began processes of unlearning machismo.

This process was greatly influenced by Marcela Lagarde, a Mexican anthropologist and expert on gender and development who visited CANTERA in mid-1993 to run a workshop that focused partly on male gender identities. The workshop served to widen the intellectual debate on gender theory and its practical applications in community development with women and men. Marcela Lagarde's visit to CANTERA represents, in effect, an external catalytic input that helped to dissipate fears, especially within men, and that contributed substantially to the breaking down of intellectual and emotional resistances to gender.

As a result of Marcela Lagarde's visit, a small group of men in CAN-TERA began to visualize with greater clarity the contradictions between their discourse on popular education and social justice, and their personal and professional day-to-day practice, and thus began to accept the arguments put to them by women within the CANTERA technical team. On a rational level, gender was becoming recognized as an imperative of popular education; on an emotional level, its inclusion in popular education became a means for improving the quality of life of women and men and human relationships in general.

Courses on Masculinity and Popular Education

After a year of deliberation it was decided to organize a one-day encounter with the aim of bringing together men from other organizations and from different parts of the country to reflect on gender and masculinity. A total of forty-one men took part in a day-long encounter of soul-searching analysis and critical appraisal of their own attitudes, values and behaviour as men, focusing on personal and family histories. Perhaps one of the most important discoveries of the encounter was the fact that changes in traditional male ways of thinking, being and doing bring positive consequences not only for women but also for men. Much of the debate and sharing of experiences centred upon the social restrictions placed upon men, especially in relation to the expression of fears and doubts, feelings and emotions. The men who took part in this encounter were articulating their aspirations to be different, for the first time, in their own personal and collective histories and while recognizing the rights and privileges that traditional masculinity bestows on men, they were also discovering its dehumanizing effects on the majority of men.

The overwhelming response of the participants in this first encounter and their demand for follow up paved the way for the development of a course entitled 'Masculinity and Popular Education' which has been run every year since 1995 and which is now a permanent part of CANTERA's global programme. While modifications have been incorporated into the course each year based upon the evaluations (of each workshop and at the end of the year of each course), and processes of systemization carried out, the course currently consists of four workshops, each one of three-and-a-half days' duration. To facilitate the assimilation of the (un)learning in each workshop and to give sufficient time for the implementation of proposed changes, there is usually a period of two to three months between the workshops. The course is conceived of as a process and each individual workshop builds on the previous one in terms of content, methodology and intensity, covering issues such as the social construction of masculinity, male identities, gender theory, violence (types, causes and effects), sex and sexuality, homosexuality and homophobia, relationships with women, self-image and self-esteem, discrimination, fatherhood, HIV/AIDS, inter-personal communication, the pressures of having to always be in charge, mental health, fears and prejudices.

The fourth and final workshop, entitled 'Forging Just Relations', brings men together with the women who take part in CANTERA's 'Popular Education Between Women' course which runs parallel to the course on masculinity. This shared space permits the joint discussion of aspirations and expectations, fears and doubts, proposals and strategies. Given that the ultimate aim of CANTERA's work on gender and popular education is to contribute to greater gender equity and justice between men and women (and between men, and between women) within the family, at work, within the community and on a political level, this workshop is seen as a vital, strategic component for both women and men. For many women it represents the first time that they are able to express their gender needs in the presence of men and feel that they are being listened to. The first time, too, that they come face to face with men who are unlearning machismo. For many men, it is the moment that they have been waiting for since the course on masculinity began. At this stage, however, more than eight months after the first workshop, they have new experiences, perceptions and conceptions to share with women and, in general, are more sensitive and better equipped to listen.

Since CANTERA began to work on issues of masculinity in 1994, around 450 men have taken part in the national courses. Most have been Nicaraguans but men from Costa Rica, Honduras, Panama, Guatemala, El Salvador, Spain, Haiti, the USA and England have also participated. As well as enabling men to instigate journeys of self-discovery and unravel the social processes that influence their formation as men and propose concrete changes, they also equip them with the necessary methodological and pedagogical tools to replicate the course (or elements of it) with other men in their workplaces and communities.

The methodological focus of the courses has proved to be of vital importance in the facilitation of processes of transformation in attitudes, values and behaviour. Men are not taught about gender, masculinity or violence in a traditional way. Rather they are nurtured into processes of critical analysis of the socialization processes that they live through in the different periods of their personal development (infancy, childhood, adolescence, youth, adulthood). Major emphasis is put on the recalling of personal experiences which, when reflected upon, can be reinterpreted and seen in a different light. Men slowly begin to discover the existence in society of a hegemonic model of masculinity towards which all men are pushed from early infancy, and to which all must aspire. The realization that each individual man is moulded in the image and likeness of this paradigmatic super macho enables participants to discover the social, learned nature of their own individual masculine identity and arrive at the conclusion that unlearning machismo is not only possible but also necessary and beneficial. As part of this process it is not enough for men only to learn theories of gender and masculinity. They first and foremost have to delve into the realms of their own subjectivity and uncover the layers of myths, prejudices and discriminatory concepts and practices in which their inner selves are shrouded. By exposing culturally accepted norms of traditional masculinity as harmful and destructive, and rejecting them, new concepts, attitudes and values can be internalized and changes in external behaviour nurtured. Unlearning machismo is not just an intellectual, rational exercise, it also involves the exteriorization of feelings and emotions and the working through of fears.

The methodology developed by CANTERA promotes the challenging of stereotypes and prejudices and places particular importance on the articulation and expression of feelings, fears, sentiments and aspirations. Awareness of subjective reality is in itself knowledge, is recognized as such and is valued. It is also a source of 'power', which for men willing to unlearn machismo means the relinquishing of the mechanisms and structures they have learned and used to dominate, exploit and control other people, especially women. In essence, unlearning machismo is the conscious and systematic stripping down of the internal and external manifestations of patriarchal power and the assimilation of new attributes and values: tenderness, affection, compassion, co-operation, communication.

In educational terms, one of the major implications of this type of learning is that each individual man sets his own agenda, since the (un)learning process itself is intrinsically related to each one's personal history and the extent to which the paradigm of masculinity has been incorporated into individual identity. As previously stated, the course represents the beginning of a new journey for each man, one that will be dictated to a major degree by the past experiences that have moulded and formed his particular vision of himself and his world. One man's starting point may entail the realization that violence is a psychological phenomenon as well as a physical one. Thus he may discover that the control he wields over his partner's social mobility constitutes the violation of basic rights and as such is an act of violence. Another man may come to terms for the first time with the homophobic attitudes and conduct that he has learned and begin to take measures to eradicate discrimination practices towards gays, lesbians, bisexuals and transvestites. The predominant principle is that each man must take responsibility for his own process of critical analysis and subsequent transformation, a task that requires honesty, sincerity and a large amount of courage.

Measuring Change

In 1998, CANTERA carried out an impact study with the principal aim of measuring the changes that men were instigating in their lives. The results, published in January 1999, were very positive and allowed men's own appreciation of the changes they were experiencing to be contrasted with those that women (partners, sisters, mothers) were observing. In general, women confirmed the changes that men said they were experiencing, albeit to a slightly lesser degree. For example, both men and women stated that after participating in the course on masculinity men showed greater solidarity with women, gays and lesbians, demonstrated greater responsibility as fathers and partners, had increased their participation in domestic chores and were less violent.

Special emphasis was put on conjugal violence and analysis revealed that 54.5 per cent of the men included in the study registered the use of violence (physical and/or psychological) against their partner on at least one occasion, before, during or after the course on masculinity. Comparing the registered incidents of violence before and after participation in the courses, the study also detected that incidents of psychological/emotional violence dropped by 36 per cent and of physical violence by 56 per cent.

It is notoriously hard, however, to measure change in attitudes, values and behaviour and any interpretation of these figures should bear in mind their subjective character. While reductions in levels of violence should indeed be welcomed, many men, in the year following their participation in the CANTERA courses, were still resorting to both psychological and physical violence in their conjugal relationships. Rather than hard and fast figures, the 'results' of the impact study strongly suggest that men are indeed embarking upon processes of change that undoubtedly, in the future, need to be strengthened. There are no magical solutions to gender-based violence.

CANTERA's work on masculinity has been developed within a pro-feminist framework that builds upon women's own processes of awareness-raising and training in gender. Experience teaches that men's own reality is the most appropriate starting point for unlearning machismo and the popular education methodology implemented by CANTERA enables men to analyse, together, their own life experiences and to make proposals for changes that they feel they are able to undertake. Many men, however, who have taken part in workshops and seminars on gender theory, family violence or feminism, usually given by women, have been ill-equipped to deal with their content and focus. Some come away feeling confused, others on the defensive and angry at the accusative character of feminist discourse. This is not to say, however, that women do not have a role to play in men's processes of unlearning machismo and, indeed, the mixed workshop 'Forging Just Relations' clearly demonstrates the need for men and women to come together, not only as participants but also as facilitators. If men are to be willing to enter into processes of reflection, analysis and change, it is of paramount importance that their initial contact with gender theory be a positive one. Reflection and analysis of lived experiences, rather than an academic class on feminism, have proven to be a good starting point to set these processes in motion. As they develop, however, analysis and sharing of personal experience can be complemented by the facilitation of theoretical materials, the use of documentaries and commercial films and formal talks by experts (women and men) on relevant issues. This enables men not only to interpret their own experience within the conceptual framework of feminism and gender theory, but also to conceptualize and understand that framework in their own words.

Within development circles in Nicaragua and Central America, work on gender and masculinity has, in general, been welcomed and even hailed as 'pioneering'. Since its conception, however, many legitimate concerns have also been articulated within NGOs, within the women's movement and, of course, by international funding agencies that sponsor the work. These have ranged from cynical doubts that men could in fact change (who would voluntarily give up so much power?) to concerns regarding the effectiveness of the methodology. Fears have also been expressed that masculinity has become a fashionable fad and that already limited funds for gender work with women is being channelled into work with men, with very limited guarantees that this will in effect contribute to greater gender equity. Furthermore, some women are apprehensive that work on masculinity could lead to some men developing even subtler ways of oppressing women. These concerns, doubts and fears are legitimate and further underline the urgent need to develop programmes of gender awareness-raising with men within a pro-feminist framework. Steps must be taken to facilitate the inclusion of women in their development and to ensure the construction of strategic alliances between women and men orientated towards positive contributions by men to gender equity.

The Association of Men Against Violence (AMAV)

One such step that men in Nicaragua have taken towards achieving this goal has been the setting up of the Association of Men Against Violence (AMAV), founded in March 2000 by the members of the GMAV in Managua. A membership organization, the AMAV is open to all men in Nicaragua committed to eradicating gender-based violence. Women too can become 'members in solidarity'. By the time the AMAV's offices were inaugurated in Managua in September of the same year, membership had risen to over 100 (including twenty women) from all parts of Nicaragua and new men's groups were being set up. The AMAV's main focus is on the promotion of educational and organizational processes with men on issues of masculinity and violence, the development of a psycho-educational programme for men who use violence against women and the setting up and strengthening of appropriate structures to enable the work to be carried out with efficiency and efficacy.

A management committee, incorporating seven men from different parts of the country, has been set up as has a consultative committee that includes prominent men and women from civil society organizations (NNWAV, PAHO [Panamerican Health Organization], feminist NGOs) and government entities (Procurator for Human Rights, army, police). Its members have been selected on the basis of their personal qualities and professional expertise and their role will be to advise the AMAV on specific issues related to institutional development, strategic planning, transparency and social responsibility and gender issues.

In the near future the AMAV aims to increase its membership and to encourage its active, democratic participation in activities and on issues at both a local and national level. A profeminist focus is central to the philosophy of the AMAV and steps are being taken to create formal channels of communication and co-ordination with the NNWAV and other feminist NGOs in order to support women's political and social agendas. Current examples of this are the presence of members of the AMAV in public demonstrations organized by the NNWAV to protest against proposals to criminalize therapeutic abortion; and a public pronouncement made by the GMAV on the issue, supporting the NNWAV's stance and inviting men to recognize their role and take responsibility in relation to therapeutic abortion. Furthermore, members of the AMAV continue to participate in the efforts of the NNWAV and Zoilamérica Narváez to strip Daniel Ortega of his diplomatic immunity and face the legal charges of sexual abuse that have been brought against him.

In Nicaragua, work with men on issues of gender, masculinity, violence and sexuality endeavours to contribute to the improvement in the quality of life of both men and women. To do this men must commit themselves to integral educational processes that enable them to continuously unlearn machismo. In doing so, they reclaim the human dimension of their beings, challenging the hegemonic model of masculinity that deforms men and that subordinates and exploits women. In post-revolutionary Nicaragua, the unlearning of machismo is a truly revolutionary endeavour capable of contributing to just gender relationships based upon equity, mutual respect and solidarity.

References

CANTERA (1998) *El Significado de Ser Hombre: Propuesta Metodología Para el Trabajo de Masculinidad con Hombres*, Managua, Nicaragua.

La Corriente (1997) *Movimiento de Mujeres en Centroamérica*, Programa Regional la Corriente, Managua, Nicaragua.

Montoya Tellería, Oswaldo (1998) 'Nadando Contra Corriente', Managua: Puntos de Encuentro.

Randall, M. (1994) *Sandino's Daughters Revisited: Feminism in Nicaragua*, New Brunswick, NJ: Rutgers Press.

13

Moving Beyond Mateship: Reconstructing Australian Men's Practices

Bob Pease

In this chapter I will explore the implications of the definitively Australian style of masculine behaviour called 'mateship' for gender relations in Australia. Mateship is part of the Australian male heritage; it originated in colonial days and was glorified in war and sport. The feminist movement in Australia has challenged the dominant form of masculinity inherent in mateship and the basic rationale for gender relations that flow from it. In this context, I will discuss Australian profeminist men's attempts to challenge patriarchal gender relations and construct non-patriarchal subjectivities and practices.

Theorizing about masculinity in Australia has tended to be derivative of overseas literature. This is partly because publishers are looking for overseas markets for their books so they discourage writers on masculinity from grounding men's practices in a specifically Australian context. While there are benefits in generalizing about western masculinities, such writing misses the uniqueness of the lived experiences of Australian men. It is this uniqueness that I will address in this chapter. As McGrane and Patience (1995: 15) note, 'Australian masculinism has a history of its own that needs to be recognized at the same time as it can be usefully compared to the masculinisms of similar cultures'.

Colonial Masculinities

To understand Australian masculinities, we have to locate Australian men's lives historically. The start of male dominated society in Australia can be traced to 1788 with the arrival of the first 'convict settlers' (Bell 1973: 1–2). The myth of the peaceful settlement of Australia has been a pervading theme in Australian history. The proposition was that the European incursion encountered no resistance from the Aboriginal inhabitants of this continent. This premise has been powerfully challenged by Reynolds

(2000) who demonstrates that generations of Australians grew up with a distorted version of the past.

Stealing land from the Aborigines became a factor in constructing a typically Australian male identity. If the Aborigines resisted, the whites were forced to rely upon each other for help (Colling 1992: 6). Also, the harsh physical environment of colonial Australia meant that the men had to depend on each other for economic survival. Thus a particular form of male bonding developed 'to meet the needs of coping with the environment and the demands of economic survival' (Bell 1973: 2). In the context of such an alien hostile environment, they developed what Colling (1992: 6) describes as a 'frontier survival mentality'.

As Tacey notes:

We are speaking of a frontier society where men gather together to provide mutual support and security, where women are held at a distance ... where hostile relations exist between the colonizing settlers and the indigenous people ... In this situation, the famous Australian mateship is born, that particular kind of behavioural code in which a man will do anything to protect or support a mate. (Tacey 1997: 135)

An important element of mateship has always been that the company of other men is preferred to the company of women (Bell 1973: 10). Thus Australian mateship developed in the context of the harsh reality of bush life for men without female companionship. The central elements are that mates are 'exclusively male, not female, they share a particular sceptical camaraderie in doing things together [and] there is a lack of emotional expression other than sharing jokes' (Edgar 1997: 79).

The First World War introduced a new stage of mateship. Men had to be moulded together into an effective fighting force (Webb 1998: 74–5). In fact, as Garton (1998: 94) has noted, war played a significant role in 'constructing particular masculine ideals in Australian culture'. Perhaps, more than any other event, it was the Gallipoli campaign that enshrined mateship as a significant part of the Australian male self-image. This mythologizing began immediately after the landing in 1915. The Anzac legend of mateship, anti-authoritarianism, larrikinism and fortitude, became translated into a national ethos (Garton 1998: 94). It is telling that the strongest bonds between men are forged in war.

Second-wave Feminism Comes to Australia

The second wave of the feminist movement that emerged in Australia in the early 1970s challenged the foundations of male–female relations upon which mateship was based. However, most Australian men were

unable to grasp the feminist analysis of gender-based injustices. Because
most Australian men did not beat their wives or rape women, they believed
that the feminist analysis did not apply to them (Colling 1992: 33). Nevertheless, they felt the impact of feminism's challenge to the institutionalized
power of men.

The women's movement in Australia grew in strength through the late
1970s to the 1980s. Its organizational forms were mainly represented
through political groups such as Women's Liberation and Women's Electoral Lobby (WEL) (Cuthoys 1994: 18). Women's Liberation took more of
a socialist and radical feminist analysis of women's position and activists
were involved in community-based services such as women's refuges and
rape crisis centres, while WEL was more involved in electoral and
bureaucratic politics within the state. In fact, many Australian feminists
endeavoured to use the state to redistribute resources between men and
women (Lake 1999: 253). Many women were appointed to positions specifically to bring about gender reform. In this regard, feminists were able to
influence the political agenda and achieve a variety of policy reforms
(Kenway 1996: 452). Such women were called 'femocrats'.

The strength of Australian men's resistance to even the more liberal
feminist campaigns for equal opportunity and affirmative action encouraged
a feminist distrust of men as potential allies in the struggle for gender
equality. Thus the organized women's movement became more separatist
in Australia than it did in many other western countries. By the time men
were ready to respond more positively to the feminist challenge, many
women had given up on them.

Academic writing on gender that began in Australia in the 1970s understandably focused on women's experiences. Feminist historians offered new
interpretations of Australian history (for example, Summers 1975; Dixon
1982), and a series of anthologies on Australian feminism appeared (for
example, Mercer 1975; Watson and Pringle 1990; Grieve and Burns 1994;
Caine 1998).

In relation to Australian masculinities research, Bob Connell's work is
best known internationally. In 1982 he explored the relationship between
men and socialism and in 1983 he examined the relationship between class,
sex and culture. A groundbreaking paper was published in 1985 (with
Carrington and Lee) that developed an elaborate critique of sex-role theory.
He is perhaps best known, however, for his book *Gender and Power*, first
published in 1987, in which he constructs a three-fold model of the
structure of gender involving power relations, production relations and
cathexis (emotional attachment). His book *Masculinities*, with its case
studies of four groups of Australian men, was published in 1995. Although
it concentrates on Australian men, the book has an international focus, in

National Contexts   194

part because 'Australian debates on masculinity have followed a trajectory
broadly similar to that of other English speaking countries' (Connell 1997:
29). As noted earlier, however, there are costs involved in adopting this
global western tradition.

While there was little public debate about masculinity in Australia in
the 1970s, some men's consciousness-raising groups were formed at this
time. I was involved in a group called Men Against Sexism that was first
established in 1977 and I continued this involvement throughout the next
twelve years as the group underwent various changes before disbanding in
1989. The group endeavoured to balance consciousness-raising and support
with emerging forms of profeminist social action and public education.
The development of profeminist politics in the public arena was taken
further through the founding of Men Against Sexual Assault (MASA) in
Melbourne in 1989.[1]

My doctoral research (Pease 2000) explored the politics and practices
of profeminist men and the limitations and potential of groups like MASA
in developing and extending a profeminist commitment among Australian
men. The collaborative enquiry examined the attempts of profeminist men
to construct a public profeminist politics and how they positioned their
work in the context of progressive social movements and the men's movement in Australia.

I concluded that the men's movement in Australia has no potential to
develop into a progressive social movement because it is dominated by
mythopoetic and men's rights perspectives on the issues facing Australian
men. The mythopoetic perspective of Robert Bly (1990) has been popu-
larized in Australia by Steve Biddulph (1994), a self-appointed men's
movement leader who has had an enormous influence on debates about men
and masculinity. His therapeutic orientation to men's issues with its focus
on healing and personal change, in the absence of any analysis of gender
power, has in recent years been linked more with men's rights and fathers'
rights groups.[2] The celebration of masculinity and the pro-male orientation
of Biddulph's work has not challenged the premises of Australian mateship
and has fitted comfortably with the forms of male bonding developed in
men's rights discourses.

The Myths of Mateship

There are many positive dimensions claimed for mateship. Bruce Ruxton, president of the Returned Soldiers League in Australia, says it means
'supporting one another in life or death situations. Your mate is someone
you can rely upon. It is a bond between persons made in war or in civilian
life' (cited in *The Age*, 24 March 1999). While historian Geoffrey Blainey

says it 'primarily means personal or group loyalty' (ibid.). As Edgar (1997: 79) notes, 'mateship implies a deep and unspoken understanding that a mate will always stick by you'. Thus your mates should never 'dob' you in to the police no matter what crimes you may have committed. For many Australian men, mateship implies that loyalty to one's mate is a higher virtue than observance of the law.

While bonds between men have often been used as a basis for male solidarity in many countries, Australia is perhaps the only country where 'the romanticizing of male bonding provided so useful a basis for national ideology' (Altman 1987: 167). So it is more than just the Australian version of male bonding. Rather, such bonding has formed the basis of myths of national identity among Australian men. Bell (1973: 8–9) noted that while male comradeship is common in most cultures, the Australian version seems to exaggerate this institution 'almost as if Australian men were constantly in a state of emergency where they needed one another'.

As we move into the new millennium, the Anzac period has continued to establish a particular version of Australian national identity. When Australia prepared for a referendum on the option of becoming a republic in 1999, Prime Minister John Howard proposed a preamble to the Australian constitution that extolled the virtue of mateship and numerous references were made to the war years.

While mateship is often presented and promoted as healthy and positive, Marston (1994: 12) has drawn attention to a number of aspects of mateship that are 'unhealthy, oppressive and ultimately destructive'. While the idea of mates staying together is presented as one of the virtues of mateship, it can be used to justify violence against women, gays and indigenous people. In fact, Australian manhood and masculinity were constructed against the image of 'others' who were different.

In this context, Bell (1973: 24) argued almost thirty years ago that an understanding of mateship is important to an understanding of female and male relationships in Australian society. He said that frequently 'the interpersonal satisfactions of mateship for the husband are achieved at the cost of marital dissatisfaction for the wife'. Marston (1994: 14) similarly argues that mateship 'cripples the full potential of men and their relationships'.

A number of writers have commented upon the emotional poverty of Australian masculinity. Colling (1992: 50), for example, says that mateship embodies toughness and a disdain for 'weak' emotion. Meanwhile, Webb (1998: 11–12) regards the celebrated culture of silence and emotional repression as the main issue facing Australian men. In fact, silence is seen by many as the essence of traditional mateship, as evidenced in the nature of men's relationships that emphasize sport and communal drinking.

Sport and alcohol: the great Australian pastimes Australians are renowned for their alleged commitment to social equality. In this context, sport is often cited as 'the exemplar' of Australia's egalitarian character. However, in Australia, as in other countries, sport is predominantly a masculine activity. In fact, competitive sport in Australia is one of the key sites for developing and affirming masculinity for many Australian men. Members of winning football and cricket teams become national heroes.

Jim McKay (1991) has analysed the role of hegemonic masculinity in commercial sports and mass media in Australia. He demonstrates how it 'reproduces hegemonic structures by keeping women in their place' (McKay 1991: 54), while Lewis (1983: 17) also notes how Australian sport 'has been ruthlessly exploited to sell patriotism, masculinity and political images'.

Australian men are also renowned for their dedication to drinking beer. An international survey by Templer et al. (1993) has shown that Australian men have one of the highest alcoholism rates in the world. Drinking in the company of other sporty and gambling men has come to be seen as being archetypally Australian. Dixon (1982: 169) says that 'heavy drinking is a symbol of mateship and social solidarity'. Thus drinking has become part of the mateship subculture.

Drinking to the point of drunkenness is particularly common in Australia among working-class men. Many such men often gain prestige in the eyes of other men for how much they drink and how drunk they get (Bell 1973: 11) and many men drink specifically for the purpose of getting drunk.

Furthermore, many men feel that they cannot refuse an invitation to drink. There are various rules governing 'shouting', the practice of buying drinks for members of the drinking group. The rules demand that a man join the group when invited and remain with the group until all members (including himself) have bought one round of drinks for the group. One Australian study showed that 94 per cent of men thought that once an individual joined the group, it was unacceptable to leave without 'shouting', while 74 per cent believed it was important to remain in the group until everyone had 'shouted' at least once (Folland 1986: 82).

Drinking in pubs is one of the factors that establish a masculine pattern of high alcohol consumption in Australia. The Australian pub functions as a working-class male preserve for the performance of male solidarity (Chambers 1989: 12). Thus drinking in pubs plays a role in segregating men and women and in affirming men's superior status and rights (Dempsey 1992: 48). Originally, Aboriginal people and women were forbidden to drink in pubs. Drinking beer with other men was represented as the way of defining one's masculinity. National identity and masculinity were thus interwoven with pub culture (Kirkby 1997: 2).

Beyond the expression of mateship in sport and communal drinking, however, there are more troubling aspects to this Australian form of male bonding

Mateship and violence against women Pack rape is more prevalent in Australia than in America or Britain. Looker (1994; 217–18) suggests that this is connected to the intricacies of relationships between men in Australia and the affirmation of an aggressive form of masculinity. She cites a convicted rapist: 'There's ... a sense of camaraderie about a gang bang, where you have a good mate, and you will share a woman with a good mate. It's ... a very binding act with you and your friend, with you and your mate. The sense of camaraderie would be possibly the biggest aspect of it. You do everything together' (Looker 1994: 218).

A recent Australian study found that young men were more likely to sexually assault women in groups than alone (cited in Carrington 1998. 160). The research demonstrates the critical influence the peer group plays in the commission of sexual assault. Most boys at puberty experience peer pressure to demonstrate their sexual prowess.

This aspect of male culture is elucidated in a recent book by Carrington (1998), who retraces the police investigation into the rape and murder of a fourteen-year-old girl at a beach party in an Australian town in 1989. The book describes vividly what happens when shame and mateship mix with a small-town mentality. The police responsible for the murder investigation reported that a 'wall of silence' hampered their investigation. This silence was seen to be related to 'a rigorous adherence to the ethic of not dobbing in a mate' (Carrington 1998: 99).

Homophobia and mateship Homophobia is also a dominant feature of Australian masculinity, with widespread condemnation of homosexuality by men evidenced by the hostility and violence shown towards gay men (see, for example, GLAD 1994; Sandroussi and Thompson 1995; Tomsen 1998). Tacey (1997: 135) says that homophobia is the most recently discovered shadow aspect of Australian mateship. While 'men adore their mates, there will be no obvious caring, no touching, no outward display'.

Thus, while male bonding is an important prerequisite for the development of masculine identity in Australia, many men fear that if that bonding is too close, it will destroy heterosexual identity and become confused with homosexuality (Webb 1998: 114). Nevertheless, mateship and homosexuality have a very close homosocial proximity. Certainly, there are affinities between mateship as a social relationship and homosexuality as a sexual relationship. Dixon (1982: 81) even suggests that mateship involves 'powerful sublimated homosexuality'.

As Kimmel (1994: 130) has noted, homophobia involves suppression of homoerotic desire and men's attempts to 'purify' relationships with other men of sexual connotations. Male heterosexual identity, implicit in mateship, is thus reproduced by fear and hatred of gay men (Donaldson 1993: 648). It is important to acknowledge that homophobia and patriarchy are inextricably linked, with the former serving as a function in reproducing the latter and in promoting misogyny and sexism among men.

Mateship as racialized masculinity Australian mateship is constructed against the image of indigenous men, immigrant males and non-caucasian males. The 'virtues' of mateship are thus reserved for native-born white men. Furthermore, there is a presumption of whiteness in most discussions of men's lives in Australia. In spite of the multicultural nature of Australian society, issues of race and culture have played little part in Australian masculinity literature. There has been no attempt to analyse the changing modes of masculinity resulting from migration to Australia and we know little about the effects of migration on men's work, leisure and domestic relations (Chambers 1989: 13).

Most significantly, however, there has been no analysis of the changing modes of masculinity among Aboriginal men from hunter-gatherers to members of an urban capitalist society. However, it is clear that Aboriginal men have lost their traditional power and authority since colonization and many have embraced alcoholism and become recipients of welfare (Flynn 1986: 38).[3]

Reconstructing Australian Men's Practices

In light of the power of the mateship tradition in Australian society, what are the possibilities of reconstructing men's subjectivities and practices? There are a number of important developments where interventions aimed at addressing gender-based inequality have been implemented. There are tensions in many of these policy and practice arenas, however, as feminist women and profeminist men engage critically with therapeutic and backlash responses to men's issues.

Working with perpetrators of violence against women in the home In the last fifteen years in Australia, we have witnessed a dramatic increase in the development of education and counselling programmes for violent men. The provision of services to violent men has proved controversial. While they have been seen by some as constituting a viable alternative to legal sanctions, they have been condemned by others as decriminalizing men's violence. Many of the early programmes focused on childhood precedents of violent behaviour, anger management and communication in relationships and failed to address adequately issues of gender inequality, women's safety and accountability. More recently, explicitly profeminist educational programmes that challenge patriarchal belief systems have predominated. Government accreditation guidelines and competency standards have ensured that such programmes are linked to the criminal justice system and have lines of accountability to ensure that their work does not endanger the safety of women.

Challenging the culture of violence A national study of 5,000 young people aged between twelve and twenty found that 12 per cent of male respondents said it was acceptable to 'make a girl have sex' (Gray 2000). Men Against Sexual Assault (MASA) was formed at a public meeting in Melbourne in December 1989 to challenge these attitudes that legitimate sexual violence, by encouraging men to take action against sexual assault through community education, social action, public media work and sexism awareness workshops. The primary purpose of MASA is rape awareness education for all men. This is based on the premise that there is a relationship between the dominant model of masculine sexuality in Australian society and the prevalence of sexual assault. MASA has been involved in organizing public forums on the societal factors that perpetuate and maintain sexual assault, facilitating patriarchy awareness workshops, organizing marches and a White Ribbon campaign against men's violence and commenting in the public media on sexism in popular culture.

Working with boys in schools In the last few years there has been active public debate about boys' education and the role of masculinities in schools. Concerns have been expressed 'that boys generally are unmotivated, badly behaved and underachieving and that girls are outperforming them' (Kenway 1996: 447). This pro-boys' movement has led to major changes in gender reform policies in Australia. As Kenway (1996: 448) has pointed out, 'the danger of the boys' movement ... threatens to pit girls' interests against boys'. In contrast, profeminist programmes in schools focus on the construction of masculinities and encourage boys to take responsibility for the abuse perpetrated by them as well as examining the emotional costs of adhering to traditional masculinity (Lingard and Douglas 1999: 141).

Challenging men's sexism in relationships and families Research demonstrates that women's involvement in the paid labour force does not significantly affect the amount of unpaid work they do in the home. An Australian study published in 1997 showed that women in full-time paid employment completed over 65 per cent of the household's unpaid labour (Dempsey 1997: 209).

Resentment and disputes over various forms of marital inequality such as these are among the factors that men and women cite as contributing to the breakdown of their marriages (Dempsey 1997: 226). One-third of all marriages in Australia end in divorce. Many women want their husbands to do more housework and child-care, they want more opportunities for leisure and they want a greater say in decision-making (Dempsey 1997: 169). Thus it would seem that marital breakdown is directly related to men's sense of marital entitlement and their sexism. In response to these issues, the Commonwealth government recently allocated $6 million over four years to forty-six organizations for projects aimed at addressing issues facing men in families. Very few of these projects, however, have an explicit profeminist focus and there is much work to be done to encourage human service workers who work with men in families to engage with feminist analyses of masculinity to understand the real issues facing men and women.[4]

There is, for example, a prevalent view in the human services literature in Australia that greater involvement of men in child-care is important to heal the 'father wound' which is caused by fathers' remoteness and absence (Biddulph 1994). However, while this literature advocates greater involvement of men with their children, it also encourages clear distinctions between men's and women's roles. For example, fathers are expected to be the main transmitters of culturally approved masculinity to their sons. McMahon (1999) has pointed out in his analysis of 'new father' writing that only a minority of such texts argue for equity in child-care work.

Furthermore, there is often an inference that *any* father involvement in child-care is better than none. This tends to gloss over the fact that men are over-represented as perpetrators of child abuse in families, compared with their level of involvement. While we should be encouraging the involvement of non-patriarchal nurturing fathers, we should be mindful of the dangers of increasing the involvement of violent and abusive fathers.

Rethinking men's health Issues of men's health in Australia started to surface publicly in the early 1990s. Men's health status was used by some segments of the men's movement to claim that men are a disadvantaged group and are discriminated against in health services compared with women. Men's health conferences and men's health policy documents often ignored the social divisions between men and the relationship between men's health status and their relationship to gender-based power. Profeminist approaches to men's health have emphasized diversity and difference in men's lives and the costs of men's adherence to forms of social domination.[5]

Challenging the commitment to paid work Men have been socialized to pursue work as the central life interest and consequently regard child-rearing and domestic responsibilities as secondary. Work-related behaviours influence men's personalities and carry over into the home setting. The competitive world of work encourages men to estrange themselves from their feelings as a way of surviving. Furthermore, given the masculinized nature of some men's work, the aura of masculinity is sustained by keeping women out or 'keeping them in their place' if they get in.

Some men are 'now less willing to spend endless hours at work, to subordinate their family life to the interests of the corporation, to lead an unbalanced life in which personal well-being comes last' (Edgar 1998: 3). Thus there is pressure on workplaces to become more family-friendly. In response to these issues, in recent years we have seen the development of anti-sexist educational programmes targeted at men in the workplace.[6] The purpose of these workshops is to encourage male managers to work more co-operatively with people and to place a higher value on family issues.

If more egalitarian relationships between women and men are to emerge in Australia, however, significant alterations to the nature and structure of paid employment are required. Such alterations should include the flexible restructuring of work to take account of child-care needs, parental leave which leaves either partner the option of selecting child-care as a priority, increased availability of job-sharing and part time work and changes in the nature of career values.

Conclusion

The women's movement and profeminist masculinity politics have played a significant role in challenging mateship and putting men's violence and gender-based inequalities on the political agenda in Australia. The introduction of women's studies and gender studies in the university sector, affirmative action and equal opportunity legislation within the state, community-based initiatives tackling men's violence and campaigns challenging patriarchal ideologies and belief systems underlying mateship have all contributed towards more egalitarian gender relations. There have been major changes in women's employment rates, an increase in women in senior positions within the state and corporate sectors, an increased recognition of violence against women in the home as a crime that should not be tolerated and a increased confidence among young women who demand equality with men.

At the same time, each step towards gender equality elicits defensive reactions from men and women who have internalized domination and oppression into their psyches. Men's limited participation in housework and child-care, sexist harassment towards women who have moved into traditional 'men's jobs', a predominance of women in part-time work, sexually aggressive behaviour towards young women and misogynistic male bonding under the guise of mateship, are constant reminders of the resilience of patriarchal structures and abusive belief systems among Australian men. The focus on men as 'victims' in public discourses about masculinity and the organized backlash of men's rights organizations pose continual threats to the gains that have been made in the last twenty years. Australia has a long way to go before its claimed commitment to the principles of social equality, as they relate to gender relations, can become more than rhetoric.

Notes

1. A chronicle of my involvement in profeminist politics during the 1980s and 1990s is outlined in the essays in Pease (1997).

2. See Johnson (1999) for an example of the men's rights backlash in Australia.

3. See Pease (2001) for an interview I conducted with Graham Atkinson, an Aboriginal activist, on the impact of colonization on indigenous men's lives.

4. I have recently co-edited a book on pro-feminist approaches to working with men in the human services. See Pease and Camilleri (2001).

5. See Pease (1999) for an example of a profeminist approach to men's health in Australia.

6. Graeme Russell has worked extensively in this area. See Russell (1998).

References

Altman, D. (1987) 'The Myth of Mateship', *Meanjin*, Vol. 46, No. 2: 163–72.

Bell, C. (1973) *Mateship in Australia: Some Implications for Male–Female Relationships*, Melbourne: La Trobe University Working Papers.

Biddulph, S. (1994) *Manhood*, Sydney: Finch.

Bly, R. (1990) *Iron John: A Book About Men*, New York: Addison.

Caine, B. (ed.) (1998) *Australian Feminism: A Companion*, Melbourne: Oxford University Press.

Carrington, K. (1998) *Who Killed Leigh Leigh?: A Story of Shame and Mateship in an Australian Town*, Sydney: Random House.

Carrington, T., R. Connell and J. Lee (1985) 'Towards a New Sociology of Masculinity', *Theory and Society*, Vol. 14: 551–604.

Chambers, D. (1989) 'Contemporary Problems in the Study of Masculinities: A Comparison Between Australia and Britain', paper presented at the Australian Sociological Assocation Conference, La Trobe University, Melbourne.

Colling, T. (1992) *Beyond Mateship: Understanding Australian Men*, Sydney: Simon and Schuster.

Connell, R. (1982) 'Men and Socialism', in G. Evans and J. Reeves (eds), *Labour Essays*, Melbourne: Drummond.

— (1983) *Which Way Is Up? Essays on Class, Sex and Culture*, Sydney: Allen and Unwin.

— (1987) *Gender and Power*, Sydney: Allen and Unwin.

— (1995) *Masculinities*, Sydney: Allen and Unwin.

— (1997) 'Australian Research on Men and Masculinity', *International Association of Studies of Men Newsletter*, Vol. 4, No. 1: 29–30.

Cuthoys, A. (1994) 'Australian Feminism since 1970', in Grieve and Burns (eds), *Australian Women*.

Dempsey, K. (1992) *A Man's Town: Inequality Between Women and Men in Rural Australia*, Melbourne: Oxford University Press.

— (1997) *Inequalities in Marriage: Australia and Beyond*, Melbourne: Oxford University Press.

Dixon, M. (1982) *The Real Matilda: Women and Identity in Australia*, Melbourne: Penguin.

Donaldson, M. (1993) 'What is Hegemonic Masculinity?', *Theory and Society*, No. 22: 643–57.

Edgar, D. (1997) *Men, Mateship, Marriage*, Sydney: HarperCollins.

— (1998) 'Reclaiming Care for Men: Family and Work Futures', in *National Forum on Men and Family Relationships*, Canberra: Commonwealth Department of Family and Community Services.

Flynn, S. (1986) 'Issues for Aboriginal Men', in *Linking Men's Services*, Adelaide: Noarlunga Health Services.

Folland, G. (1986) 'Men and Alcoholism', in *Linking Men's Services*, Adelaide: Noarlunga Health Services.

Garton, S. (1998) 'War and Masculinity in Twentieth Century Australia', *Journal of Australian Studies*, No. 56: 86–95.

GLAD (1994) *Not a Day Goes By: Report on the GLAD Survey into Discrimination and Violence Against Lesbians and Gay Men in Victoria*, Melbourne: Gay Men and Lesbians Against Discrimination.

Gray, D. (2000) 'Alarming Picture of Teenage Sexual Violence in Report', *The Age*, 26 April.

Grieve, N. and A. Burns (eds) (1994) *Australian Women: Contemporary Feminist Thought*, Melbourne: Oxford University Press.

Johnson, T. (1999) *No Man's Land*, Sydney: Halstead Press.

Kenway, J. (1996) 'Reasserting Masculinity in Australian Schools', *Women's Studies International Forum*, Vol. 19, No. 4: 447–66.

Kimmell, M. (1994) 'Masculinity as Homophobia: Fear, Shame and Silence in the Construction of Masculinity', in H. Brod and M. Kaufman (eds), *Theorizing Masculinities*, Thousand Oaks, CA: Sage.

Kirkby, D. (1997) *Barmaids: A History of Women's Work in Pubs*, Melbourne: Cambridge University Press.

Lake, M. (1999) *Getting Equal: The History of Australian Feminism*, Sydney: Allen and Unwin.

Lewis, G. (1983) *Real Men Like Violence: Australian Men, Media and Violence*, Sydney: Kangaroo Press.

Lingard, B. and P. Douglas (1999) *Men Engaging Feminisms: Pro-feminism, Backlashes and Schooling*, Buckingham: Open University Press.

Looker, P. (1994) 'Doing It with Your Mates: Connecting Aspects of Modern Australian Masculinity', in D. Headon, J. Hooton and D. Horne (eds), *The Abundant Culture: Meaning and Significance in Everyday Australia*, Sydney: Allen and Unwin.

McGrane, T. and A. Patience (1995) 'Masculinity: Consequences for Adolescent Sexuality in Australia', *On the Level*, Vol. 3, No. 4: 12–23.

McKay, J. (1991) *No Pain, No Gain: Sport and Australian Culture*, Sydney: Prentice Hall.

McMahon, A. (1999) *Taking Care of Men: Sexual Politics in the Public Mind*, Melbourne: Cambridge University Press.

Marston, G. (1994) 'Invisible boundaries', *XY: Men, Sex, Politics*, Vol. 4, No. 2: 12–14.

Mercer, J. (ed.) (1975) *The Other Half: Women in Australian Society*, Melbourne: Penguin.

Moore, C. (1998) 'Australian Masculinities', *Journal of Australian Studies*, No. 56: 1–16.

Pease, B. (1997) *Men and Sexual Politics: Towards a Pro-feminist Practice*, Adelaide: Dulwich Centre Publications.

— (1999) 'The Politics of Men's Health Promotion', *Just Policy*, Vol. 15: 29–35.

— (2000) *Recreating Men: Postmodern Masculinity Politics*, London: Sage.

— (2001) 'The Changing Role of Indigenous Men in Community and Family Life: An Interview with Graham Atkinson', in Pease and Camilleri (eds) (forthcoming) *Working with Men in the Human Services*.

Pease, B. and P. Camilleri (eds) (2001) *Working with Men in the Human Services*, Allen and Unwin, Sydney.

Reynolds, H. (2000) *Why weren't We Told?*, Melbourne: Penguin.

Russell, G. (1998) 'Reaching Fathers Through the Corporate World', in *National Forum on Men and Family Relationships*, Canberra: Commonwealth Department Family and Community Services.

Sandroussi, J. and S. Thompson (1995) *Out of the Blue: A Survey of Violence and Harassment Against Gay Men and Lesbians*, Sydney: NSW Police Force.

Summers, A. (1975) *Damned Whores and God's Police: The Colonization of Women in Australia*, Melbourne: Penguin.

Tacey, D. (1997) *Remaking Men: Jung, Spirituality and Social Change*, London: Routledge.

Templer, D., P. Griffin and J. Hintze (1993) 'Gender Life Expectancy and Alcohol: An International Perspective', *International Journal of Addictions*, Vol. 24, No. 14: 1613–20.

Tomsen, S. (1998) '"He had to be a poofter or something": Violence, Male Honour and Heterosexual Panic', *Journal of Interdisciplinary Gender Studies*, Vol. 3, No. 2: 44–57.

Watson, S. and R. Pringle (eds) (1990) *Playing the State: Australian Feminist Intervention*, Sydney: Allen and Unwin.

Webb, J. (1998) *Junk Male: Reflections on Australian Masculinity*, Sydney: HarperCollins.

14

Gendering Men's Services in Hong Kong: Backlash or Pursuit of Gender Equality?

Chan Kam Wah

Although the indigenous feminist movement in Hong Kong has been growing since the early 1980s, the profeminist men's movement is virtually non-existent. This partly reflects the reality that it is much more difficult to change men than change women, something that is especially true in a strong patriarchal culture such as Hong Kong. At the same time, it also indicates that the feminist movement in Hong Kong is still relatively under-developed. Although explicitly profeminist men's practice does not exist, social services for men have started to develop in recent years. While most of these services are insensitive to gender issues, some of them are ambivalent or even sympathetic to feminist approaches.

This chapter aims to sketch the pattern of existing social services for men in Hong Kong, and to raise issues and debates on related practices. In order to have a more thorough understanding of the situation, I conducted a small-scale research project on social services for men in Hong Kong in mid-1999.[1] Discussion on the development of men's services in Hong Kong is mainly based on data collected in this research, unless otherwise stated.

The chapter starts with a brief review of the development and different approaches of the men's movement in western countries so as to provide a framework for classifying related practices in Hong Kong. I then outline the existing profile of men's services and go on to trace the social background leading to the under-development of a profeminist orientation. Finally, I raise some issues related to the development of men's services in Hong Kong.

The Men's Movement and Men's Services

First of all, we must clarify what we mean by men's services. In this chapter, men's services refers to services offered by social work or social services agencies, government or non-government organizations, specifically for men, with an emphasis on men's problems in the context of fatherhood, gender relations and gender equality, men's violence towards women and children, and the social and psychological pressures on men.

Men's services in the West evolved from men's movements with very diverse orientations and focuses. Messner (1997) has identified three major terrains for the men's movement: first, the institutionalized privileges of men; second, the cost of masculinity or the negative impact of a narrow conception of masculinity on men; and third, the differences and inequalities among men. Different men's movements build on different terrains or different combinations of terrains.

The men's movement started in United States and the United Kingdom as a profeminist movement in the 1960s and early 1970s (Snodgrass 1977). This movement builds on the critique of institutionalized privileges of men, and questions the existing patriarchal culture, masculinity and gender inequality in society at large (Hearn 1987; Brod 1987; Brod and Kaufman 1994; Connell 1995). Like feminism, the profeminist men's movement challenges the institutionalized power of men over women. Unlike some traditional feminists who emphasized only the suffering of women in the patriarchal system, profeminist men's studies point out that the patriarchal system is paradoxical. On one hand, men benefit from the institutionalized power, but on the other hand they also suffer from gender-role segregation and stereotyping. The aim of calling attention to men's dilemma is to develop more equal, fair and harmonious gender relations.

However, in the mid- and late 1970s, this concern about men's dilemmas developed into an essentialist, mythopoetic men's movement and a men's liberation movement emphasizing the costs of masculinity. Examples of these are Robert Bly's (1990) mythopoetic men's movement, the religion-based Promise Keepers movement, the men's liberation movement as advocated by Farrell (1975), and the anti-feminist men's rights movement (Goldberg 1979; Baumli 1985) that emphasizes men's 'disadvantages' under the cover of a feminist movement. These movements emphasize the cost or negative impact of traditional masculinity on men. The solution is to revitalize 'true masculinity', to develop a new form of manhood for modern society, or to focus on fighting for men's interests under the 'oppression of feminism'. In general, these approaches put too much emphasis on individual changes without paying enough attention to institutionalized power inequality between the two genders.

In recent years, another approach has arisen within the men's movement, with an emphasis on the differences between men. This approach is concerned with the politics of racial and sexual identity, and aims to put racial discrimination and discrimination against sexuality on the agenda of the men's movement (Douglas 1994). The Million Man March (Karenga 1995) in the USA, and gay liberation are typical examples.

The men's movement in Hong Kong did not go through the same stages as that in western countries. In fact, it is still too early to talk of a men's movement as such.

In Search of Men's Services in Hong Kong

In order to understand the development of men's services in Hong Kong, I conducted a small-scale research project in mid-1999. A questionnaire was sent to all social services agencies that were members of the Hong Kong Council of Social Service, asking them to identify and report any services for men. I then approached those projects and the particular social worker organizing the programme, requesting an in-depth interview. During the research process, I also identified some service projects for men that were not reported in the questionnaire. These newly identified projects were also examined. Altogether I have identified twelve social service agencies or service units (see Table 14.1 for a list of projects interviewed and some of their basic characteristics), and was able to interview the workers organizing the programme.

Programmes and services Strictly speaking, there are only two established service projects for men in Hong Kong. The one with the longest history is the Breakthrough project, which is part of the activities of a religious organization. Since 1991 Breakthrough organized seminars, workshops, talks and training courses on men's changing role and fatherhood, and has published widely on this topic (Choi and Au 1998; Au 1996). This project is close to the mythopoetic movement or the Promise Keepers movement in the West. The second project is the Men's Centre[2] launched in 1998 by the Caritas, one of the largest social service NGOs in Hong Kong. This is a multi-service centre specifically designed for men, offering services such as social and developmental groups, seminars, talks, training courses, interest groups and family life education programmes. All other men's services are less established or much smaller in scale and most of the started only in recent years. Eight out of twelve projects started in 1998 or 1999, three started in the mid-1990s.

The contents of the programme fall mainly into two categories: men with specific problems and the changing role of men in general. Services for the former category address problems such as men perpetrating domestic violence, men who have extra-marital affairs, men whose wives suffer post-natal depression, and men in unemployment. Five out of twelve projects are in this group. The others could be classified as the latter

TABLE 14.1 Agencies or service units interviewed

Agency/service unit	Major services	Remarks
1. Family Welfare Society domestic	Group and counselling for men involving violence	Started 1995
2. Christian Family Service Centre	Group for unemployed men	Started 1998
3. Yang's Social Service Centre	Support group for men whose wives suffer post-natal depression	Not yet started, recruiting members
4. Christian Service	Men's developmental group; cases mainly referred from family services	Started 1996
5. Catholic Marriage Advisory Council	Developmental group for married men, part of Family Life Education programme	Started 1998
6. Couple Co-creation Society Limited	Workshops on men's changing role; religious background	Started 1995
7. Breakthrough Counselling Centre	Workshops, seminars, talks on changing roles of men; religious background	Started 1991, popular programme
8. Caritas, Shatin, Personal Growth Centre for Men	Multi-services including developmental group, courses, workshops, publications	Started 1998, the only men's centre in Hong Kong
9. Caritas Community Centre, Tsuen Wan	Group for unemployed men, mainly manual workers	Started 1999, group terminated prematurely
10. Caritas, Tung Tau Estate community development project	Men's group evolved from a community-based residents' organization	Started 1999, a self-help group independent of Caritas
11. Hong Kong Children and Youth Service, Northern District and Tai Po	Mainly summer programme on fatherhood, parenting and spousal relationship, some open to family members	Summer programme in 1998, 1999
12. SKH Tung Chung Social Service Centre	Started as an unemployed men's group, evolving into a developmental group	Started 1998

category, which deal with the changing role of men, masculinity, fatherhood or family relations in general.

The format of the services varies greatly, ranging from therapeutic groups for violent men, mutual support groups for the unemployed, seminars, workshops or training courses, social groups for men in the community, men's drop-in centres, and summer programmes for fathers and their children. However, it should be clarified that this categorization is not clear-cut or rigid. Some groups, like that of the SKH Tung Chung Project, started with a group of unemployed men and eventually evolved into a long-term social and developmental group.

Some projects are experimenting with different strategies, such as working with men and their spouses in a group setting, or involving all family members, or employing a female social worker as group facilitator, or joint male and female facilitators to run groups. The experiences of the front-line social workers indicate that there is more chance of success if they can involve a participant's spouse. In some services, a significant proportion of male participants are referred by their wives who used the services for women at the centre.

These programme formats are still very limited in comparison to the existing welfare services in Hong Kong. Men's services in Hong Kong are mainly initiated by counselling and family services. This should be further developed to group and community settings, rehabilitation and services for the elderly. We should explore new means of working with men, and learn from the experience of other social services.

Service target: middle class v. working class A controversial issue in the early stages of developing men's services in the West concerned whether such services were mainly for middle-class men (Brod 1983), or more exactly, middle-class white men. In Hong Kong, the middle class is also a significant target group for men's services. Nine out of the twelve projects studied mainly serve middle- or lower-middle-income men with upper secondary or tertiary education. Only three projects run men's groups in working-class communities involving manual workers or men from lower-income strata. Of course, we should bear in mind that it is often difficult to categorize the social class of service recipients, and very often the target groups are of mixed social background.

Although the lower-income groups, the oppressed and the disadvantaged should be given higher priority in the allocation of social resources, this should not exclude the middle- and lower-middle-income group from receiving services. There are at least two reasons. First, some men's issues cut across the class boundary. For example, both working-class and middle class men could be involved in violence against women and children.

Second, we should not restrict social services only to the most vulnerable, otherwise we fall into the trap of marginalizing social services and limiting services to the 'deserving poor' as advocated by conservatives (Murray 1990; see critique by Dean and Taylor-Gooby 1992; and Leung and Chan 1998 for the debate in the Hong Kong context). On the other hand, we should bear in mind that men's services in Hong Kong are still in their infancy. We can see that the varieties of service targets are gradually expanding, while some projects are exploring strategies of reaching out to manual workers and lower-income groups in working-class communities.

Having said that, I need to emphasize that we should pay more attention to men in different disadvantaged positions, such as working-class men, manual workers displaced by globalization and economic restructuring, lone fathers, gay men, middle-aged and older men, new immigrant men from mainland China, men in ethnic minorities, men with physical or mental disabilities, male sex offenders or criminals. As in the UK and the USA, some anti-patriarchal men's movements are being challenged for neglecting sexual and racial politics; men's movements sometimes neglect the differences and inequalities among men (Pease 1999). This echoes the debate on diversity and differences in feminist politics as raised by post-modernists (Williams 1996; Weedon 1997).

Men-centred v. family-centred services To a large extent, men's services in Hong Kong evolved from family services, counselling and family life education. Therefore, it is not surprising to see that a significant proportion of the services are family-centred rather than men-centred. Five of the projects we interviewed explicitly stated that their objective of changing men is to improve family relationships. Their programmes focus on fatherhood, parenting, spousal relations and family relations in general. Six projects claimed that their main objective is to change men; therefore, their focus is on men's particular problems such as unemployment, work pressures, or the changing role of men. The remaining project said that it is important to change both men and their families, and their programme includes both men's problems and family problems.

This somewhat resembles the debate about women-centred versus family-centred social work that has taken place among social workers in Hong Kong in recent years (Hung and Fung 1995). Many traditional social workers still insist that women should be treated as a part of their family, not as individuals. Their focus in working with women is on improving home management skills, parenting skills and spousal relations. In other words, the prime responsibility of a woman is to be a good mother and a good wife.

Many concerns about men's welfare in Hong Kong seem to be repeating the problem of traditional family-centred women's services, in which changing men is regarded as a means of changing the family. Men are being targeted as fathers and husbands, while their own problems and needs are neglected. That is why much of the research on men in Hong Kong is focused on their role as fathers (Lit et al. 1991; BGCA 1990).

However, we should not equate the debate on women-centred services with that on men-centred services. In the traditional gender division of labour, women's prime responsibility is to the family while that of men is to work. Family-centred women's services further confine women in the family instead of liberating them. On the other hand, traditionally, men are discouraged or excluded from taking an active part in the family. Family-centred men's services contribute to opening up new arenas for men's development, and challenging traditional masculinity. Strategically, it is not necessarily problematic for men's services to focus partly on men's roles as fathers and husbands. Of course, this does not dismiss the need to pay more attention to men's individual or particular needs.

We can thus see that it is more complicated to discuss men-centred services as compared to women-centred services. The meaning of 'men-centred' is elusive or can be very misleading. Over-emphasizing 'men-centred', the 'rights' of men and the portrait of men as victims may lead to an anti-feminist men's rights movement. This does not only fail to promote gender equality, but reinforces the domination of men. The important issue is not whether this is men-centred or family-centred, but pro-feminist or anti-feminist as I discuss in the following section.

Profeminist v. anti-feminist services As I pointed out in the previous section, most men's services in Hong Kong are initiated by family services or family life education projects, which are rarely profeminist. In our studies, nine out of the twelve projects can be classified as non-feminist; each stated clearly that its service was not related to gender equality. Among these nine projects, three are non-feminist in the sense that the social workers are unaware of issues of gender equality or have never thought of applying a feminist perspective in their services. Six of the projects could be classified as anti-feminist because they did not think that a feminist approach would be useful; some even believe that the pursuit of women's rights antagonizes gender relations. For these non-feminist projects, men's services are just 'value-free' social services meeting the needs or solving the problems of their clients. They are unaware that traditional 'value-free' social work is value-laden, and that the men's services they are providing could reinforce existing gender inequality.

Of the remaining three projects, two of them could be regarded as sympathetic to feminist approaches. Although they were aware of feminist debates and accepted that gender equality should be one of the main themes of men's services, they admitted that they were not systematically applying a profeminist approach. Only one of the social workers interviewed explicitly stated that his practice pursued gender equality; this reflects only the orientation of the social worker, not that of the social service agency. This is not surprising or unexpected in Hong Kong, where ideological and theoretical approaches are rarely the concern of social service delivery. Pragmatism, utilitarianism and traditional values are the taken-for-granted foundation for most social work practice.

The Under-development of Profeminist Men's Services

Why is it that profeminist men's services are so under-developed in Hong Kong? Pursuing gender equality is generally regarded as women's business, even in western countries where feminist movements are relatively developed; in Hong Kong, patriarchal Chinese culture is still the prevailing ethos. To explain the lack of profeminist men's services in Hong Kong, this section focuses on the under-development of the women's movement, the lack of gender consciousness in welfare services in Hong Kong, and the domination of patriarchal Chinese culture.

The under-development of the women's movement Since there is a lack of a strong women's movement here, it is not surprising to see that a profeminist men's movement is virtually non-existent in Hong Kong. A prominent feminist activist starts her paper on the women's movement in Hong Kong by asking '[I]s there indeed a women's movement to speak of?' (Tsang 1995: 276). She goes on to point out that 'the women's movement in Hong Kong is too young to invite an authoritative balance sheet' (ibid.).

The 'first wave' of the women's movement can be traced back to the 1950s, when the Hong Kong Council of Women (established in 1947) raised issues such as equal pay for women and the abolition of the traditional Chinese concubinage system. After this movement had won the day, very sadly, it also lost its impetus.

It was not until the 1970s that the 'second wave' of a women's movement emerged in Hong Kong. Inspired by the 'second-wave' women's movement, the student movement and the civil rights movement in the West, some expatriate women joined the Hong Kong Council of Women and revitalized it. Although feminists in this stage launched a much broader challenge to the social and political system, they failed to base their movement firmly in the grassroots and community level due to the limitations of their middle-class and expatriate backgrounds.

The 'third wave' of the women's movement in Hong Kong started to develop in the mid-1980s with the establishment of the Association for the Advancement of Feminism, a locally based, grassroots-oriented and explicitly feminist organization. This period is characterized by indigenization and diversification of women's groups. Many groups were established in the 1980s and 1990s, such as the Hong Kong Women's Christian Council, the Hong Kong Women Workers Association, the Association Concerning Sexual Violence Against Women, and Zi Teng (a group for female prostitutes). Political parties and labour unions have also founded their own women's branches, not to mention the many community-based women's groups. The heated debate about extending the United Nations' Convention for the Elimination of All Forms of Discrimination Against Women (CEDAW) to Hong Kong in the early 1990s, and the subsequent establishment of the Equal Opportunities Commission in 1996 have placed gender issues on the political agenda.

Although the women's movement started to indigenize in the 1980s and flourish in the 1990s, a profeminist men's movement is yet to be seen in Hong Kong. One of the reasons is that men's involvement in the women's movement in Hong Kong is extremely scarce. Gender equality is still largely regarded as women's business. Another reason may be that the scale and impact of the women's movement in Hong Kong is far less extensive and strong when compared to that of the West. Anyway, in spite of the diversifying concerns of the women's movement in Hong Kong, a men's movement is still not on the agenda. Most feminist groups do not have a clear attitude towards the men's movement, or may even be unaware of this development.

Gender-blind Social Welfare Services

The under-development of men's services can also be traced to the lack of gender consciousness in social welfare services in Hong Kong. Unlike some western countries where working with men is an increasing concern in social work practice (Cavanagh and Cree 1996; Pringle 1995; Pease 1999), this discussion does not exist in Hong Kong. Welfare services and policy in Hong Kong are dominated by family-centred approaches that emphasize traditional patriarchal values. Research by feminist groups in Hong Kong documents this problem in detail (AAF 1990; 1993), and so there is no need to duplicate the arguments here.

The Hong Kong Council of Social Service, an organization representing social service NGOs in Hong Kong, has been promoting women-centred services since the 1980s (HKCSS 1997). Yet, up to the present, there is no direct subsidy from the government for women's service projects, men's service projects, or projects related to promotion of gender equality. All these services are funded by voluntary donation, or informally by an internal transfer of resources within a social welfare agency. According to a survey by the Hong Kong Council of Social Service on women services in Hong Kong, 67.1 per cent of the welfare agencies think that the government's support is inadequate, while only 3.1 per cent think that it is adequate; the remaining 30 per cent had no opinion or do not want to comment (HKCSS 1996: 25).

Besides the lack of resources, many social welfare agencies providing women's services focus mainly on the improvement of family relationships and the promotion of community participation, instead of on women's rights and gender equality. According to the survey of the Hong Kong Council of Social Service, only a small percentage of welfare agencies providing women's services are concerned with the promotion of women's rights. Only 17.3 per cent of them included 'promoting women's social status' as one of their aims, 13.6 per cent included 'promoting gender equality and justice', and 9.1 per cent included 'eliminating unequal treatment for women' (HKCSS 1996: 24).

For many social service agencies, providing women's services is not related to the promotion of gender equality; it is simply a service for a vulnerable group. The focus is on individual change or amelioration of individual difficulties, not on the pursuit of gender equality or social justice. In this context, it is not surprising to see that most of the newly developed men's services in Hong Kong are non-feminist or even anti-feminist.

Even some of the academics advocating men's services in Hong Kong are not conscious of gender issues. For example, Chan (forthcoming), in arguing for more support for men services, tends to adopt a non-feminist stance. He argues that a lot of resources in the social service system are channelled to solve women's problems, while men's welfare is almost completely neglected. And he goes on to raise some anti-feminist issues such as banning affirmative action for women's employment, arguing that men are more likely to be injured by women instead of the other way round as is commonly believed, and that fathers are usually discriminated against in divorce cases.

This conception is problematic. We need to point out that women are not getting a lot of social resources as is generally perceived. At present, most services for women are family-centred rather than women-centred. Women as family carers receive the services for their family members, not exclusively for themselves. Of course, we should pay more attention to and provide more resources for men's services. However, it is wrong to say that we have spent too much on women. Both men's and women's services are under-developed and should receive more support. The purpose of developing men's services is not to seize resources from women.

No matter what the reasons are for the lack of both men's and women's services, it comes down to the question of a balance of forces between an anti-patriarchal feminist movement and the domination of traditional patri-archal Chinese culture. Domination of patriarchal culture in Hong Kong is so strong that it is difficult for both types of service to develop.

Domination of Patriarchal Chinese Culture and the Backlash

The UK and the USA share a background that includes civil rights movements and a belief in individual liberty. Hong Kong, by contrast, was a British colony until 1997. At the time of writing, we are still not allowed to elect our governor (called the Chief Executive since 1997). Conceptions such as liberty, rights and equality are not part of the Hong Kong culture. Instead we are dominated by laissez-faire capitalist logic (Chan et al. 1999) and traditional patriarchal Chinese culture. The phenomenal economic growth of Hong Kong in the past decades, the globalization and economic restructuring, and the decolonization after 1997 do not automatically improve the situation.

While a profeminist men's movement is still non-existent in Hong Kong, the backlash against the feminist movement has already developed rapidly. The establishment of the Equal Opportunities Commission (EOC) in 1996 has attracted criticism from the business sector, which expresses concern about its impact on Hong Kong's economic competitiveness.

In fact, some men are conscious of and skilful at making use of the EOC to fight for their interests. For example, when the EOC was estab-lished in 1996, the first issue it took up was a complaint from a man against a restaurant offering special discounts for women but not for men (Leung 1999: 339). The EOC adopted a simplistic symmetrical approach, stating that both men and women are vulnerable to discrimination, so it was protecting both men and women.

Recently, there was another ruthless attack on profeminist arguments. A professor of philosophy published an article in a local journal, arguing that we are abusing the concept of equal opportunities. He thinks that women and disabled persons are born inferior, and they are being 'pro-tected' or taken care of on humanitarian grounds, not because of equal opportunities (Lee 1999).

In 1999, a website[3] on men's issues was established, probably the first in Hong Kong. This website is closely linked to the National Coalition of Free Men (NCFM) in North America, and represents the argument of the anti-feminist men's rights movement. They are concerned about the 'rising of women power', and depict men as the victims. They call for Hong Kong men to fight against women, and 'demystify' feminist arguments.

I could continue to give examples of the anti-feminist backlash in Hong Kong. In such a patriarchal society, modest progress in gender equality results in strong repercussions. Under these circumstances, it is extremely difficult for the feminist movement and the profeminist men's movement to develop.

Conclusion: Gendering Men's Services

Up to the present, men's services in Hong Kong are still very under-developed. Although many social service NGOs have launched various men's services in recent years, most of these projects regard themselves as a form of social service helping vulnerable individuals or reinforcing the family, instead of an anti-sexist and anti-oppressive practice. In general, their major concern is the cost of masculinity or the negative impact on men of gender-role stereotyping, not the institutionalized gender inequality or racial and sexual politics. Most of the services can be regarded as non-feminist or even anti-feminist, with just a few exceptions being sympathetic to the agenda of the feminist movement. The under-development of pro-feminist men's services can be attributed to the lack of a strong feminist movement and the lack of gender consciousness in social welfare services in Hong Kong. Pragmatism and the lack of concern for ideology in social services could lead to reinforcing of traditional patriarchal values, con-sciously or unconsciously.

Is the existing development of non-feminist men's services a backlash and a shifting of resources from women to men? This is a complicated question. The answer could be both yes and no, depending on developments in the coming years. First, we should be aware that different approaches in the men's movement, for example, mythopoetic and profeminist, are not necessarily mutually exclusive. It is possible that different men's move-ments could collaborate with each other in the pursuit of anti-sexist and anti-oppressive policy (Kimmel 1995). Second, the orientation and ideology underpinning the social services are not static but are always developing; just as in the early years of the development of women's services in Hong Kong, family-centred and gender-blind approaches were dominant. After continuous debates and challenges from feminists, more women-centred and gender-conscious approaches are developing. Therefore, in the develop-ment of men's services, we need to pay more attention to the problems of ideology and theoretical orientation.

Changing men is one of the major focuses of the feminist movement. Dismissing all forms of the men's movement as a backlash would lose an important arena of anti-sexist struggle. On the other hand, assuming that all forms of the men's movement could lead to a more just society is equally naïve. What we need to do is not only pay more attention to men's issues, but also develop a more thorough debate and reflection on the orientation of men's services.

Notes

1. This research was funded by the Department of Applied Social Studies of Hong Kong Polytechnic University. The author is grateful for the support of the department.

2. Website: http://home4u.hongkong.com/arts/graphics/oniondesign/ONION/men/index.htm

3. Website: http://members.xoom.com/_XMCM/hkmin/index.htm

References

AAF (ed.) (Association for the Advancement of Feminism) (1990) *Women and Social Welfare Policy in Hong Kong*, Hong Kong: AAF (in Chinese).

— (ed.) (1993) *Hong Kong Women's File*, Hong Kong: AAF (in Chinese).

Au, R. (1996) *Growth Journey of Men*, Hong Kong: Breakthrough (in Chinese).

Baumli, F. (ed.) (1985) *Men Freeing Men: Exploding the Myth of the Traditional Male*, Jersey City, NJ: New Atlantis.

BGCA (Boys' and Girls' Clubs Association of Hong Kong) (1990) *The Role of Father in the Family in Hong Kong*, Hong Kong: BGCA (in Chinese).

Bly, R. (1990) *Iron John: A Book About Men*, Reading, MA: Addison-Wesley.

Brod, H. (1983) 'Work Clothes and Leisure Suits: The Class Basis and Bias of the Men's Movement', *Changing Men*, No. 11: 10–12 and 38 40.

— (ed.) (1987) *The Making of Masculinities: The New Men's Studies*, Boston, MA: Allen and Unwin.

Brod, H. and M. Kaufman (eds) (1994) *Theorizing Masculinities*, London: Sage.

Cavanagh, K. and V. Cree (eds) (1996) *Working with Men: Feminism and Social Work*, London: Routledge.

Chan, K. H. (forthcoming) 'Menism and the Men's Movement', in Hong Kong Council of Social Service (ed.) *Community Development Division Resource Book: 1999–2000*, Hong Kong: Hong Kong Council of Social Service, Community Development Division (in Chinese).

Chan, K. W., J. Lee and K. L. Ho (1999) *Hegemony of Rationality: Conception of Welfare Policy Making in Hong Kong*, Research Monograph No. 1, Hong Kong: Department of Applied Social Studies, Hong Kong Polytechnic University.

Choi, P. and R. Au (1998) *Men Behind the Masks*, Hong Kong: Breakthrough (in Chinese).

Connell, R. W. (1995) *Masculinities*, Berkeley, CA: University of California Press.

Dean, H. and P. Taylor-Gooby (1992) *Dependency Culture*, Hemel Hempstead: Harvester Wheatsheaf.

Douglas, P. (1994) '"New Men" and the Tensions of Profeminism', *Social Alternatives*, Vol. 12, No. 4: 32–5.

Farrell, W. (1975) *The Liberated Man*, New York: Bantam Books.

Goldberg, S. (1979) *The New Male: From Macho to Sensitive but Still All Male*, New York: Signet.

Hearn, J. (1987) *The Gender of Oppression: Men, Masculinity and Social Theory*, London: Unwin Hyman.

HKCSS (Hong Kong Council of Social Service) (1996) *Women Services in Hong Kong: A Survey Report*, Hong Kong: Hong Kong Council of Social Service, Working Group on Women Service, February (in Chinese).

— (1997) *A Consultative Paper on 'The Future Development of Women Services in Hong Kong'*, Hong Kong: Hong Kong Council of Social Service.

Hung, S. L. and K. K. Fung (1995) 'Women-Centred Practice', in Association for the Advancement of Feminism and Hong Kong Council of Social Service (ed.), *Women's Services in Hong Kong: Theory and Practice*, Hong Kong: Association for the Advancement of Feminism (in Chinese).

Karenga, M. (1995) 'The Million Man March/Day of Absence Mission', *Black Scholar*, Vol. 25: 2–11.

Kimmel, M. (ed.) (1995) *The Politics of Manhood: Pro-feminist Men Respond to the Mythopoetic Men's Movement (And the Mythopoetic Leaders Answer)*, Philadelphia: Temple University Press.

Lee, T. M. (1999) 'The Fallacy of Human Rights', *Ming Pao Monthly*, August: 25–33 (in Chinese).

Leung, L. C. (1999) 'Gender Discrimination and Social Policy', in K. C. Lee, W. S. Chui, L. C. Leung and K. W. Chan (eds), *New Social Policy*, Hong Kong: Chinese University Press (in Chinese).

Leung, L. C. and K. W. Chan (1998) 'The New Opium War: Welfare Dependency of Lone Mothers in Hong Kong', *Hong Kong Journal of Social Work*, Vol. 32, No. 2: 117–29.

Lit, K.Y, S. Y. Fok and Y. M. Ip Yim (1991) *Fatherhood in the 90s: Implications for Service Needs*, Hong Kong: Department of Applied Social Studies, City Polytechnic of Hong Kong.

Messner, M. (1997) *Politics of Masculinities: Men in Movements*, Thousand Oaks, CA: Sage.

Murray, C. (1990) *The Emerging British Underclass*, London: Institute of Economic Affairs.

Pease, B. (1999) 'Deconstructing Masculinity – Reconstructing Men', in B. Pease and J. Fook (eds), *Transforming Social Work Practice: Postmodern Critical Perspectives*, London: Routledge.

Pringle, K. (1995) *Men, Masculinities and Social Welfare*, London: UCL Press.

Snodgrass, J. (ed.) (1977) *A Book of Readings for Men Against Sexism*, Albion, CA: Times Change Press.

Tsang, G.-Y. (1995) 'The Women's Movement at the Crossroads', in V. Pearson and B. Leung (ed.), *Women in Hong Kong*, Hong Kong: Oxford University Press.

Weedon, C. (1997) *Feminist Practice and Poststructuralist Theory*, 2nd edn, London: Basil Blackwell.

Williams, F. (1996) 'Postmodernism, Feminism and the Question of Difference', in N. Parton (ed.), *Social Theory, Social Change and Social Work*, London: Routledge.

15

Saris, Men and Non-violence: Reflections on Indian Masculinity

Siddhartha

When I began working on this chapter, I discovered I could not find an article with a profeminist perspective written by an Indian man. The librarian at a reasonably good documentation centre in Bangalore provided me with several bulky files on women's issues but only a slim one on men's responses. The latter contained a few newspaper clippings from western contexts, but almost nothing from India. I am aware there are some small efforts to remedy this situation in parts of the country, but they do not add up to much as yet. In the pages that follow I have focused on Hindu tradition, but patriarchal attitudes equally permeate the whole of Indian society regardless of religious persuasion. I hope that similar papers will be attempted from Muslim, Christian, Sikh and other minority perspectives.

Early Perceptions of Men and Women

By way of introduction, I will begin with myself. I was brought up to believe that women were inferior to men. Nobody actually said it, but it was in the air. The pattern of relations within the family and the privileges and power accorded to men were all part of the unspoken script. The men believed in it. So did the women. In my college years, before feminist ideas began to trickle in, I remember proposing the daring idea that both sexes are equal. A tall well-built medical student shot back that I was talking nonsense and she believed women were inferior. It must have secretly pleased me to hear that.

I felt close to my mother in my childhood. She was the one I could throw tantrums at, cuddle and cling to when I felt low, or when my father had thundered at one of us. My father was a kindly man but was mildly bi-polar, which is the name given to the illness that produces mood fluctuations. He could be morose and depressed for weeks, when he hardly spoke, followed by periods when he was irritable and yelled with an intensity that would make us shrivel with fear. When I was three, I remember him throwing a plate at my mother. The plate missed her, crashed against the wall and a ricocheting fragment slashed her arm. She bled profusely and I was terrified. There was little she could do but weep. From an early age I understood that women were meant quietly to accept battering from their husbands and not retaliate.

Wife-battering and the Honour of Men

Wife-battering cuts across all social classes and is deeply engrained in all our communities and religious groups. Let me mention a case that readily comes to mind. Ramasamy, who lives in a slum nearby, is an unskilled worker, excavating earth for construction, mixing cement and shifting bricks on his head. It is hard work and he is not too strong, frequently developing kidney stones. When he returns home in the evening, he expects his wife Lakshmi to have a hot meal of rice and dhal (lentil gruel) ready. This does not always happen as Lakshmi works as a maid in three houses and is often asked to do extra time. Every once in a while Ramasamy goes to a nearby hooch joint after work and gets drunk on illicit arrack. He is usually in a foul mood when he returns and Lakshmi has to take his hectoring. If she reacts he beats her up, not too badly, mercifully, as she is the stronger of the two and can sometimes retaliate in equal measure. She would leave Ramasamy for good if she knew how to cope financially on one income and if she received assistance from her parents and siblings in bringing up her three children. On a couple of occasions she did leave Ramasamy briefly, taking her children with her. But Ramasamy was heartbroken each time and pleaded for her to return. He wanted her back because he did love her very much, even if he never admitted that his attitude was unjust. Without her there was no longer any household, no one to cook his meals and look after his children. He once told me, 'When a wife does something wrong it is the husband's duty to correct her. If I don't beat her who else will!' Ramasamy's attitude is in keeping with mainstream cultural values in India, while Lakshmi is part of a fledgling non-conformism. But even Lakshmi's desire to quit her husband is ambivalent. A part of her is militant, influenced by the values of a women's organization working in the area, while another part craves for traditional social acceptance in the community.

What angers Ramasamy is that his wife answers back. She rarely breaks down and cries when he insults her, which infuriates him even further. If she cried it would show she was penitent and vulnerable, that his words had found their mark. It would help him re-establish authority over her, allow him to be stern and gentle in turn. He grew up believing a woman should be patient, hard-working, devoted and long-suffering, attitudes deeply engrained in the Indian psyche, women believing in them as much as men. Another useful case is that of Kanan, the carpenter, who threatens his wife Andalamma every now and then when he is drunk. Once Andalamma tried to drown herself because Kanan, in a fit of drunken rage, asked her to go and kill herself. I later asked Andalamma why she had attempted such a foolish act. Brimming with pride she told me, 'When your husband asks you to do something you must do it.'

I knew Andalamma well and was sure she had no intention of dying, that her attempt to drown herself was done in full view of her neighbours, with the knowledge she would be rescued before completing the act. She was the secretary of the neighbourhood unit of a political party. She was not a battered woman in the strict sense, for Kannan was a weak man even in his drunken state. He did not have the courage to stand up to her and generally went along with whatever she wished. But Andalamma was in need of redeeming her reputation and showing she was within the cultural matrix, where it is meritorious for a woman to obey her husband's wish. Kannan was even more proud of his wife after that day and Andalamma's standing in the community went up.

The Indian Bride: Duties without Rights

The notion that a woman's role is to be utterly devoted to her husband is an old one and has been well stated by a western woman Sr. Nivedita, earlier known as Margaret Noble, who became an ardent disciple of the well-known Indian monk Swami Vivekananda. Writing at the beginning of the twentieth century, she wholeheartedly restated his view on being feminine:

> The Indian bride comes to her husband much as the Western woman might enter a church ... For the woman supreme love is ... a duty. Only to the man his mother must always stand first. In some sense, therefore, the relation is not mutual. And this is in full accordance with the national sentiment, which stigmatizes affection that asks for equal return as 'shopkeeping' ... As a disciple might, she prostrates herself before him, touching his feet with her head before receiving his blessing. It is not equality. No. But who talks of a vulgar equality, asks the Hindu wife, when she may have instead the unspeakable blessedness of offering worship? (Roy 1999: 116)

The frame of reference for male attitudes to women in Indian society is culturally sanctioned and comes from ancient religious scriptures. In the Manusmriti, an important text on Hindu law dating from 200 B.C., Manu the law-giver states that women are weak and fickle in nature and should not be given independence (Manu 1991: ch. 9, translated by Doniger and Smith). Although she must be held in respect she should be under the control of her father first, then her husband and later her son. A good woman is one who goes about her domestic duties with devotion and bears male offspring for her husband. The importance of the male child is underlined by Manu when he states:

> The husband enters the wife, becomes an embryo, and is born here on earth. That is why the wife is called a wife, because he is born again in her. The wife brings forth a son who is just like the man she makes love with; that is why he should guard his wife zealously, in order to keep his progeny clean. (Manu 1991: 197)

(The bias towards the male child is still cruelly evident today with female infanticide and female foeticide being widely practised.)[1]

The Hindu epic *Ramayana*, in the popular version written by the sage Valmiki, is another good source for exploring traditional gender attitudes. Sita, the wife of the god Rama, follows her husband into the forest where he is exiled. Kidnapped from the forest she is taken to the palace of the demon king Ravana, who is enamoured of her beauty. Rama eventually rescues Sita after slaying Ravana. But Rama insists that Sita has to endure an ordeal by fire to prove her chastity. Sita comes through victorious, proving she is beyond reproach. Eventually Rama returns with Sita to Ayodhya, where he becomes king. But Sita's trauma is far from over as rumours concerning her chastity still abound. In accordance with tradition, Rama unwillingly banishes Sita from the palace. Understandably, most Indian men prefer to see Sita as beautiful, dutiful and loyal. Women would also agree, although some might argue that Sita did not take her humiliation lying down. In some versions of the *Ramayana* she defends herself some-what more vigorously against her husband's unfair suspicions.

The Quest for Manhood

Many modern Indians will believe that to be a man means to be strong and gutsy. I had a sense of this when I was at university. Our college, run by the Jesuits, refused to take part in a city-wide demonstration against what some southerners perceived as the unjust imposition of Hindi as the national language by the central government in Delhi. Most of the men's colleges in the city of Tiruchirapalli went on strike. When they realized that our college was still working, a delegation of students appeared at the gate to present us with saris (the traditional attire of Indian women). The saris signified that we were women, lacking in courage. The provocation was sufficient for the students to storm out of the campus and join the rest of the protesters. In the past, Indian men were seen to be effeminate. Consider what Lord Macaulay, who became Viceroy in nineteenth-century colonial India, had to say. According to him the Indian is:

> feeble even to effeminacy. He lives in a constant vapour bath. His pursuits are sedentary, his limbs delicate, his movements languid. During many ages he has been trampled upon by men of bolder and more hardy breeds ... His mind bears a singular analogy to his body. It is weak even to helplessness for purposes of manly resistance; but its suppleness and tact move the children of sterner climates to admiration not unmingled with contempt. (Rudolph and Rudolph 1969: 164)

Even Mahatma Gandhi, as a young man, was traumatized by his own perceived weakness. He wrote, 'It must at the outset be admitted that the Hindus as a rule are notoriously weak' (Rudolph and Rudolph 1969: 167).[2]

Swami Vivekananda, the popular late-nineteenth-century Hindu monk, referred to Indian men as an unattractive 'nation of women'. Photographs of Vivekananda were probably calculated to show him as strong and manly, unlike his own guru Ramakrishna who emphasized the feminine dimension. Ramakrishna, who saw himself as the handmaid of God, said, 'I spent many days as the handmaid of God. I dressed myself in women's clothes, put on ornaments, and covered the upper part of my body with a scarf, just like a woman' (Roy 1999: 97).[3] No wonder that Vivekananda, caught in the throes of nascent nationalism, wished to distance himself from this feminine image of his guru. For him, 'Ramakrishna's unlettered, intuitive, otherworldly ecstasy was not merely reproducible, it was not a fit model to emulate' (Roy 1999: 107). Vivekananda made this explicit when he said, 'The older I grow, the more everything seems to me to be in manliness. This is my new gospel. Do even evil like a man! Be wicked, if you must, on a grand scale' (Roy 1999: 106). I might add that Vivekananda, despite these views, is a revered figure in the collective consciousness of Indians, both Hindu and non-Hindu. He founded the Ramakrishna mission that is today the most significant Hindu body concerned with theology, education, health and charitable activities.

Gandhi: Non-violence as Feminine Energy

Mahatma Gandhi appears to have rejected Vivekananda's masculine ideal and actively associated the feminine with peaceful and communitarian values. For him women were the incarnation of *ahimsa* (non-violence and love; see Rudolph and Rudolph 1969: 215). Gandhi himself did not hold these views to begin with. In his youth his Muslim friend Mehtab told him that Hindus were weak because they did not eat meat; Mehtab ascribed his superior strength and athletic prowess to being a meat-eater. Many of the local people also believed that meat-eating made an Englishman strong and allowed him to rule India. When Gandhi later went to England to study law he continued to imitate Englishmen, but his attempts at Anglicization failed and he began slowly to return to the way of life he was accustomed to, one that was ascetic and self-denying (Rudolph and Rudolph 1969: 179). It was only a question of time before non-violence became the central pillar of his social and political life. Gandhi saw non-violence as representing the potency of women: 'Has she not greater intuition, is she not more self-sacrificing, has she not greater powers of endurance, has she not greater courage?' (Rudolph and Rudolph 1969: 192). Gandhi believed that the essence of femininity was superior to that of masculinity and that masculinity was better than cowardice (see Nandy 1999: 53).

Gandhi's appreciation of women is nevertheless within a patriarchal context. He wrote:

> It is not for women to go out and work, as men do. If we send them to the factories who will look after our domestic and social affairs? If women go out and work our social life will be ruined and moral standards will decline … I am convinced that for men and women to go out for work together will mean the fall of both. (Baldt 2000: 81)

Gandhi was also a believer in 'conscience' and the 'inner voice', and if these made a woman flout social norms it would be acceptable. He insisted that 'The wife has a perfect right to take her own course, and meekly brave the consequences when she knows herself to be in the right, and when her resistance is for a nobler cause' (Baldt 2000: 81). Although he believed that a woman's place was in the home, he shrewdly used them to agitate against the British to great political effect. Suresh R. Baldt (2000) argues that Gandhi realized the impact on world opinion if women peacefully demonstrated against the policies of their colonial rulers. For Gandhi, the issue of women's liberation was possibly secondary to the goal of winning independence from the British. Gandhi suffers in hindsight but for that period he was seen as a radical reformer and played a significant role in the emancipation of women. His belief that women could be active in public life and still be good housewives continues to be the norm today.

Gandhian non-violence and the glorification of the woman (however inconsistent) were slowly eroded by the rising tide of cultural nationalism towards the end of the twentieth century. Vivekananda's notions of masculinity were more apt for the purpose. In promoting an aggressive nationalism, some political organizations went further than Vivekananda and articulated an inimical policy towards minorities such as Muslims and Christians. These organizations are unfortunately no longer marginal and arc today part of the ruling political establishment. Today a coalition government led by Hindu nationalists rules the country. The seminal ideas of this nationalism largely emanated from the ideas of Vinayak Damodar Savarkar who wanted 'the undying vitality of Hindu manhood' to strengthen a movement that would 'make the enemies of Hindudom shudder' (Jurgensmeyer 1994: 84).

Jolted into Awareness

The passage from patriarchy to an awareness of the oppression of women is not an easy one for most Indian men and I have still to come across one who has made a painless transition. Take my own case. I was twenty-six when I was jolted into angry humiliation by Véronique, a young French woman, at an educational workshop in Paris. That afternoon we were discussing women's issues. Typically, the men remained silent while the women discussed patriarchy and the oppression they experienced. I was not new to women's issues and I was upset that my point of view was not solicited. After all I was a champion in espousing women's issues and several Indian women were regularly present at the sessions I had organized back home. (Obviously I had not then considered that patriarchy could also manifest in men in the garb of women's liberation.) The women who led the discussion at the Paris workshop went about as if the men were not present in the room, although I was certain they wanted us to register every word they said. After politely listening to them for more than an hour, several of us were dying to slip out of the room but we didn't dare, for it would have been construed as a further sign of male chauvinism. Since none of us wanted trouble, we patiently sat it out. Towards the end an unconscious smirk appeared on my face. Véronique noticed the smirk and was quick to grab the opportunity. 'Why are you smiling?' she asked menacingly. I was momentarily thrown off guard since I was not even aware I was smiling. 'Men always grin or laugh when women's issues are discussed!' she bellowed. I was angry she had picked on me for what I thought was a pardonable misdemeanour, if in fact it was one. Later, largely to keep the peace, I went up to her and apologized without feeling remorseful. 'It's easy for men to apologize,' she continued, unwilling to get off the moral high ground. At the time I genuinely believed she was being ungracious, although I did not say anything. As punishment Véronique asked me to go and make tea for all the women in the room. She told me I was being let off lightly. I made the tea and put on a mask of meek gentleness, although I was mortified at what I perceived to be needless aggression. It was an important lesson. Thereafter, I never smiled when women's issues were discussed. On the whole, for many years I avoided such discussions when I could, although, thankfully, I did not regress into rigid male attitudes. I reluctantly continued to develop an appreciation of the rights of women. I think I came to dislike feminists who challenged men. Years later I came to accept the truth of Véronique's intervention and was grateful to her for it.

Cultural Nationalism: Reinforcing Patriarchal Attitudes

Today we are confronted by the twin dangers of aggressive cultural nationalism and a new global macho culture reinforcing traditional male attitudes. The former sees Hinduism as the true religion of India and portrays Muslims and Christians as outsiders. When four Christian nuns were raped in Jhabua recently, the general secretary of the Vishwa Hindu Parishad, a powerful Hindu nationalist outfit, dismissed the incident as the natural outcome of Christian attempts to convert Hindus. Well-known women leaders like Uma Bharati and Sadhvi Rithambara and women's organizations like Durga Vahini have actively contributed to instigating violence against minorities (Marik 1999). Today, Hindu nationalism has a two-pronged and seemingly contradictory approach to women. On the one hand it attempts to reinforce the subordinate position of women and on the other it uses women to join in the chorus of intimidation and violence against Muslims and Christians. According to the Hindu right, the main factor behind rape is the demand of women for equal and democratic rights. In 1983, Mridula Sharma, the president of Mahila Morcha, a women's organization, rationalized wife-beating and dowry (Marik 1999).

Most men with whom I have discussed these issues would like to believe that there are some qualities that are essentially masculine and others that are feminine. They would feel very threatened by the proposition that the sexes are essentially the same (allowing for biological differences) and that role differences are only historical and cultural constructions. For example, Indians seem to agree with Mahatma Gandhi and do not feel that former prime minister Indira Gandhi was setting a bad example by being active in public life. As Ashis Nandy (1999: 42) puts it, 'public success does not seem to detract from private womanliness'. A woman like Indira Gandhi may have assimilated aggressive models of leadership that are competitive and non-giving but she also projected a feminine essence related to dress and other behaviour. Aggressive and competitive patterns are not seen as inherently masculine. In mythology and folklore they are also qualities associated with women (Nandy 1999). Indira Gandhi herself did not want to be known as a feminist, and Madhu Kiswar, the editor of *Manushi*, a women's journal, sees feminism as a loaded eurocentric term (Roy 1999: 206). Most men would agree, for other reasons, and advocate a perspective that would support complementarity and difference rather than sameness and equality.

Bollywood and the New Man

Aggressive male machismo, fuelled by Hollywood, has progressively seeped into the cultural scene over the last two decades. India's Bollywood (as the hugely popular Bombay Indian film industry is referred to) has caught up fast and Indian actors like Salman Khan now imitate 'Rambo' (Sylvester Stallone) in strutting about bare-chested displaying muscular torsos. The aggressive individualism promoted by the global market has also played a decisive role in legitimizing violence and a particular conception of masculinity. The last twenty years have accelerated efforts at women's empowerment but we are also witnessing the hardening of male attitudes and an increase in violence against women. While exact figures are not available, a cautious estimate would suggest that around a thousand women are killed each month in the country. Dowry killings have been in the news regularly for the past two decades. They reveal the new commercial attitudes of sections of the middle class who would see dowry as more worthy than the wife. If the woman's family refuses to pay the full dowry they had promised, or reject fresh demands, an unforeseen 'accident' might well end her young life or she may be subjected to continual battering by the husband and his family. Many women's movements in the country have been highlighting dowry deaths and other violence against women. As a result, there is probably some fear about indulging in these acts, although even this is doubtful as it is well known that most cases are written off as suicide and hardly any of the perpetrators end up behind bars. Even when they are arrested, the unsympathetic attitude of the police and the judiciary see to it that they are acquitted.

A large number of non-governmental organizations are playing important roles in the empowerment of women all over the country. This has led to women becoming more assertive. But the changing attitudes of women have not led to any significant increase in the capacity of men to appreciate the new feminism. Men have felt threatened and in many cases have reacted with increased ferocity. I remember the case of a couple who worked with me in a village outside Bangalore. As social workers, they were both exposed to ideas about the empowerment of women, but the man beat up his wife whenever she returned late from women's meetings in the villages. He wanted her home early so that the evening meal would be ready on time and there would 'be someone at home when I return'. (For the traditional male, the feminine is associated with 'home' and the masculine with 'outside'.) Despite being a social worker he was unable to overcome these old cultural archetypes and only paid lip-service to the rights of women.

Gender Sensitivity: Are Men in Need of Help?

It is increasingly clear that the empowerment of women must go along with the 'alternative' empowerment of men if it is not to lead to major conflicts in the family and outside. This new empowerment has little to do with the old brute power that men often exercised over women. The alternative empowerment must replace the old attitudes of authority and domination with equality and complementarity. This process necessitates looking into the cultural archetypes that are deeply embedded in the consciousness of both men and women. It also means that Indian men must accord the same dignity to the wife that they give to the mother. In the end we must work towards women and men who are both humane and empowered. It will benefit nobody to have many men permanently reacting against feminism or conversely being debilitated by the questions it raises.

Most men are so culturally conditioned that they are not deeply aware of the distress and harm they cause women. Even men who are exposed to feminism plead their inability to change in too radical a fashion as they lack, in the words of one male friend, 'the skills to be non-patriarchic'. They prefer a benign and humane patriarchy where they are not radically destabilized. But can women be really empowered with attitudes such as these? Or should women accept that society should move incrementally, a step at a time, and content themselves with the idea that some empowerment is better than none at all? For men this is an easier prospect to digest than a sudden overturning of power relations and the bitter and irrational conflicts that follow. Some men understandably feel that a dialogical approach may allow them to deal more confidently with their fears and undergo a greater degree of positive transformation than the proposals put forward by radical feminists. The majority of Indian women are also probably of a similar disposition. Better to advance towards an increase of liberties and fulfilment than face a broken marriage and isolation. Perhaps if the social conditions were right, a fair number of middle-class women might prefer outright divorce to being the objects of violence. But it would be a lonely furrow for most and many women prefer to remain within marriage than face social exclusion, the degree of which would depend on her social class and job qualifications. Despite these considerations, many middle-class women are now opting for divorce in the urban contexts and the number is likely to rise steadily. At one end of the continuum is the woman who fuses the traditional notion of the home with modern roles outside the home and at the other we find the new feminism which is convinced of the unfairness of traditional roles and opts for the outside. There is obviously no a priori clarity possible except the touchstone of dialogue and negotiation. Whatever the approach, one pre-condition is the openness needed on the part of the psychologically defensive Indian male, simultaneously struggling to protect his privileges and deal with the pain that comes with creative change.

Indian men are, however, not beyond redemption. To make their marriages work, middle-class men are learning to negotiate new patterns of relationship with their wives. A small minority of men understand the need for both partners to share in household chores, particularly where the woman is also employed. Even in more traditional contexts it would be misleading to assume that the situation is bleak and that conjugal happiness is entirely absent. In a large number of families women are respected and play decisive roles in family affairs even if they do not outwardly appear to be doing so. In recent years expressions such as 'gender sensitivity', 'gender parity' and 'gender audit' have become not uncommon among university-educated people and in private and public institutions. The efforts of some non-governmental organizations have helped immensely to foster a new awareness through gender training sessions. These have helped some men to become aware of daily happenings that should be obvious but are not: that most women wake up much earlier than men, eat later than men, are busier than men and go to sleep later than men. In addition there is an emerging recognition that women in villages and slums (where toilets are not usually available) have to go out to relieve themselves under cover of darkness either before daybreak or at night. The not-too-threatening atmosphere of these training sessions helps men to see the suffering women undergo on a daily basis. It has helped remove some of their smugness and many men who have gone through these sessions come away with a desire to change their attitudes and behaviour.

Notes

1. A study published by the National Law School of India University entitled *Female Infanticide and Foeticide* reveals some of the causes and the extent of the problem.

2. Rudolph and Rudolph's *The Modernity of Tradition* (1969) contains an excellent chapter on Gandhi's struggle to become more manly and courageous and his subsequent adherence to a 'feminine' non-violence.

3. Ramakrishna advised his disciples to avoid the company of women, except when they could be seen as maternal figures. He spoke of several kinds of sexual intercourse, including: listening to a woman, speaking about her, whispering to her privately, keeping something belonging to her and touching her. Parama Roy states: 'Sexual desire could not however be kept in check by mere abstinence; it could only be transcended by becoming this troubling object of desire. The only way to shun women (as seductive figure) was to become woman (of another kind).'

References

Baldt, S. R. (2000) 'The Politics of Gandhi's Feminism', in S. Ranchold-Nilsson and M. Tetreault (eds), *Women, States and Nationalism*, London: Routledge.

Jurgensmeyer, M. (1994) *Religious Nationalism Confronts the Secular State*, Oxford: Oxford University Press.

Manu (1991) *The Laws of Manu*, trans. W. Doniger and B. Smith, London: Penguin.

Marik, S. (1999) 'He for God only, she for God in him', *The Telegraph* (Calcutta), 29 November.

Nandy, A. (1999) *Exiled at Home*, Oxford: Oxford University Press.

Roy, P. (1999) *Indian Traffic*, New Delhi: Vistaar Publications.

Rudolph, L. I. and S. Rudolph (1969) *The Modernity of Tradition*, New Delhi: Orient Longmans.

16

Cultural Practices of Masculinity in Post-apartheid South Africa

Ira Horowitz

Prior to the demise of apartheid in South Africa, the focus for liberation was understandably on overthrowing that tyrannical system. As a result, little attention seemed to be available to address the needs of other oppressed groups, including women. This meant that when the country ushered in its new democracy in 1994, traditional patterns of patriarchy flourished.[1]

Just how deeply these patterns were engrained was brought home to me in 1996 in the description of an incident told by a female Masters student during the first workshop on gender I facilitated in South Africa. The student, who had been an activist during her undergraduate days, related how one night in the late 1980s while she and some men were on the run from the police, she noticed that the man who was driving seemed to be very tired. Since she was the only other person in the van with a driver's licence, she offered at least six times to drive so that he could get some sleep. She was repeatedly ignored until the driver finally exclaimed: 'I'm not going to be driven by a f***ing woman!' Shortly thereafter, he fell asleep at the wheel and drove off the road, at which point the van rolled over. The woman concluded her tale by saying she still suffers from whiplash and could have died because of that 'sexist pig'. In effect, they could be 'comrades' at the barricade, but this man could not bear the embarrassment of being in a car with a woman driving!

It is beyond the scope of this chapter to explore in depth the roots of such attitudes and behaviours. A good start on that task has recently been undertaken in a book, *Changing Men in South Africa*. In his introductory chapter, the editor, Robert Morrell, describes how masculine identity in South Africa has been shaped by the many diverse forces and events in the country's complicated and violent history. Among the factors he discusses are: traditional African, agrarian culture; Afrikaner nationalism and the Boer wars; British colonialism and imperialism; the resulting impoverishment of indigenous peoples on their farms which led to the movement of male labour first to the mines and then to the cities; the imposition of the repressive apartheid system accompanied by international isolation; and finally the overthrow of that system after a protracted, and often violent, struggle.

What will be attempted here is much more limited. This chapter will look at how the early experiences of some contemporary South African men have shaped their attitudes and behaviour. This will be done by examining anecdotal information from gender-awareness-raising workshops for men held over the last three years.[2] Particular emphasis will be placed on cultural practices, especially those of black people since they comprise over 80 per cent of South Africa's population and black men comprised the largest group at the workshops. The role religions play, primarily Christianity and Islam, will also be examined. The chapter will then describe how the workshop participants decided to challenge their early socialization in an attempt to develop new concepts of masculinity while preserving the positive elements of their traditions. Finally, the chapter will describe how these men have begun to join with others in a series of fledgling efforts to bring about the type of gender equality enshrined in the South African constitution and recent implementing legislation.[3]

Before beginning the main section of this chapter, it should be helpful to most readers to have a brief overview of the racial and cultural setting in which the workshops took place. Also, it is important to at least mention where women in South Africa are situated with regard to this struggle.

Issues of race and culture remain extremely diverse and contentious here. Under apartheid, there was strict and complete separation of the four main 'racial' classifications: white, coloured, Indian and black. Thus they had separate areas where they could live; schools and universities; media outlets such as newspapers and radio stations. The extent (and horror) of this separation was brought to my attention by a white woman married to a black man who told me that aside from there being no legal place for their family to live, she feared being in a car accident with her husband and children because the injured would be taken to three different hospitals based on their racial classification! (Her children would be classified as 'coloured'.) Whites obviously controlled everything while 'coloureds' and Indians were given limited privilege on such issues as travel (only black people had to carry 'passes', for example), the right to conduct certain businesses and a superior form of education.

Although groups were classified together, there was considerable diversity within each of the four classifications. Among the whites, the two largest groups are the descendants of the original Dutch settlers known as Afrikaners, and the English who began to settle here in the mid- to late eighteenth century. Unlike other colonial people including the English, the Afrikaners cut all ties to the mother country and saw South Africa as their home. In many ways the 'coloureds' who are centred in the Western Cape are the most problematic grouping. They are seen as mixed-race people but they are actually descendants of three primary groups: the Khoi and San, light-skinned African tribes who lived in the western half of the country when the Europeans arrived and who suffered genocide as a result of wars and western diseases; imported slaves from other Dutch colonies, primarily Malaysia and Indonesia; and the children of mixed parentage which resulted from the sexual exploitation of women of colour and natural inter-breeding. The majority of these people, who are sometimes referred to as 'brown Afrikaners', are generally first language Afrikaans speakers and members of the Dutch Reformed Church. The Indians were also imported, having been brought here as indentured labourers in the latter half of the nine teenth century to work the sugar plantations of the English-controlled area known as Natal. Other Indians came as 'free traders' to supply the new market. Finally, the diversity among the darker-skinned black communities is much too complex to describe here. One way to get a sense of it is to recognize that of the eleven official languages in the 'new' South Africa, nine are African and the other two are Afrikaans and English.

Turning to the issue of how women are dealing with issues of patriarchy, I obtained a sense of the changing female consciousness on these issues, about a year after I arrived here, during a gender-awareness-raising work-shop for shop stewards convened by a local affiliate of the Congress of South African Trade Unions (COSATU). Near the beginning of the workshop, participants were separated by gender to complete an activity on early socialization. Since there were fewer of us, I went with the men to work in a smaller room nearby. When we returned to the main room, we were greeted by the women singing one of the moving songs from the apartheid struggle. It was clear that they were now singing as part of a new struggle – the one for gender equality![4]

The Role of Early Socialization

There are two exercises early in the men's workshops that require the participants to reflect upon their early socialization: one a brainstorm of the rules they learned about how boys and men are supposed to behave; the other, a story-telling activity of significant incidents from which they learned one or more of the rules. It is during this portion of the workshops that the participants reflect upon the fact that their gendered behaviour is learned and that among the major influences shaping those actions are religion and culture.

Initially, what is perhaps most striking about the data generated from these activities is the similarity between the rules across the different cultures. Thus in every workshop, regardless of the composition of the participants, there were always rules to the effect that the man had to protect others; be the breadwinner; be strong; continuously compete and not lose, especially to a girl; make the decisions and be a leader; and above all, not to cry or show emotions. The near universality of these rules was particularly noted in several workshops. In one, a participant who was temporarily working in South Africa for an international funding organization was surprised at how even though he grew up in Europe, 'the rules were the same'. He wondered why the pattern was world-wide. Similarly, in the workshop held in the Western Cape, which was the only one with a significant number of 'coloured' participants, a man said he 'could relate to all of what's been said. There are differences in culture and language, but so much is the same.'

Even when there were cultural variations in practice, the underlying messages were often similar. Thus, in a workshop held in a government agency, an Afrikaner man indicated that he was taught, 'ladies first'. An African man who came from the Xhosa community then said in his culture, the rule was 'men first'. The reason, he explained, was to protect the family from an animal or the enemy. In the discussion of these apparently opposite rules, it was noted that both are based on an assumption that women are weaker and need either protection or assistance.

Despite the apparent universality of the rules, many cultural variations appeared in the workshops. For example, it was noted that in Muslim weddings the bride is not present at the ceremony, and that in the Venda or Pedi communities it is believed that eating from a cooking pot could change a man's sex. One of the more unusual stories was told by a man who was the last child born in his family where there were five girls. Previously, several other boys had died at a young age. Therefore when he was young, he was dressed like a girl so that the *tokoloshes* (evil gnome-like spirits) would not take him as they had taken the other males. He also played with dolls with his sisters because that is what they played with. This lasted until one day when his father, after seeing him playing with dolls, became furious and forbade him from doing so ever again.

Of course, some of the different practices had more of an impact on behaviour than others. Perhaps the most significant in the majority of African communities was the requirement that a teenage boy should attend circumcision school and silently endure the pain from that procedure. One participant explained that the word for this training was '*mopat*' in Sesotho, the place that 'transformed you from a boy to a man'. For those who did not attend or who did not satisfactorily meet this test of their 'manhood', there were significant sanctions such as 'girls would not marry you', or, as stated in another workshop, your son would be called a 'boy's son'.

Perhaps the most discussed cultural practice was the payment of *lobola*, or bride-price, that is still common even among urban, educated African men. Indeed, at one workshop several men strongly challenged another who had two daughters and announced that, if they married, he would not ask their future husbands to pay *lobola*. The participant then backtracked to saying he would accept a gift if offered, but would not require one. Formerly the standard payment was eleven cows, if the man could afford that much, although now the means of exchange has expanded to include cash for those living in urban areas. Some parts of this modernization were lamented by participants who saw them as the 'commercialization' of the practice. The example was given of a man having to pay R100,000 (about US$16,000) for an educated woman.

Although no consistent rationale was provided for why *lobola* was first paid, the most common explanations offered were that it served as 'a gift exchange between families to make them a part of each other' or a 'thanksgiving' to the bride's family. In some private discussions, a further explanation was provided that it served to recognize that the bride's family was losing a valuable worker. Like circumcision school, the requirement to pay *lobola* remains a test of manhood today for many men. Thus, at one workshop, a participant told how an acquaintance of his who had been unable to pay *lobola* was shunned by his peers who said: 'What can you discuss with us?'

Judging by the justifications offered at the workshops for patriarchal behaviour, religious principles were almost the equal of culture as an influence on many of the men present. Perhaps the most striking example of the depth of religious belief here is the repeated use of the biblical story of the Creation to demonstrate why men are meant to be superior to women. At one workshop, a man simply explained in a matter-of-fact way that God created Adam and told Eve she was to be dominated by him. What is most significant about this is that while such statements were often challenged within a religious debate, not one participant in any of the workshops ever used theories of evolution to contest the validity of this biblical rationale for male superiority. It is, of course, possible that some people did not take the Bible literally but were just seeing the story of Adam and Eve as an expression of God's intention as to the roles of women and men. But at least for those who spoke, there seemed to be no question of how humans were created. And Christianity was not the only religion discussed in this manner. At one workshop, a man who was a devout Muslim explained that the Koran 'says women and men ... have different roles in society, for example, men will always be the leaders'.

Challenging the Effects of Early Socialization

The second segment of the workshops shows how our early socialization results in men being privileged and women oppressed in current society. This situation is contrasted with the goal of South Africa to transform itself into a human rights culture. Analogies are often drawn between the struggle to end apartheid and women's struggle for gender equality. For example, during a discussion of what 'gender equality' really meant, one participant made the emotional comment that:

> We took away equal opportunity, perhaps unconsciously. It's like the old regime taking away opportunities from certain people ... For me as a white man, I am feeling very sad ... I now understand equality of opportunity and choice for women. I thought I had the right answers, but I see I was acting on my own conditioning. I was still an oppressor even though I thought I was doing something different.

After looking at how women are currently being treated, the key section of the workshops focuses on uncovering the tremendous price men pay for their so-called privilege. In one of the last of the activities in this section, the participants summarize what has gone before by listing the costs to men for conforming to the rules they learned as boys. Among the responses listed in the first workshop in the series were: stress and health problems that shorten your life; depression; aggression, i.e. you hurt yourself (suicide) or others; substance abuse (alcohol and drugs); isolation from family and friends; the loss of emotions such as compassion and co-operation; and the loss of self-esteem. One additional cost raised at other workshops is 'premature death', whether it be as a result of wars or other violent clashes or from working at a dangerous job such as in the mines (still a major form of employment in South Africa).

It is during this stage of the workshop that cultural and religious prescriptions are often critically examined. One example concerns the payment of *lobola* discussed earlier. A belief sometimes expressed by Africans (and, based on social interactions, one shared by many whites) is that it is OK 'in our culture' for a husband to hit his wife. When probed, this position seems to be based at least in part on the fact that the husband has paid *lobola* and therefore his wife is his possession. But other men strongly disagree, such as one who argued that he 'did not see anything wrong with our traditions ... We must go back and ask "Why did you do this?" Then we can decide whether to accept or reject that tradition.' Lobola was not 'buying a woman', according to him, it was paid to strengthen the relationship between the families. 'Men have misused culture. It does not mean you can accept beating. That is not our culture. We have a saying: "Beating does not build a home".'

Another way in which cultural issues were contested concerns the encroachment of outside influences. In the workshops this usually was expressed as disapproval of the trend, especially among young urban people, to adopt western lifestyles. Thus, after watching a video depicting the negative stereotypes of women in advertising, someone commented that 'the African Renaissance will do away with all of this. As long as we follow western life styles, these things will exist.' But such thinking touches on the question of gender equality when it is extended to label feminism 'un-African' as a way of trying to maintain traditional gender roles. For example, during the same discussion, a participant argued that the reason women are starting to take over and push men aside is 'because we don't stick to our culture. Western culture is on TV, the Internet, etc ... That's why we are having a big problem.' For some men, however, it was not acceptable to use a dislike for the West in this way. Thus one man responded to the earlier comments by labelling them: 'a political statement from the ANC which says that western lifestyle is harmful. But in the African lifestyle, it was OK to beat your wife. I think that irrespective of lifestyle and culture, we have a choice of how to act.' A similar sentiment that culture should not interfere with the fight for gender equality was offered in another workshop: 'I learned today that there is a common element between white and black cultures and that we can fight together because we have common ground.'

A key argument repeatedly offered to rebut the use of culture to justify maintenance of male privilege is that culture is not static. Thus one participant explained that some practices continued to be followed even though the reason they were introduced may no longer be there. An example he gave was the cultural prescription against throwing out rubbish at night. Originally there was a reason for this because it was dark and you might throw something important away. Now with electricity it is no longer totally dark at night but many people still follow the custom. Later in the same discussion, someone remarked that as things change, for example, moving to urban areas, the rules change also. He claimed that 'culture becomes diluted'. But as a facilitator at the first men's workshops who is Zulu used to point out, there may be good reasons for the changes. For example, he expressed approval of the termination of certain former practices in Zulu culture, such as killing one member of a set of twins or killing one of his lieutenants when the king died 'so that he would not travel alone'. He claimed that these changes reflect the fact that we have become more humane and enlightened.

Parallel to the above discussions were ones that challenged the religious justifications for retaining the status quo in gender relations. For example, during the discussion in which the above reference to the story of Adam and Eve was made, another man argued that by saying 'something is divine means we are disempowering ourselves. It is saying we can't change it.' He was supported by another participant who exclaimed: 'I'm shocked that some people seem to justify the domination of women by men on the Bible. Those were philosophers who wanted to perpetuate a certain class.'

Resistance to Change

It should be noted that while tremendous progress in increasing gender awareness was made by virtually all men who attended the workshops, in some instances a line was reached which at least some of those present would not cross. A review of these examples indicates where the socialization is the strongest and therefore where attention must be paid in future.

The only example of resistance that appeared in multiple workshops was the belief that there cannot be full equality at home. In two workshops in particular, several participants insisted the man must be the head of the household based on the teachings of the Bible and the Koran. Under pressure from colleagues, these men were willing to grant a greater say to women, but they would never be equal. Just how convoluted the arguments became is represented by one man's statement that 'if man is the head, then woman is the neck which will turn the head where it wants'. In another workshop, the line was drawn on cultural grounds. Thus, after a comment to the effect that a couple should agree on the surname, not take the husband's automatically, someone asked whether this meant that he might have to go to his wife's home if she insisted. The immediate response from one man was that the questioner 'was romanticizing the whole thing. The woman goes to the in-laws. This is not negotiable.'

Near the end of another workshop, a line was drawn concerning the degree to which men could express their emotions. This occurred after the participants had jointly developed a vision for a new masculinity that included men being able to show their feelings. While there seemed to be a reluctant but almost unanimous consensus that it was acceptable for men to express grief such as when a loved one died, most remained unwilling to agree that it was OK for men to cry when they were in physical pain. The major example focused upon was the circumcision ritual. It remained important to the participants that men show their strength in such instances primarily so they could remain calm and effective and would be a model for others. The argument was that if they showed their pain in a difficult situation, others might panic or their children would not feel safe. Although counter-arguments were raised, few men seemed willing to change their minds. This discussion was one of the most honest and demonstrated just how much the men were struggling with gender issues.

Somewhat more surprisingly, there was great resistance in another workshop to ending the corporal punishment of children as a form of discipline that seemed common to several different cultures. Some participants made a distinction between 'being beaten' by a parent and 'getting a hiding'. The former is 'violence' while the latter is 'discipline'. This position was challenged by the facilitators who asked whether there was a connection between using corporal punishment to discipline children and the general high level of violence in South African society. Several men stuck to their position, however, such as one who said: 'When my dad disciplined me with a stick or belt, he was not hitting out of anger; it was an attempt to correct behaviour.' A facilitator then asked whether this distinction held for times when you wanted to correct your wife's behaviour, i.e. was it ever OK to strike her? The general consensus seemed to be 'no', it was different when you struck another adult. One man reasoned that, since you choose your spouse, 'You have to negotiate with her about how you will relate to each other. You chose each other and both can walk away. But you have a responsibility to raise your child.'

Related to the places where they personally drew the line against change, men who attended the workshops also recognized the places where others were most resistant. These constituted further indications that the struggle for gender equality would be a long and painful one. Among the obstacles to be faced were the strength of the early socialization for both genders, the continued pervasiveness of sexist images in the media and within other institutions, and most importantly, the resistance to change produced by fears of isolation and ridicule. Samples from discussions of two key obstacles – the roles played by women acting out of their internalized oppression and by organized religion – are provided.

Throughout the workshops the men noted that their actions were not the only problem. For example, one person described how in his culture, the way that a woman is supposed to act as a wife (i.e. dedicated to serving her husband) is taught to her by her mother and grandmother just prior to her marriage. 'How will we deal with those problems?' he asked. Also, in a story-telling activity, a participant told of how as a boy he was slapped by his aunt and told to sit down while he was washing the dishes because of what the girls would think of him.

As for the role of organized religion, several men noted, during a discussion which advocated doing away with hierarchies at work based on gender, that no one from a religious institution was present. This was significant because, as one man pointed out, all the major religions in South Africa have hierarchies with males on top that are based on religious doctrine. The next comment was to the effect that what makes it very difficult for us are our traditions and culture: 'The tradition says men dominate, men have the responsibility for providing for the family. And religion is the most problematic. It has been used to continue the oppression of women.'

Signs of Hope

Despite the fact that during the workshops everyone realized that both personal and societal resistance to reaching full equality for women were still very strong, ultimately more signs of hope than discouragement were provided. First of all many participants expressed a renewed commitment to bringing about gender justice: 'This is the first time I have been able to draw parallels between race and gender oppression. I will take the gender issue more seriously, and I see the need to eradicate gender oppression.'

They also asserted a changed attitude towards women: 'My father taught me to never let a woman on top. Beat her instead. Now I realize that was wrong.' And men realized that they were trapped by their socialization, including some of the rules established by their culture and religion: 'Men have been hiding behind religion and culture to some extent. Now I see that those values are not a part of culture. They were supported because we benefited ... Culture and religion are innocent. It's really us, the conditioning, the brainwashing.'

In sum, as one man expressed it: 'The goal is not to make everyone the same in relations between men and women. There will be different cultural practices except for the overriding principle of equal human rights for all.'

It was also hopeful that men repeatedly expressed the need to support each other. In one instance, a man who had gone through a divorce completely on his own explained: 'There is no support for black men and we need to build a culture of support for each other.' In another, a man who has since founded a group to end violence against women in his township said: 'I personally feel that something is happening in South Africa – for men; for the whole country. Violence against women is an epidemic which has been treated only from one side. Now women are no longer alone. They will have men as allies ... We need to support each other during difficult times.'

And in the same workshop, a man concluded:

I got a new vision here ... Talking about these subjects is meaningless unless we make changes in our attitudes and in our families ... We will be euphoric for a week, then it will be hard. We will be ridiculed; we can't do it on our own. We need to maintain the brotherhood we created. I pledge my support to the men here.

Further, what is probably most important for the long-term commitment of men to the struggle for gender equality is their realization that winning that struggle is in their interests as well as women's. Perhaps this was exemplified best by an elderly man who had been sent to a workshop by his tribal council in a rural area, and who said: 'Today I see I do not have to do everything, make all the decisions in the family. I feel relieved, a free man.' In effect, he had reversed the whole paradigm of what men fear in terms of women's liberation, fear of the loss of their own power. Instead, he realized that by giving up his so-called exclusive right to make decisions in the family, he became free.

Overall, the degree to which the men at these workshops indicated a heightened consciousness on gender issues surprised everyone involved. Yet it would be naïve to expect major changes in behaviour immediately. Gender roles are so pervasive in society and are so engrained in all of us at an early age, that everyone realizes that this will continue to be a long and painful struggle. It is expected that even the men who attend the workshops will experience numerous setbacks as they return to the environments that shaped their behaviours in the first place. Even more importantly, these workshops have reached only a handful of men and much more work is obviously needed. As indicated in the next section, though, the results from these workshops have left all who participated with a much greater sense of hope that once men in South Africa realize how much *both* genders have to gain from gender equality, they will be eager to join the struggle to reach it.

Organized Efforts to Support Change in South Africa

As mentioned at the outset of this chapter, patriarchy and sexism and all of the negative consequences of such systems of belief and behaviour still flourish in South Africa. Indeed, although some figures have recently been disputed, it cannot be denied that the country's rates of rape and domestic violence are among the highest, if not the highest, in the world. And as the men in the workshops discovered, the harm is not limited to women. For example, there seem to be accounts several times a week in the local media of the suicides of prominent men such as police officers who often murder other family members along with themselves. Suicide is the ultimate way of 'dropping out' to avoid the shame and the pain; and although male gender socialization cannot be seen as the sole cause of such behaviour, it is likely to be a contributing factor.

Just as the story about the female shop stewards indicates a changed consciousness among a growing number of women in South Africa, however, there are signs that a limited number of men now are also working to end the gender imbalances here. From a personal standpoint, by far the most gratifying example is the creation of an organization called Men for Change (MFC) by a man in his twenties who attended the first GETNET men's workshop in November 1996 and the first Training of Trainers a year later. He formed MFC after working at a domestic abuse prevention centre in Alexandra Township outside Johannesburg, and he has now raised international funding to support a wide variety of activities and programmes. These include a recurring series of three one-day men's gender awareness workshops in four townships in the region; an ongoing young men's support group in his home township; and a men's counselling service which has been running for about a year and has helped more than ninety local men better to understand their emotions and be able to settle disputes peacefully. Further, MFC is negotiating with the country's professional soccer league to include messages against violence against women on advertising billboards at all soccer matches; with the Office of Prosecutors within the national Department of Justice to provide a gender awareness component to the training of prosecutors; and with the Provincial Department of Education to conduct weekend workshops for male high-school students.

As an example of how much MFC has accomplished in so short a time, recently I co-facilitated a Training of Trainers for the young men who will be leading the high-school workshops. What was so remarkable to me, as the week of training went on, was the fact that the focus was solely on how they could master the content and improve their facilitation skills so as to become better trainers. There was no controversy whatsoever around the fact that men are privileged or that we as men had a responsibility to work to end the mistreatment of women in South Africa.

Other efforts to work with men to end violence against women and bring about equality were recently surveyed by the National Commission on Gender Equality (CGE).[5] While this survey is probably not exhaustive, it does give an indication of the range of groups and activities currently underway in South Africa to involve men in this struggle.

At one end of the spectrum in terms of size and aspiration is the South African Men's Forum, currently based in Johannesburg but with a goal to be national in scope. Among its activities is the hosting of regular 'Men's Indabas' (Zulu for 'gathering') whose goal is to achieve a moral revival among men which would end violence against women among other concerns. At the other end of this spectrum is the Embizweni Voluntary Association which, as its name states, is a voluntary men's organization based in Khayelitsha, Cape Town, that conducts family enrichment workshops, lay counselling and training for men in the township.

In between these poles are more traditional types of organizations that have begun to work with men in one way or another. First, there are two non-governmental organizations that conduct workshops to sensitize men on gender-related issues among extensive other activities. These are GETNET, which has already been discussed, and the Men as Partners programme of the Planned Parenthood Association. Besides MFC, there are two other organizations whose sole function is to work with men. One is the 5 in 6 Project which was the first group to focus solely on men and which conducts mass actions and media campaigns in addition to workshops. The other is Change Moves, which includes healing among its goals and creative arts-based tools in its programmes. There also are three multidimensional domestic abuse prevention agencies which have incorporated men's programmes into their activities, and two organizations which run rehabilitation and support programmes for perpetrators of domestic violence who are either referred by the justice system or come on a voluntary basis. Finally, the CGE survey lists the National Organization for Gay and Lesbian Equality, which focuses on supporting gay men; and the University of the Western Cape Gender Equity Unit, which runs programmes for men on that campus.

Mention should also be made here of the Men's March to End Violence Against Women which attracted close to 3,000 men including then President Mandela to Pretoria in 1998. Organized by the National NGO Coalition and inspired by an earlier march held in Alexandra, this march received significant publicity and as a result brought to greater public awareness the fact that men were also concerned about these issues. This awareness was further raised when the primary feminist journal in South Africa, *AGENDA*, devoted its April 1998 issue to the topic 'The New Men?' This issue included, among others, articles that described the various efforts by men to take part in the struggle for gender equality both in South Africa and elsewhere in the world.

Just as significant as these formal indicators that the tide may be beginning to turn in this country (so notorious for its male chauvinism and violence), are informal pieces of evidence such as a story recently told to me by a colleague who works at GETNET. He is a black man who recently moved into a traditionally more conservative white area where he attended a neighbourhood improvement meeting. Near the end, under the heading of 'new business', an elderly Afrikaner man rose to say in a somewhat halting fashion that 'we need to address this domestic violence matter'. A few days later, a parallel story was told to me by a black woman activist who was working with a community-based group in a peri-urban area outside Durban.

All in all, when you add stories such as these to the reactions of the men to the GETNET workshops and the formal activities of a growing number of organized groups, there does seem to be reason to hope that the people who achieved perhaps the greatest peaceful overthrow of an oppressive regime in history will also be able to win the even tougher and longer struggle of achieving the truly egalitarian society aspired to in their remarkable constitution.

Notes

1. In a book entitled *Changing Men in South Africa* (London: Zed Books, 2001), resulting from a colloquium entitled 'Masculinities in Southern Africa' held at the University of Natal in July 1997, its editor, Robert Morrell, opens his introductory chapter by quoting a November 1994 newspaper story in which South Africa's most renowned playwright, Athol Fugard, calls his country 'one of the last bastions of male chauvinism'.

2. These workshops, which number fifteen, were held in every province in South Africa with men from a smattering of both governmental and non-governmental organizations and one private corporation. There were participants from all or most of the various cultural groupings in the country, but the majority of men in most of the sessions were black. The workshops were either co-ordinated by or grew out of the efforts of an NGO in Cape Town known as the Gender Education and Training Network (GET-NET). The author was a facilitator at each of these workshops and wrote detailed reports of their content that are unpublished but available from GETNET.

3. In Chapter 2 of the South African constitution entitled 'Bill of Rights', paragraph 9 (3) prohibits unfair discrimination by the state on the basis of numerous classifications including 'gender, sex, pregnancy, marital status and sexual orientation'. Examples of recent legislation which seeks to promote rights, often of particular concern to women, include the considerable additional protections provided in the Domestic Violence Act of 1998; the inclusion of women as a 'designated group' whose employment is to be promoted by the provisions in the Employment Equity Act; and the provision for maternity and family leave in the Basic Conditions of Employment Act.

4. While not discussed in detail below, participants at the workshops noted many changes in South Africa relating to the status, attitudes and behaviours of women.

5. The survey was conducted from the Western Cape office of the CGE, which is significant because the responses seem to include a disproportionate number of groups from that province. For example, the only voluntary, community-based organization listed is from a township near Cape Town. It would be hard for the CGE to know of similar groups elsewhere even though it sent out requests for information nationally. Thus, it is very likely that the survey under-counts the actual efforts to work with men on gender issues.

17

Afterword: A Man's World? Rethinking Commonality and Diversity in Men's Practices

Keith Pringle and Bob Pease

In this concluding chapter we do not attempt to provide a detailed analysis of the rich material contained in the preceding chapters. Instead, we will draw upon that material to identify some key issues which we believe arise and which may prove to be fruitful lines of future enquiry in ongoing debates about men's practices transnationally. The two issues which we choose to focus upon here are: first, the complex patterning of diversity and commonality which we observe in men's practices transnationally; and second, flowing from the first point, the theme of men's practices and globalization.

Men's Practices: Diversities and Commonalities

Of course each reader of this volume will draw her/his own conclusions about the relative balance of diversities and commonalities to be discovered in the material contained within. Our reading of the texts in this volume is necessarily a personal one. It is presented here mainly as a marker against which readers can measure their own judgements.

From the material it is clear to us that there is a very high degree of transnational commonality around some important aspects of men's practices. At its most obvious this commonality can be observed in the 'patriarchal dividend' (Connell 1995) that seems to apply, one way or another, in all the social formations surveyed in this study. It occurs both in clearly patriarchal and hierarchical societies such as the United Kingdom or the United States as well as in societies more closely associated with gender and class equality such as Finland and Sweden. It is also observable in societies with an 'imperial' history (Sweden, United Kingdom) as well as in those that were shaped in important ways by other nations' colonial ambitions (for instance, Australia, Brazil, Finland, Hong Kong, India, Ireland, Nicaragua, South Africa, United States). The same is true both in countries which are heavily urbanized (Hong Kong, United Kingdom, United States) and in those where rural economies remain of more significance to some extent (Brazil, Finland, Ireland, India, Nicaragua, South Africa). Nor does the dominance of any religious grouping in a particular country seem to reduce significantly the pervasiveness of the patriarchal dividend. Indeed, as Ira Horowitz points out in his chapter on South Africa, the various religious affiliations there share at least one feature – their adherence to patriarchal values which result in 'dividends' to men.

Perhaps many of us in the academic world have become so familiar with the concept of the patriarchal dividend that we are no longer astonished at such commonality. Yet in putting together this book, it has shocked us afresh just how globally pervasive that pay-off is. And of course this pervasiveness speaks of other, particularly pernicious, transnational commonalities. The most important of these is the broad and global extent of men's violence towards women, children and other men. Indeed, this is identified as a major issue, in one form or another, in all the chapters within this book. In other words, it is a central feature of men's practices not only geographically but also thematically. Thus Jeff Hearn has charted the linkages with fatherhood in both an overtly patriarchal society such as Britain and in the allegedly more gender-equal milieu of Finland. And, as Lesley Doyal has recently pointed out (Doyal 1999), men's violence is one of the most central causes of women's ill-health world-wide. Thus the material in this book contributes in a major way to our awareness of an often neglected but absolutely essential fact: men's violence represents one of the most massive global social problems. In terms of future academic, policy and practice work around the social issue of men, one of the 'messages' to us from this book is that such endeavours always have to be developed within a global context.

On a more positive note, this volume also attests to the commonality of developing responses by men across the world challenging patriarchal power relations – a commonality which Michael Kimmel particularly emphasizes in his chapter. A relatively well-known response is the White Ribbon Campaign (WRC) that, as Michael Kaufman points out, has taken on global proportions. Furthermore, other chapters provide numerous and varied examples of organized positive responses around the world: grassroots profeminist activism in Australia and among African American men in the United States; profeminist training and awareness work with men in Nicaragua and South Africa; significant legislative changes on prostitution in Sweden; developing profeminist research centres in Brazil; dedicated programmes aimed at challenging the violence of individual men in Ireland and the United Kingdom. However, it also has to be said that the evidence presented here demonstrates the ongoing struggle which inevitably accompanies such positive initiatives: 'backlash' organizations (for example, United Kingdom); the resistance of entrenched political interests, sometimes from the right (for example, Hong Kong), sometimes from the left (for example, Nicaragua); over-reliance on charitable and 'voluntary' activity rather than clear state commitment (for example, Ireland); and of course the resistance of individual men to change (for example, Hong Kong, India, Nicaragua, Australia). Moreover, Michael Kimmel instances an especially virulent form of resistance, the right-wing militias in the United States. As Kimmel puts it so graphically, 'masculine reclamation and the restoration of public and domestic patriarchies' are central objectives for those militias.

If commonality of issues is one theme emerging from this book, then it is inextricably and paradoxically bound together in a complex interaction with a contrary theme: the extraordinary diversity occurring in men's practices across the world. Wherever one finds commonality, almost invariably one also finds diversity. Gary Lemons's chapter on profeminism and African American men in the United States is particularly helpful in this respect. For at the same time as he clearly demonstrates the commonality of patriarchal relations across black and white communities, and the need for a common profeminist response, Lemons also brings into focus the particularity of the cultural, social and historical contexts within which the practices of some African American men need to be understood: for instance, the hegemonic models of masculinity and sexuality presented by white men in the context of slavery during the colonial and post-colonial eras. In this example, one may also see both resistance to, and identification with, colonial white norms occurring simultaneously. Likewise, Harry Ferguson reveals the developing patriarchal commonalities for Irish men within a global perspective; while at the same time interrogating the particular historical context of hegemonic forms of masculinity associated in Ireland with the priesthood and celibacy. Siddhartha, in his chapter, notes that patriarchal considerations permeate all religious groupings in India, while helping us to understand the specific forms in relation to Hindu tradition. Or, again, Ira Horowitz underlines the patriarchal commonalities running across diverse religious boundaries in South Africa while also stressing the particularities associated with some of those boundaries. His chapter is also important in helping us to remember the crucial point that diversity occurs both within and across national boundaries.

In Bob Pease's contribution, Australia presents as another very interesting case. He notes that studies of Australian men have sometimes been used (Connell 1995) as the basis for general analyses of masculinity worldwide. Although these analyses have made vital contributions to pro-feminist understandings of (and responses to) men's practices, they have not necessarily taken into account the particularity of the Australian context; an absence which Pease begins to rectify by means of his study of Australian 'mateship'.

What of course the United States, South Africa, Ireland and Australia (as well as Hong Kong and India) also have in common is a history of British imperialism and colonialism. As regards this theme, in the preceding chapters it is once again possible to see both potential commonalities of experience in relation to men's practices and possible disjunctures. In terms of commonality, one could argue from the evidence presented in this volume that in several cases (Ireland, Australia) hegemonic forms of masculinity were partly shaped by a determined 'otherness' in the face of such colonialism. On the other hand, as already noted, some hegemonic forms of African American masculinity in the United States may, at least partially, have been influenced by colonial and post-colonial white models.

Sometimes, as in the case of Hong Kong, the authors attribute specific resistances regarding feminism and profeminism to local cultural and historical features. Hearn's comparative analysis of Britain and Finland demonstrates how complex may be the influence of such features. He reveals the historical and cultural trajectories which have resulted in contrasting social contexts: overtly patriarchal and hierarchical in Britain; more committed to ideas of gender equality in Finland. Yet at the same time he not only points out evidence for similar (and high) levels of violence towards women by men in both countries but also in some respects a greater awareness of such issues in Britain. In fact, one of the editors of this volume has recently suggested that the very same social and cultural factors influence both Britain's relative welfare negativity and its positive awareness of gendered violence compared to the Nordic countries (Pringle 1998; Pringle and Harder 1999).

Thus, for ourselves as editors of this book, another significant 'message' emerging here is not simply that men's practices across the world manifest striking commonalities and diversities; but that these two features are intertwined in a paradoxical, and indeed often a contradictory, fashion. In terms of academic study, policy formation and practice implementation this means that we must always be alert to the negatives which may accompany apparently positive developments and likewise the unintended regressive outcomes which can sometimes result from apparently progressive measures.

Of course the issue of commonalities and diversities across the world has important implications for debates about globalization and men's practices. Indeed, this is a theme which has surfaced at many points in the volume. Consequently, in the second half of this chapter we want to comment on that theme in the light of the material which the contributors have presented.

Globalization and Men's Practices

In the course of the preceding chapters a considerable number of issues have been raised which seem to conform to the literature arguing in favour of the globalization thesis generally and, more specifically, to Connell's (1995; 1998) arguments regarding masculinities and globalization. We now discuss some of these issues and then offer a limited critique of Connell's work on globalization based on the material in this book.

There seems no doubt to us that many features which appear in the preceding chapters benefit from the analysis suggested by Bob Connell in his 1998 article on masculinities and globalization. For instance, the neo-liberal shadow of a 'transnational business masculinity' can be seen in many of the contributions, generally exerting a regressive influence on attempts to challenge patriarchal power relations or actually promoting such power relations transnationally.

This is very clear, for example, in relation to Brazilian advertisements as analysed in the chapter by Benedito Medrado, Jorge Lyra and Marko Monteiro. Or again, Harry Ferguson makes clear reference to the con-textualization of present-day Ireland in global capitalism and the complex gendered implications of the country's new international economic growth. Similarly, Chan Kam Wah underlines the powerful resistance of business in Hong Kong to the nascent feminist movement there.

Broadening the perspective slightly, Alastair Christie contextualizes some of the central changes occurring in relation to gender and the social work profession in Britain by reference to globalization processes and the conditions of late modernity, not least in relation to 'risk'. The two points that Sven-Axel Månsson makes in his chapter on Sweden relating to the 'trafficking' of women and to the use of the internet for pornographic purposes both benefit from contextualizing his analysis within globalization processes. Thus the internet has transformed the 'business' of pornography globally both in terms of scale and of individuals' access to it. In relation to 'trafficking', Månsson notes that the global effects flow from both 'periphery' to 'metropole' and vice versa; a characteristic of the globalizing processes analysed more broadly by Connell (1998). Regarding a very different topic, fatherhood, and from the vantage point of Finland and Britain rather than Sweden, Jeff Hearn also highlights the complexities arising from greater global interchange in the form of cross-border popula-tion movements. Moreover, taking a wider geographical view on fatherhood, Graeme Russell in his chapter makes explicit the potential negatives arising from processes of globalization. As he says, while expectations regarding fatherhood expand, 'increased work demands within a global environment will necessarily lead to higher levels of conflict and provide new challenges for men seeking to establish an identity as an involved and committed father'.

While we can acknowledge the analytic value of Connell's globalization framework for globalization and masculinities, the material in this book also suggests to us that his model has some limitations. In many respects those limitations parallel the critiques aimed at globalization theory more generally. Some of these critiques were outlined in Chapter 1 and Alastair Christie also comments upon them in his chapter. A recent sceptical review of the globalization literature relating to social policy summarizes these general critiques well: 'Some of the claims surrounding the process and impact of globalization on states, social policy and welfare states are simplistic and exaggerated. The "constraints" that are placed on social policy development are primarily ideological and thus susceptible to political manipulation' (Yeates 2000: 53). And the author continues: 'While it is necessary to recognize the global context of social policy development, global economic forces are contested and mediated by states whose political responses are conditioned by local, internal factors, such as historical and institutional arrangements, cultural and religious values and traditions, political and social forces and the balance of political power' (ibid.).

As this last quotation implies, her critique of 'strong' globalization theories in relation to social policy is focused on issues of time and space. Time, because many alleged globalization processes seem to be observable in one form or another as far back as the fifteenth century, if not earlier. Space, because the local contestations and mediations of globalization processes frequently seem both highly profound and diverse.

The same arguments, as evidenced from material in this book, cause us to recommend some caution in relation to Connell's globalization model (Connell 1998). Of course, Connell himself acknowledges the chronological and local dimensions. In terms of time, he traces 'globalizing masculinities' through processes of conquest and settlement; empire; post-colonialism and neo-liberalism. In terms of space, Connell acknowledges the complex interplay between the local and the global. However, the question is: at what point does the chronological elongation of globalization processes and the depth of local mediations/contestations render those processes meaningless as analytical tools? As a way of looking at that question, let us examine some of the evidence to be found in this book, much of which we have already reviewed earlier in the chapter.

As regards time, we have already noted that many of the countries in this study have long histories of colonialism and imperialism, generally at the hands of various European conquerors such as Britain, Portugal and Spain. Moreover, it is clear that the transnational processes associated with those histories, not least migrations of conquerors or slaves, have had a profound impact on processes of masculinity formation in some of those countries. However, whether those historical *transnational* linkages can be regarded as processes of *globalization* is more debatable; unless we stretch 'globalization' to a point where its conceptual usefulness becomes strained. Let us take one example. In his chapter on Ireland, Harry Ferguson suggests that: 'Because of the profound historical significance of emigration and the impact of colonization within the British Empire, identity in Ireland has always been constructed on a global stage, although the terms of that engagement have shifted over time, not least today with the emergence of globalization processes.' This passage makes a crucial distinction between two figures of thought: on the one hand, the historical reality that Irish gender and identity constructions have always occurred in a global context; on the other hand, the more recent impact on such constructions arising from globalization processes. The distinction is between a long historical state of affairs where the 'global' or the 'transnational' has played a part; and a much more recent suggested phenomenon labelled 'globalization'. It is the confusion of these two in some writings that we believe partly clouds the issue about 'globalization'.

That is, of course, not the whole story. For, leaving aside the issue of time, we must also consider the question of space: the extent to which globalization processes in relation to men's practices are mediated and/or contested by local processes. In this chapter we have already acknowledged that: (1) there are striking commonalities across the world in terms of patriarchal power relations; (2) in that context, Connell's globalization framework provides important analytic connections in explaining a range of gender issues highlighted throughout the book. At the same time, we have also noted the massive degree of diversity in men's practices globally – a diversity between nation-states and within nation-states. Of course, as Connell's model would indeed suggest, there seems to be a complex interaction between the local and the global in many of those cases. However, given the extent of local diversity across the world charted in this book, we may doubt whether one can quite place the weight on globalizing forces that Connell does when he says:

> There is already a move beyond strictly local studies in the direction of comparative studies from different parts of the world ... My argument suggests moving beyond this again, to study the global arena itself, both as a venue for the social construction of masculinities, and as a powerful force in local gender dynamics. Such a move will require a reconsideration of research methods, since the life-history and ethnographic methods that have been central to recent work on masculinities give limited grasp on the very large scale institutions, markets, and mass communications that are in play

on the world scale. Finally, the typical researcher of recent years – the individual scholar with a personal research project – will need to be supplemented by international teams, able to work together for significant periods, to investigate issues of the scale and complexity we must now address. (Connell 1998: 19)

Based on the evidence from this book, it probably is the case that masculinity construction and gendered power relations have, in recent years, involved globalized and globalizing processes to a degree which marks them out from previous transnational phenomena. And therefore the study of these processes is no doubt important. Whether the changes are quite so dramatic, and whether therefore the research agenda needs to change quite so dramatically as Connell suggests, is, in our view, more debatable.

For instance, in this volume Graeme Russell notes that in some respects there has been a paucity of comparative studies regarding fatherhood, certainly beyond the so-called 'developed' societies. And yet, as is clear from his chapter, the benefits of such an extended comparative approach are immense. This in itself suggests that before we accept the relative redundancy of comparative analysis in favour of an explicit focus on Connell's 'global arena', we should first of all take advantage of the potential offered by comparative study – a potential which, we would argue, has been largely untapped regarding the issue of men's practices. In Chapter 1 we demonstrated that, in terms of the common struggle to challenge patriarchal power relations, broad comparative profeminist study has seriously fallen behind path-breaking feminist analyses of women's situation transnationally. We believe that this book is an important contribution to such profeminist study – and itself is a testimony to the hitherto unfulfilled potential of comparative analysis in this field.

References

Connell, R. W. (1995) *Masculinities*, Sydney: Allen and Unwin.

— (1998) 'Masculinities and Globalization', *Men and Masculinities*, Vol. 1, No. 1: 3–23.

Doyal, L. (1999) 'Sex, Gender and Health', in S. Watson and L. Doyal (eds), *Engendering Social Policy*, Milton Keynes: Open University Press.

Pringle, K. (1998) *Children and Social Welfare in Europe*, Milton Keynes: Open University Press.

Pringle, K. and M. Harder (1999) *Through Two Pairs of Eyes: A Comparative Study of Danish Social Policy and Child Welfare Practice*, Aalborg: Aalborg University Press.

Yeates, N. (2000) 'Social Politics and Policy in an Era of Globalization: Critical Reflections', in N. Manning and I. Shaw (eds), *New Risks, New Welfare: Signposts for Social Policy*, Oxford: Basil Blackwell.

Index